REVIE'S BOYS

David Saffer

VERTICAL EDITIONS

www.verticaleditions.com

First published in the United Kingdom in 2011 by Vertical Editions, Unit 4a, Snaygill Industrial Estate, Skipton, North Yorkshire BD23 2QR

www.verticaleditions.com

ISBN 978–1–904091–58–5

A CIP catalogue record for this book is available from the British Library

Cover design by HBA Design, York

Printed and bound by MPG Books, Bodmin

ACKNOWLEDGEMENTS

I would like to thank Norman Hunter for providing the foreword for *Revie's Boys*, statistician Gary Shepherd for painstakingly amalgamating all the player details, Paul Dews at Leeds United Football Club for his continued support on my writing escapades and Karl Waddicor together with Diane Evans at Vertical Editions.

With reference to the pictures in Revie's Boy's a sincere thanks to Jim Cadman for his help. A contribution has been made to the Don Revie tribute.

David Saffer left a career in the computer industry to become a full time author and journalist in 2002. His writing exploits began five years earlier when impulsively he penned a book on Leeds United winning the FA Cup for the only time in the Centenary final 1972. and over a decade on he has now written over 20 sports-related books, *Revie's Boys* being his latest offering. Among his other publications are authorised biographies of Allan 'Sniffer' Clarke, Celtic hero Bobby Collins and histories of a number of clubs in addition to an account through player memories of FA Cup finals (1953–69).

Married to Debbie, with three children and two cocker spaniels, life is never dull for the Leeds-born writer. He relaxes by listening to jazz and commentating on football for Hospital Radio.

CONTENTS

FOREWORD

In March 1961 when Don Revie was appointed player-manager at Leeds United, I was wondering if I would be taken on as a full time professional. Don made me his second signing and after giving me my debut at Swansea Town seven games into the 1962–63 season. I will never forget what he did for me in the 1960s and 1970s.

Don would become a great manager and terrific motivator who possessed a wealth of football knowledge but when he took the hot seat it was his first managerial post so had to earn the respect of established players such as Freddie Goodwin and Jack Charlton along with talented youngsters like Billy Bremner.

Slowly, Don introduced players from the juniors. I made my debut when Gary Sprake, Paul Reaney and Rod Johnson also got their big chance, and over the coming seasons he blooded the likes of Terry Cooper, Jimmy Greenhoff, Peter Lorimer, Paul Madeley and Eddie Gray. Don also made shrewd signings in Bobby Collins, Johnny Giles, Alan Peacock, Mick Jones, Allan Clarke, Joe Jordan, Gordon McQueen and Trevor Cherry.

As the team developed after winning the Division 2 title in 1963–64 we didn't win major honours to begin with but, after going close on a number of occasions, finally triumphed in the League Cup when my great mate TC struck the winning goal. Following a Fairs Cup triumph, we clinched the Division 1 championship on a never-to-be forgotten night against Liverpool at Anfield when the Kop acclaimed us as champions.

In the coming years we suffered plenty of heartache, especially in 1969–70 when we chased the treble and against Sunderland at Wembley in '73. We also endured our fair share of bad refereeing decisions. Who will ever forget Peter's last minute disallowed goal against Chelsea in an FA Cup semi-final in '67? Or Ray Tinkler allowing an 'offside' goal for West Brom in a vital league clash in '71? Or our defeat to AC Milan when I witnessed the worst officiating in my professional career two years later?

Winning trophies and suffering defeat though is all part and parcel of football, and I experienced both. But for every bad day there were many more glorious occasions. None of the lads who played in the Centenary Cup final in '72 will ever forget it and when Don decided to take on the England job he left on a high as we claimed a second Division 1 title in a record-breaking season. Whenever we won big games we knew how to celebrate and on days of defeat, Don was at his best picking us up to go again. Away from the action the lads were great mates and remain so today. We always enjoy getting together and I find it incredible that 50 years have passed since Don took the helm at Leeds.

This book though is more than just about the lads I played with who won league titles and cups domestically and in Europe. Many books have been written about Don's time at Elland Road but none has concentrated solely on players of his era as manager. Some played hundreds of games but many more had shorter spells or struggled to make the first team. Every player though has one thing in common; we were all selected to play for Leeds United by the greatest manager of them all, Don Revie.

I'm sure you will enjoy reading each player's individual journey.

Norman Hunter, October 2011

INTRODUCTION

The date 17 MARCH 1961 is etched into the history of Leeds United Football Club.

Don Revie was appointed player-manager and introduced by United director Harry Reynolds as the new boss to squad members in the home dressing room before training. The background is well documented that Reynolds penned a letter of reference about Revie's capabilities for the manager's post at Bournemouth FC and realising he had the person his own club required tore up the letter and spoke with fellow directors, who unanimously agreed to appoint Revie.

On 18 March 1961, the Revie era started with a 3–1 defeat at Portsmouth. Revie's initial United XI of Humphreys, Jones, Kilford, Cameron, Goodwin, McConnell, Francis, Fitzgerald, Charlton, Bremner and Grainger is bound in club history.

Over 13 seasons in the manager's hot seat at Elland Road, Revie selected 75 players, apart from himself, for a few games, to represent the club. From a team struggling at the foot of Division 2, Revie's boys would rewrite club history. During his time at the helm, Leeds won Division 1 and Division 2 titles, the FA Cup, League Cup, Inter-Cities Fairs Cup and Charity Shield aside 10 runners-up finishes domestically and in European competition. The most feared British club side of its generation, United's consistency for a decade was unmatched.

Every era however must come to an end and when Leeds lined up as Division 1 champions to salute the Loftus Road crowd at Queens Park Rangers on 17 April 1974, United's XI—Harvey, Reaney, Cherry, Bremner, McQueen, Hunter, Lorimer, Clarke, Jordan, Giles, Madeley (substitute Yorath) would be Revie's last selection. The line up, like his first, is detailed in club record books ending a remarkable era.

During the intervening years, Revie moulded a side still respected decades on. Of course, much has been written about legends such as Billy Bremner, the only first team player to straddle the period, Bobby Collins, Jack Charlton, Norman Hunter, Peter Lorimer and Johnny Giles but what about less celebrated players like Mike Addy, Nigel Davey,

Gerry Francis, Chris Galvin, Glan Letheren and Barrie Wright? Some of Revie's boys were inherited, others were jettisoned and many failed to win major honours, while others became internationals and household names. Whatever their successes or misfortunes, every one was selected by Revie to play a part in the rise of the club during the most memorable period in the club's history.

Don asked 75 footballers to pull on the white shirt of Leeds United. To a man they gave everything to the cause as United developed from a side scrapping for Division 2 survival to the most feared in Division 1 and among the elite in European football. Each biopic documents a player's role whether for 19 minutes, a handful of matches, a few seasons or over a decade of loyal service during a glorious period associated with The Don.

Each player has a tale to tell and it is in that spirit that Revie's boys has been crafted.

David Saffer, October 2011

DON REVIE:
AN APPRECIATION

Don Revie is a name synonymous with Leeds United.

Manager during the club's glory years, Revie developed a team heading for obscurity into one of European football's most feared outfits. Appearance-wise the club's top 10 is filled with Revie's players. Winning every domestic honour and enjoying European success, United produced sublime football or battled when required. In terms of consistency, for a decade Revie's boys set a benchmark that has not been matched at Elland Road.

Born in Middlesbrough on 10 July 1927, Revie began his playing career at Leicester City in 1944 before a £20,000 fee took him to Hull City five years later.

A cultured footballer, Manchester City paid £25,000 in 1951 for him and he made his name there as a 'deep-lying' centre-forward. Revie's distribution skills were perfect for a system that became known as the 'Revie plan'. Football Writers' Player of the Year in 1954–55 when City lost to Newcastle United in the FA Cup final, Revie was back at Wembley 12 months later to star as City defeated Birmingham City.

Revie played twice for the Football League representative side and won six caps for England. A £22,000 transfer then took him to Sunderland within 18 months and as captain he faced Leeds in John Charles' final game before his record transfer to Juventus in 1957.

Revie moved to Elland Road in a £12,000 transfer in November 1958. Following his debut in a 3–2 win against Newcastle United, Revie was then appointed captain. His appointment as player-manager came in March 1961 where his opening game resulted in a 3–1 defeat at Portsmouth. After an inauspicious start the first victory came in a 7–0 win against Lincoln City, before the end of the season.

Looking to the future, Revie replaced the first team strip with the all-white of Real Madrid and built on the club's youth policy. Retiring as a player in 1961–62, with United bottom of Division 2 and 11 games remaining, Revie signed a number of players including Bobby Collins who inspired his struggling team to safety in the final game at Newcastle United.

In 1962–63, Revie introduced talented teenagers alongside Collins, Jack Charlton, Billy Bremner, Willie Bell and Albert Johanneson. Progress was swift as Gary Sprake, Paul Reaney and Norman Hunter cemented places before Johnny Giles and Alan Peacock's arrival helped secure the Division 2 title in 1963–64.

Leeds' pursuit of success brought accusations of a 'win-at-all-costs' philosophy and some games were certainly not for the faint hearted. Dubbed 'Dirty Leeds' by the media, this title seemed outrageous in an era when every team had 'hard' players. However, the tag stuck for years.

The 'double' was tantalisingly close in 1964–65 as Leeds finished runners-up in both Division 1 and the FA Cup. And the coming seasons saw stars emerge in Terry Cooper, Paul Madeley, Peter Lorimer, Eddie Gray and Mike O'Grady as Leeds chased honours finishing runners-up in Division 1 again and the Fairs Cup. United also fell in FA Cup and Fairs Cup semi-finals.

Having appointed Les Cocker, Syd Owen, Maurice Lindley and Cyril Partridge as his backroom team, Revie, though overly superstitious and over cautious at times, was tactically astute and decades ahead of his time in terms of his legendary attention to detail. Insisting on the best travel and conditions for his players, Revie utilised detailed dossiers on opponents and left nothing to chance.

A superb organiser and spotter of talent, Revie's greatest strength was arguably his man-management skills. Requiring a talented squad to battle on all fronts, fringe players included Mick Bates, David Harvey, Rod Belfitt, Jimmy Greenhoff and Terry Hibbitt. Good enough to play regularly in Division 1, a number eventually did, but each player made significant contributions in the mid-sixties. Balancing the needs of a squad packed with international stars was no easy task, however Revie received total loyalty from his players.

A few weeks into the 1967–68 season Revie strengthened his side by signing Mick Jones and Leeds finally won a major trophy when Cooper's strike against Arsenal secured the League Cup, and after Jones nudged home a goal against Hungarian giants Ferencvaros in the Fairs Cup final, an astonishing defensive effort in Budapest secured a first European trophy.

Revie's team was in its pomp and after five years' endeavour, finally claimed the Division 1 championship in 1968–69 with a record number of points and host of new benchmarks.

The acquisition of Allan Clarke prior to 1969–70 meant Leeds had a clinical strike force. And at the dawn of a new decade, Revie began to remove the defensive shackles on his team. Leeds received the plaudits their talents deserved but unprecedented fixture congestion denied them a unique League, FA Cup and European Cup treble.

United landed another Fairs Cup in 1970–71 before hitting its peak in the second half of the 1971–72 campaign, when the football displayed at times was breathtaking. Inventive, resourceful and dazzling, Leeds produced awesome displays to sweep Manchester United aside 5–1 but the performance that captured Revie's boys' capabilities came in the dying stages of a 7–0 annihilation of Southampton when Bremner and co played 'keep-ball' to chants of 'Ole Ole' from home fans in front of the *Match of the Day* cameras. To cap a memorable season 'Sniffer' Clarke's diving header secured the FA Cup.

But for all United's successes, there were also days of woe as Division 4 outfit Colchester United stunned English football in the FA Cup shock of the decade in 1971 whilst rank outsiders Sunderland broke Leeds hearts in the FA Cup final two years later. The beautiful game can be cruel and Leeds suffered appalling officialdom most notably against Chelsea at the end of an FA Cup semi-final in 1967, versus West Brom in a vital league game when they were on the wrong end of an 'offside' goal in 1971 and infamously when AC Milan won the European Cup Winners Cup on a night of shame in Salonika in 1973.

But Revie was renowned for picking up his team and with David Harvey, Trevor Cherry, Joe Jordan, Gordon McQueen and Terry Yorath breaking through, Leeds embarked on an unbeaten 29-match run to clinch another Division 1 crown in 1973–74.

Revie's tenure as England manager after accepting the post in July 1974 has been well documented. Suffice to say after securing his family's financial future with a lucrative offer from the United Arab Emirates, the manner of his resignation was lamentable but the political shenanigans at the Football Association made Revie's position impossible. Despite overturning a 10-year FA ban from working in English football, apart from a consulting role at Leeds, Revie never managed another league club.

Married to his devoted wife Elsie, the Revies settled in Kinross, Scotland in 1986. Diagnosed with motor neuron disease a year later, the city of Leeds mourned Don's death in May 1989.

The greatest manager in the club's history had put United on the football map worldwide and made household names of his star players. Winning six major trophies, plus the Charity Shield, United went close to many more honours. Becoming division 1 runners-up and cup runners-up domestically and in Europe on 10 occasions was some achievement. United also finished in the top four of Division 1 every season after gaining promotion in 1963–64. The team to beat every season, United played to packed houses and domestically was the most debated club of the era.

Revie's achievements stack up as no English club manager between 1968–74 claimed more trophies. One of the great bosses of his generation alongside Sir Matt Busby, Bill Shankly, Bill Nicholson, Joe Mercer, Harry Catterick and Bertie Mee, Revie's legendary side is acknowledged as one of the greatest post-war sides during a glorious decade of success.

And the true legacy of this remarkable football manager is to speak to football supporters around the globe of opposing teams. Those who recall the late 1960s and early 1970s when The Don was manager can name his team player by player. That is Don Revie's heritage.

Don Revie 1961–74

Football League Division 1 champions 1968–69, 1973–74
Football League Division 2 champions 1963–64
FA Cup winners 1971–72
League Cup winners 1967–68
Inter-Cities Fairs Cup winners 1967–68
Charity Shield winners 1969–70
Football League Division 1 runners-up 1964–65, 1965–66, 1969–70, 1970–71, 1971–72
FA Cup runners-up 1964–65, 1969–70, 1972–73
European Cup Winners Cup runners-up 1972–73

Inter-Cities Fairs Cup runners-up 1966–67
Football League Division 1: Top 4 from 1964–65 to 1973–74
FA Cup semi-finalists 1966–67, 1967–68
European Cup semi-finalists 1969–70
Inter-Cities Fairs Cup semi-finalists 1965–66
Football League Manager of the Year 1968–69, 1969–70 and 1971–72
Awarded the OBE 1970

PLAYERS

MIKE ADDY made four appearances for Leeds United during a brief spell at the club in the early 1960s. A promising wing half, Addy tasted first team action before signing professional forms but would ultimately line up in only one winning United XI.

Born in Knottingley on 20 February 1943, Addy was a talented schoolboy footballer and represented England at Youth level. He was among apprentices at Elland Road including Gary Sprake, Terry Cooper, Norman Hunter, Paul Reaney and Rod Johnson hoping to make the grade.

Early on in the 1961–62 season, at just 18 years of age, Addy pipped his talented colleagues to a senior debut when Don Revie handed him the number nine shirt for a fourth round League Cup replay against Rotherham United in January 1962. His opportunity came as recent signing, Bolton Wanderers striker Billy McAdams, was cup tied and United's boss was blooding youngsters in the tournament.

Leeds had earned a replay after coming from behind with a goal from stand-in centre-forward Jack Charlton in the first encounter at Millmoor that finished 1–1 but went down to a 2–1 home defeat when Revie's first signing, Albert Johanneson, scored the United goal.

Addy did not play again in the first team throughout a turbulent season as Leeds only avoided relegation on the last day of a fraught campaign with a 3–0 victory at Newcastle United. He then signed pro forms in May 1962 but had a tough task impressing the new boss as he played in the same position as a precocious youngster, Billy Bremner, who was also making his name at the club.

When United made a poor start to the 1962–63 season, Revie rang the changes with Sprake, Reaney and Hunter coming into the first team as youth was given its head. And Addy joined them with Bremner out of action for three first team games in a hectic week as the Revie revolution developed.

United drew league clashes against Luton Town and Southampton either side of a League Cup triumph over Crystal Palace at Elland Road.

But a 2–1 win over Palace would be Addy's sole victory in a United shirt. As Revie took his Division 2 champions into top-flight football Addy joined Division 4 side Barnsley at the end of the 1963–64 season prior to a spell at Corby Town where he ended his playing career.

The early years in the Revie era were tough for numerous players trying to make an impression. Addy was one of those young footballers to ultimately not make the grade at Elland Road but he witnessed first hand the dawn of the greatest period in the club's history.

* * * * *

MICK BATES fulfilled an essential role in Don Revie's legendary squad as they took on all-comers domestically and in Europe. Throughout his Leeds United career Bates was not an automatic first team choice in midfield but when called upon never let the side down. Bates played in many high profile games including four European finals and in a cracking match against Juventus in May 1971, fired home a crucial 'away' goal to help win the Fairs Cup.

Born in Doncaster on 19 September 1947, Bates represented Yorkshire Schools prior to joining the ground staff at Elland Road. The under-18 squad was packed with talent as Bates played alongside gifted teenagers including David Harvey, Peter Lorimer, Terry Hibbitt, Jimmy Greenhoff, Rod Belfitt and Eddie Gray. Indeed, only three of the 15-man squad failed to play in the first team. With extreme competition for places, Bates had to wait for a senior opportunity but 12 months after signing as a professional made his first team debut against Hartlepools United in a League Cup tie in September 1965. Revie used the competition to give players coming through the ranks a chance to impress. Bates lined up with Rod Johnson, Terry Cooper and Belfitt but the 4–2 success would be his only appearance of the campaign.

The 1966–67 season saw Revie select Bates in 12 matches including a league debut at Burnley when Gray scored in a 1–1 draw. Bates also made his European bow and it was some occasion. With a number of players injured, Bates lined up against Dinamo Zagreb in the Fairs Cup final first leg. United lost 2–0 and failed to overturn the deficit in the return but major trophies would soon arrive at Elland Road. For the young midfielder, sitting on the sidelines must have been frustrating but Revie was instilling a unique spirit in his first team squad. Competing against Billy Bremner, Johnny Giles and Paul Madeley for a midfield berth was tough but Bates' role, like Belfitt, Greenhoff, Hibbitt and eventually Terry Yorath was a signature of Revie's man-management skills. All would undoubtedly have been first team players elsewhere but Revie realised the importance of a talented pool of players with his team battling on all fronts. Diligent, competitive and a fine passer of the ball, Bates' calibre and loyalty was a vital element in Revie's strategy. And Bates' patience was soon rewarded with European honours.

In the 1967–68 season Bates played against Spora Luxembourg and Partizan Belgrade, replacing Madeley and Gray respectively, as United began another Fairs Cup campaign. Aiming this time to go all the way Leeds made it to the final where they faced Ferencvaros. In the second leg Bates sat on the bench in the white-hot atmosphere of the Nep Stadium before replacing Hibbitt after 62 minutes to bolster United's defensive effort as they battled to cling on to a 1–0 first leg advantage. Facing waves of attacks United stood firm and became the first British team to bring the trophy home. Bates had collected a first winners medal and struck his first goal for the club in a 6–1 rout over Nottingham Forest as United chased a remarkable treble in 1969–70. Making 13 starts, the majority came during the run-in including a contentious 4–1 defeat at Derby County as Revie called on his reserve players when the title chase was over.

A non-playing substitute in United's FA Cup final defeat to Chelsea, Bates would enjoy an extended first team run in 1970–71. Making 44 appearances, Bates featured in around half the games with Bremner sidelined through injury. During this spell of senior action, Bates played in an epic FA Cup shock when Colchester United stunned the football world.

But Leeds were used to battling back from adversity and after again finishing league runners-up, this time to Arsenal, Bates won another Fairs Cup winners medal. Playing in 10 of the 12 European affairs, United overcame Sarpsborg, Dynamo Dresden, Sparta Prague, Vitoria Setubal and Liverpool before an ultimate test against Juventus. In a thrilling run Dynamo were defeated on 'away' goals and Liverpool by a solitary Bremner header on aggregate but the highlight of Bates' career came in the first leg of the final at the Comunale Stadium. With United 2–1 behind, Bates replaced Mick Jones 17 minutes from time before striking home a priceless equaliser to earn a draw in Turin. In the Elland Road return, Bates came on for Madeley in a tense clash on 56 minutes and his first leg strike proved decisive as Leeds won the trophy on 'away' goals.

Bates won an FA Cup winners' medal in 1972 as a non-playing substitute against Arsenal in the Centenary final but in 1972–73, when he made 44 appearances with Bremner, Giles and Gray injured at varying times. Bates' last Cup Final ended in heartbreak during an infamous European Cup Winners Cup defeat to AC Milan.

Further silverware arrived in 1973–74 when Bates made 10 league appearances during United's Division 1 championship-winning campaign. And he scored at Manchester City and against West Ham in significant victories before an injury ended his season.

Bates joined Walsall for £25,000 at the end of 1975–76 before further spells at Bradford City in a £20,000 transfer and Doncaster Rovers.

Although not grabbing the headlines like many of his famous teammates in the Revie era Bates made 151 (36 sub) appearances and scored nine goals. Talented and loyal, Bates is justifiably recognised as a United great in a glorious period of success.

* * * * *

ROD BELFITT was part of Don Revie's powerful squad when it began to make its mark in the game and helped secure major honours. An intelligent centre-forward, Belfitt scored important goals when leading the Leeds United attack most notably a Fairs Cup semi-final hat-trick versus Kilmarnock in 1967. The only United player ever to score a semi-final treble, Belfitt also notched two goals in a League Cup semi-final against Derby County.

Born in Doncaster on 30 October 1945, Belfitt played for Doncaster United and Retford Town prior to joining United in July 1963. A member of an under-18 side brimming with talent that included strikers Peter Lorimer and Jimmy Greenhoff, Belfitt was quick to break into the first team.

Revie was blooding youngsters in the League Cup and with

experienced centre-forward Alan Peacock injured and Don Weston fading from the first team set up, Belfitt made his senior debut against Huddersfield Town in September 1964. United made light of the game fielding only five first team regulars by scoring twice early on before two bizarre goals levelled the scores. With a replay looming, Belfitt grabbed the headlines with the winner seven minutes from time in a thrilling 3–2 victory.

A league debut against Nottingham Forest followed and Belfitt enjoyed a run of seven games in the first team finding the target in consecutive home wins over Tottenham Hotspur, Sheffield United and Arsenal. But Belfitt's impact was curtailed when Revie brought another fringe striker, Rod Johnson, into the side before Peacock returned from injury to bolster United's remarkable season that saw them finish runners-up in both the league and the FA Cup.

Belfitt experienced a frustrating 1965–66 campaign as Revie gave Lorimer a first team break and recalled a fit-again Jim Storrie when Peacock picked up a long-term injury. During six appearances, Belfitt made his European debut in a stormy affair against Valencia. In a bad tempered match dubbed 'The Battle of Elland Road', the referee ordered both teams off the pitch to cool down after police intervened to separate players following a mass brawl that resulted in three dismissals including United's Jack Charlton.

A regular in the senior squad, Belfitt enjoyed his most consistent first team run in 1966–67. In the FA Cup, Belfitt scored three goals including a fifth round second replay strike against Sunderland. But in the semi-finals, Wembley hopes were dashed when United were famously denied a last minute Lorimer equaliser by a shocking refereeing decision against Chelsea.

In Europe, Belfitt played in seven Fairs Cup ties on route to the final versus Dinamo Zagreb. During a thrilling campaign, aside from experiencing United's stunning 2–0 win in Valencia and 'toss of a disc' triumph over Bologna, Belfitt enjoyed his finest hour in a United shirt when he bagged a hat-trick against Kilmarnock to seal a final place that ended in aggregate defeat.

Belfitt's chances of a regular first team spot were soon to be limited following Mick Jones' arrival in a £100,000 transfer in October 1967 as Peacock's long-term replacement. But with United's record signing cup-tied in the League Cup for the 1967–68 competition Belfitt would play his part in a major trophy arriving at Elland Road after numerous near misses. Belfitt played in wins over Luton Town, Bury and Sunderland before hitting two goals against Derby in a 3–2 semi-final victory for an aggregate triumph to take Leeds to a second Wembley final in three years. Of note historically, skipper Billy Bremner is the only Leeds player to surpass Belfitt's total of five semi-final strikes.

Against Arsenal, Belfitt made his only appearance at the Twin Towers as a second half substitute for Eddie Gray before celebrating with his teammates after Terry Cooper's winning goal. In Europe, Belfitt made four Fairs Cup starts, scoring an important goal in a 3–2 win over Partizan Belgrade as United marched to the final. Belfitt replaced Jones against Ferencvaros after his first leg goal at Elland Road before watching from the bench in Budapest as United claimed a first European title.

In his role as a squad player, Belfitt made eight appearances when United landed the Division 1 championship for the first time in 1968–69. And in a memorable campaign Belfitt scored three goals including efforts in home and away hard-fought victories versus Ipswich Town. Allan Clarke's record £165,000 transfer in the close season sidelined Belfitt further but whenever called upon demonstrated tremendous loyalty to United. Playing a handful of games as Leeds chased the treble in 1969–70, when the title race was over Belfitt played in a weakened line up that lost an infamous clash at Derby and enjoyed only one win in the final six games when Gray scored two virtuoso goals against Burnley. Used sparingly in 1970–71, 11 of Belfitt's 21 appearances were as a substitute. But fittingly, after experiencing unforgettable Fairs Cup clashes, Belfitt's final European goal came against Sparta Prague in a 3–2 win as United moved towards a second triumph.

Throughout Belfitt's time at Elland Road, he'd seen new signings take his place. And in an ironic twist on his final appearance for the club during a 1–0 win against Manchester United at Old Trafford when Lorimer scored for Leeds in October 1971, Belfitt substituted rookie centre-forward Joe Jordan who in turn would succeed Jones. Within a month Belfitt had joined Ipswich in a £55,000 transfer deal, bizarrely the last club he'd netted a goal for Leeds against earlier in the 1971–72 campaign. An £80,000 transfer then took Belfitt to Everton before Sunderland paid £70,000 for his striking abilities. Belfitt played briefly for Fulham and Huddersfield Town before winding down his career in non-league football.

During eight years at Elland Road, Belfitt made 104 (24 sub) appearances, which was a tribute to the player and Revie's man-management skills. And amongst his 33 goals during this period, Belfitt scored his semi-final efforts that took Leeds to two major cup finals. Possessing a neat touch and aptitude when leading the line Belfitt's loyalty was commendable in a pivotal period of the Revie era.

* * * * *

WILLIE BELL was an integral part of Leeds United's defensive line up as Don Revie's team developed into a formidable outfit in the mid-1960s. A forceful midfield player, Bell converted to left-back with stunning success when United pushed for top-flight football and major honours.

Born in Johnstone, Lanarkshire on 3 September 1937, Bell joined Queens Park from Neilston Juniors in 1957 and quickly impressed in the centre of the park. Winning two Scottish Amateur caps, Bell rejected a chance to join Stoke City preferring to complete an engineering apprenticeship. Bell's arrival in English football was when he became one of Leeds' manager Jack Taylor's final signings for the club in July 1960.

Taylor's decision would prove to be an inspiring one for the club in years to come. Bell made his Leeds debut against Leyton Orient in September 1960. Revie was in the United XI with the new left half—their only appearance together that season as injury restricted Bell's appearances. Also facing Orient was a developing talent in Billy Bremner and centre-back Jack Charlton who Bell would join as a backbone in defence.

After one start in six months Bell returned to the first team with Revie having taking the helm as player-boss at Elland Road. And in his first game for the new manager Bell notched his first goal for the club against Lincoln City in a 7–0 rout. The 1961–62 campaign was pivotal for Bell as he made the first steps converting to left-back but the Scot was injured for the latter part of the season as United only avoided relegation on the last day at Newcastle United with playmaker Bobby Collins pulling the midfield strings.

Revie was moulding a new team as South African winger Albert Johanneson had made his bow and the 1962–63 season brought fundamental changes in defence following a poor start. Against Swansea Town, Revie selected three teens, 'keeper Gary Sprake together with defenders Paul Reaney and Norman Hunter alongside Charlton and Cliff Mason. A 2–0 triumph heralded the Revie era although Bell would play out the campaign at left half. However, Bell succeeded stalwart left-back Grenville Hair for the 1963–64 season. Promotion as Division 2 champions ensued and in a memorable campaign Bell grabbed two special goals, the winner in a 2–1 win against Swansea followed by a 30-yard screamer against Plymouth Argyle in the penultimate game of the season.

Bell may have lacked natural pace but utilised other skills including anticipation, determination and tackling ability to form a solid defensive back four alongside Reaney, Charlton and Hunter. A workmanlike footballer, Bell also developed an understanding with flying winger Johanneson on the left flank and chipped in with memorable strikes.

Bell enjoyed a purple patch in front of goal as United stunned rivals with seven straight wins to race up the league. Always willing to join the attack, Bell slotted home a penalty to seal a win over Tottenham Hotspur before scoring the only goal in wins at Burnley and Everton. The latter clash at Goodison Park proved infamous as Sandy Brown was sent off after two minutes when he hacked down Johnny Giles. Both teams were later ordered off the pitch by the referee in order to calm down but Bell had the final word when he scored the only goal of a brutal clash that dominated the sport headlines. In a remarkable season United challenged for the title before falling short to Manchester United on goal average and in the FA Cup when Bell was ever-present, Leeds reached a first Wembley final but Liverpool claimed the trophy.

European football followed with Bell resolute in defence as United again finished Division 1 runners-up. There was no joy in either domestic cup competition but Bell made his Fairs Cup debut in a 2–1 win over SC Leipzig and his experience proved important as United reached the semi-finals before losing to Real Zaragoza in a play off.

Bell's consistent form had been impressive and belatedly in his career he won two Scotland caps as the World Cup approached. And his international debut could not have been more high profile as Bell faced Portugal star striker Eusebio followed by Brazil's Pele in warm up games before both nations competed in the finals. The 1966–67 campaign would prove to be Bell's last at Elland Road as Revie continued to develop his side with the growing maturity of Giles and budding youngsters such as Peter Lorimer, Eddie Gray and Paul Madeley.

Bell played his part as United enjoyed a top four finish. He was once more on target when the opportunity arose with strikes in home wins against West Brom, Arsenal and Stoke City. Bell's goal versus Stoke would be his last for Leeds. The League Cup ended in a humiliating 7–0 defeat at West Ham, but the FA Cup saw United reach the semi-finals before losing to Chelsea in a game that saw Bell among the Leeds posse remonstrating with the referee after a dreadful decision denied a last minute Lorimer equaliser against Chelsea. United's Fairs Cup campaign however did see Revie's team reach a first European final against Dinamo Zagreb but Bell was among injured players sidelined for the first leg. He was back for the Elland Road return but alas, United finished runners-up again.

The 1967–68 campaign saw the emergence of Terry Cooper at left-back. And in one of football's strange twists Cooper had started out on the left wing before slotting in at full back when Bell was injured the previous season. Under Revie's guidance Cooper made the position his own. Out of the first team frame, Bell joined Leicester City for £45,000 after a superb career at Elland Road that had seen him score 18 goals in 260 games. Appointed captain, injury sidelined Bell for much of 1968–69 as future Leeds star Allan Clarke fired City to an FA Cup final at Wembley although Leicester suffered relegation.

Bell joined Brighton and Hove Albion where he ended his playing days and subsequently took up a coaching post at Birmingham City alongside ex-Leeds teammate Freddie Goodwin before taking the helm as manager in the mid-1970s. Bell also managed Lincoln City briefly before coaching at Liberty Baptist College, Virginia.

Bell achieved his full potential at Leeds when the defensive quartet of Reaney-Charlton-Hunter-Bell formed the backbone on which the Revie era developed. A talented footballer, Bell was a key player that helped pave the way for the glory years to follow at Elland Road.

* * * * *

BILLY BREMNER is the most celebrated Leeds United captain in the club's history. An inspiring skipper and midfield player, King Billy drove United on throughout the Don Revie era. A world class footballer Bremner had a never-say-die spirit, exceptional ability and an eye for goal. Bremner played more games for Revie than any one else. The only player among Revie's boys to line up in his first and last game in charge, Bremner played in 649 (1 sub) of Revie's 741 games as manager. During a decade of success he held aloft the Division 1 championship trophy, FA Cup, League Cup, Fairs Cup and Charity Shield.

Born in Stirling on 9 December 1942, Bremner was a schoolboy star and played for his country versus England Schoolboys alongside future Leeds teammate Tommy Henderson. Bremner attended trials at Celtic, Arsenal and Chelsea before joining Leeds in December '59.

The following month Bremner made his debut against Chelsea on the right wing with Revie playing inside right. Impressing everyone at the club, particularly Revie, Bremner made 11 appearances in his inaugural season, scoring twice. Bremner's first Leeds goal came in a 3–3 draw against Birmingham City when Revie notched a brace. Bremner struck again in the next home game against Manchester City in a 4–3 thriller. But in a disastrous campaign United suffered relegation.

Off the field, the club's youth policy under Jack Taylor expanded following initial work by his predecessor Bill Lambton. United adapted slowly to Division 2 football while major changes were afoot at Elland Road. Following Revie's appointment as player-manager in March 1961, Bremner was in his initial starting line up at Portsmouth and struck in the club's first win under the new boss as Lincoln City were thumped 7–0. Bremner's strike was his last of nine league goals in a turbulent season but illustrated his all round ability.

Despite early setbacks due to homesickness, Leeds' new boss recognised Bremner's raw talent in spite of a fiery temperament that resulted in altercations with the Football Association. Throughout Bremner's career a desire to win never diminished, a facet illustrated in an iconic picture with Tottenham Hotspur legend Dave Mackay following an incident at White Hart Lane in the mid-1960s. Mackay is not amused as he confronts Bremner.

Before this top-flight clash, Revie's team had more pressing matters as they faced relegation in 1961–62. Bremner had opened the season with the only goal to defeat Charlton Athletic but consistently poor form saw United battling the drop. Revie, prior to his retirement as a player, and Bremner, now playing right half, scored for a last time together at Luton Town in a 3–2 defeat. Further Bremner goals came in three of four victories of a fraught period at Middlesbrough before home wins over Walsall and Liverpool. One victory in nine games saw Bobby Collins' arrival in March 1962 and an unbeaten run that included a Bremner double to see off Luton Town culminated in safety at Newcastle United. Bremner finished top scorer in the league with 11 goals and alongside Collins, Jack Charlton, Willie Bell and winger Albert Johanneson formed the basis of Revie's reshaped team.

Revie was a firm advocate of the club's youth policy and introduced 'keeper Gary Sprake alongside defenders Paul Reaney and Norman Hunter at Swansea Town in 1962–63. Another debutante at the Vetch Field was Rod Johnson who opened the scoring before Bremner sealed a 2–0 win as the Revie era ensued. During a terrific campaign Leeds finished fifth with Bremner hitting the target on 10 occasions including a brace in a 4–1 win over Preston.

When Leeds ran out against Rotherham United at Elland Road for the opening game of the 1963–64 season Bremner donned the number 4 shirt for the first time. With Charlton and Hunter already set at 5 and 6 respectively the sight of Bremner-Charlton-Hunter as the backbone of the Revie era had begun. Leeds looked solid and with the arrival of Johnny Giles and Alan Peacock, United won promotion as Division 2 champions. Bremner missed only three league games and enjoyed an influential season. Far from his most prolific season Bremner scored twice in 3–1 wins over Portsmouth and Grimsby Town.

A first divisional success for 40 years was welcome but Revie had bigger aspirations and taking Division 1 by storm Leeds astounded pundits and rivals alike by finishing runners-up in both the league and FA Cup in 1964–65. Though heartbreaking, it was a monumental achievement. United followers had seen nothing like it and Bremner relished the big occasion. With a Wembley place at stake the Scot scored in the dying moments of an unforgettable replay against Manchester United. Bremner scored again in the final before Liverpool claimed the trophy but an exciting era had dawned.

Early on in the 1965–66 campaign a long-term injury to Collins sustained in a Fairs Cup clash against Torino saw Bremner team up with Giles in central midfield. Bremner and Giles complemented each other perfectly. The duo would become the most feared midfield partnership both domestically and in Europe.

Growing in stature with the introduction of Terry Cooper, Peter Lorimer, Eddie Gray and Paul Madeley, Leeds, skippered by Bremner from 1966–67, embarked on its most successful period. Bremner was a natural leader on and off the pitch. He also enjoyed a touch of luck in European ties ending level on aggregate with no 'away' goals scored as Leeds defeated Bologna in 1966–67 and Napoli in 1968–69 on the toss of a disc. But to be successful, luck could only take United so far and Bremner was on song in '65–66 during classic encounters including away triumphs at SC Leipzig, when he notched the winner, and at Valencia against a vociferous crowd.

Initially there would be huge disappointments in cup tournaments as United lost out in a Fairs Cup semi-final play off to Real Zaragoza in 1965–66, Fairs Cup final to Dinamo Zagreb and controversially an FA Cup semi-final to Chelsea in 1966–67. But success would finally arrive in the League Cup and Fairs Cup in 1967–68 swiftly followed by the Division 1 crown within 12 months. Lifting the cup at Wembley in March 1968 after defeating Arsenal and gaining a first European honour following an unforgettable defensive display against Ferencvaros at the Nep Stadium in Budapest were memorable events but being acclaimed by Liverpool's Kop at Anfield after securing the title in 1968–69 has gone down in club folklore. Under instruction from Revie, Bremner led his team to salute the Liverpool fans. The scenes that night have been retold time and again as the Kop acclaimed the new champs.

United were now in their pomp with Mick Jones and Allan Clarke leading the line in 1969–70 although treble heartache would come in a season when Bremner was voted Footballer of the Year. One of the most recognised footballers of his era, Bremner lifted the Fairs Cup again 12 months later, the FA Cup in 1972 and Championship trophy in 1973–74.

Ever present in both title triumphs, as a player Bremner had it all. Possessing strength, stamina, an expansive passing range, shooting ability and supreme anticipation Bremner was a ball winner one moment and a goal scorer the next. He also excelled as an emergency defender, striker or sweeper but it was in midfield in tandem with Giles where he made his mark.

And for a midfield player, Bremner's haul of 115 goals was an incredible achievement, especially as many of these goals were crucial. Three FA Cup semi-final goals took Leeds to Wembley in 1965, 1970 and 1973, and a flying header against Liverpool won a classic Fairs Cup semi-final in 1971. Bremner also scored in a European Cup semi-final clash at Hampden Park against Celtic when United lost on aggregate in 1970. On five occasions Bremner hit double figures in a season, the last in 1973–74 was particularly special as most pundits had written Revie's team off after being humbled by Sunderland at Wembley in May 1973 and controversially losing out to AC Milan in the European Cup Winners Cup final days later, a match Bremner missed due to suspension.

Determined to show United were still a force to be reckoned with Bremner set the tone to a record unbeaten 29-game run that would yield the title with the opening goal of the '73–74 season after just three minutes against Everton. In a memorable campaign Bremner scored 10 goals including two in a tense run-in versus Derby County and Ipswich Town that proved vital. The season also saw Leeds play in Europe for the last time under Revie and though not the main target, Bremner enjoyed an unforgettable night in Scotland. Playing as sweeper in an injury hit UEFA Cup line up against Hibernian, Bremner drew rave reviews. To cap a memorable performance, Bremner smashed home the winning penalty in a 5–4 shoot out win over Hibs.

Capped by his country at Schoolboy and U23 level Bremner made his full Scotland debut against Spain in May 1965. Winning 54 caps, many as captain, Bremner scored three goals for his country but his finest hour was leading the Scots to the 1974 World Cup finals. However, Bremner's most famous victory saw Scotland defeat England 3–2 at Wembley to become the first team to inflict a loss on the 1966 World Cup winners.

Following Revie's departure to become England manager it was only a matter of time before Bremner moved on. One more Wembley appearance in the Charity Shield saw him sensationally sent off after an altercation with Liverpool's Kevin Keegan before a final tilt at the European Cup. And during a memorable run Bremner scored cracking goals against Anderlecht and Barcelona before the ultimate prize was snatched away by Bayern Munich. Bremner's semi-final strike versus Johan Cruyff's crack Barcelona outfit made it six semi-final goals, a club record.

Bremner made his last appearance for Leeds versus Newcastle in September 1976. A brief spell at Hull City followed before Bremner guided Doncaster Rovers to promotion twice prior to replacing Gray as Leeds boss in October 1985. Languishing in Division 2, Bremner guided Leeds to an FA Cup semi-final and Division 1 play off final before another spell at Doncaster. An accomplished after-dinner speaker, the football world mourned his death in 1997 aged 54. Of all Bremner's many accomplishments he is remembered for his time at Leeds where he made 772 (1 sub) appearances, a record he shares with Charlton. A statue of United's favourite son greets supporters to Elland Road and is a constant reminder of his fighting spirit. King Billy's achievements will never be forgotten.

* * * * *

BOBBY CAMERON scored Leeds United's first penalty in the League Cup and played in Don Revie's debut game as manager against Portsmouth. A solid inside forward, Cameron featured in a number of thrilling encounters including two of historical significance at Southampton.

Born in Greenock on 23 November 1932, Cameron developed as a youngster at Port Glasgow and won Scottish Schoolboy honours. Snapped up by Queens Park Rangers, Cameron played nine seasons for the Loftus Road club and scored 56 goals in 254 games. Signed by United manager Jack Taylor in July 1959, Cameron made his debut in the third game of the season at Luton Town when fellow striker Revie scored the only goal of the match. Playing on the wings were Jack Overfield and George Meek while Jack Charlton and Grenville Hair were stalwarts in defence. But United endured a dreadful Division 2 campaign. Cameron scored once in a shock 4–1 win at title chasing Tottenham Hotspur. And the result was certainly a surprise as Tottenham had comfortably won 4–2 at Elland Road 48 hours earlier on Boxing Day. Cameron made 22 appearances during the relegation season.

A regular in the first team as United adapted to life in Division 2,

Cameron was second top scorer alongside a young Billy Bremner, netting 10 goals in 35 appearances in 1960–61. Whilst John McCole led the scoring charts with 23 goals, Cameron was penalty taker and converted five times including twice in the League Cup. Indeed, Cameron played in all four matches of United's bow of the new competition. After defeating Blackpool in a replay Cameron slotted home the first spot kick for Leeds in the tournament in a comfortable 4–0 win over Chesterfield. Cameron also netted from the spot in the next round at Southampton as United lost a thrilling encounter 5–4 at The Dell after coming from four goals down just after half time to level at 4–4 before Saints edged an astonishing cup tie with a last minute winner.

An adaptable forward, Cameron could play either right half or inside forward and was always willing to create openings. Lining up against Pompey in Revie's managerial bow in March 1961 Cameron failed to make another appearance before the end of a tough season. And after playing in the opening fixture of 1961–62 Cameron would make six more appearances, the last when Bobby Collins made his second Leeds appearance and rookie 'keeper Gary Sprake joined up with the team for his debut just before kick off at Southampton with Tommy Younger a late casualty.

While United's 4–1 defeat entered club folklore and Collins guided Leeds to safety Cameron, who scored 11 goals in 64 matches, departed in the close season joining Gravesend and Northfleet before returning to league football briefly at Southend United in 1963–64. An experienced campaigner when he arrived at Elland Road, Cameron failed to make a lasting impression under Revie although his place in club history is assured thanks to the League Cup.

* * * * *

TERRY CARLING kept goal for Leeds United in six matches over six years at the club. Five of those appearances came at the onset of the Revie era and his last in a record season at the time for 'keepers at Elland Road.

A local lad, Carling was born in Otley on 26 February 1939, and played junior football for Dawsons PE before signing as an apprentice in November 1956. Raich Carter was manager at Elland Road and John Charles was the star player at the club. And it was an exciting time at

United because the team had just gained promotion after securing the Division 2 runners-up spot behind Sheffield Wednesday the previous season.

As Carter and Charles led Leeds to a creditable eighth place finish in 1956–57, Carling played for junior then reserve teams whilst waiting for a first team chance. His opportunity would not come until United were back in Division 2 after suffering relegation in 1959–60. By now Jack Taylor had replaced Bill Lambton as boss and selected Carling to face Chesterfield at home in the third round of the League Cup in November 1960. United were playing in the competition for the first time and had already accounted for Blackpool after a replay when Carling took over from the experienced Alan Humphreys in goal who in turn had replaced Ted Burgin the previous month after United's number one 'keeper had shipped 27 league goals in 11 league matches. Carling enjoyed a winning debut as John McCole, Bobby Cameron (pen), Billy Bremner and Noel Peyton secured United's passage into the next round in a 4–0 win.

Humphreys reclaimed the jersey until the arrival of Revie who took the opportunity to watch both 'keepers in action with United in mid-table before the end of the campaign. Carling played four league games including home and away fixtures against Scunthorpe United. Leeds failed to win any of the matches.

The coming 1961–62 season would be traumatic for United as they battled against relegation in Revie's first season at the helm. It would also be a campaign when four goalkeepers donned the number one jersey. Humphreys was the first incumbent before Carling made his sixth and last appearance for the club in a 1–1 draw at home to Brighton and Hove Albion. Humphreys would take over briefly before Revie signed another experienced 'keeper, Tommy Younger. The season also saw the debut of teenage 'keeper Gary Sprake who would go on to play over 500 games for the club. Sprake's appearance was the first time since 1948–49 that four goalkeepers had played in a season for Leeds.

Out of contention for the 'keepers jersey Carling went on to serve lower league clubs keeping goal for Lincoln City, Walsall and Chester. Whilst Carling was unable to make an impression at Elland Road, on a historical note he played in one of three seasons at the time when four 'keepers had played in the first team.

* * * * *

TERRY CASEY joined Leeds United's ground staff at the start of the 1960s. Breaking into the first team at 17 years of age, tragically off the field events would end his career prematurely after a handful of games.

Born in Abergwynfi, Swansea on 5 September 1943, Casey was a promising half back amongst a talented crop of players at Elland Road aiming to make it in the game. Teammates in a burgeoning junior set up included Gary Sprake, Terry Cooper, Norman Hunter, Paul Reaney and Rod Johnson.

After two opening wins in 1961–62 against Charlton Athletic and Brighton, when a young Billy Bremner making his name at the club scored in both games, United struggled for form, picking up a further four league victories by the New Year. In the midst of a dismal run Revie used the League Cup to blood promising players. Casey received his opportunity when he made his senior debut at Rotherham United. United earned a draw when Jack Charlton equalised during a period when he was playing as an emergency centre-forward. By the home replay a month later Casey was in the first team due to injuries so missed Leeds crash out of the competition in a 2–1 defeat.

Either side of the Rotherham replay Casey played bizarrely against Rotherham but this time away from home though the match also ended in a 2–1 loss. Retaining his place in the side when an Eric Smith goal brought a hard fought win at home to Sunderland, seven days later Newcastle United returned from Elland Road with the spoils by the same score line.

Tragically, the match what would be the teenagers' last game in professional football, his fledgling career cut short after a car crash involving a number of players at the club. Returning to South Wales, Casey played for Worcester City in non-league football. There are many tales of football careers never coming to fruition for various reasons and unfortunately Casey was a young footballer to endure such a fate at the start of the Revie era.

* * * * *

JOHN CHARLES is acknowledged to be British football's greatest 'all-round' footballer. A world class player at centre-half and centre-forward, Charles was the star attraction at Leeds United throughout his time at the club in the 1950s. He was a legend with the Italian giants Juventus until Don Revie brought 'Il Gigante Buono' back to Elland Road—although his second spell would be brief.

Born on 27 December 1931 in Cwmbwrla, Swansea, Charles was spotted by Leeds' South Wales scout, Jack Pickard. It is still astonishing to think his local club Swansea Town had not snapped him up but following his arrival at United, the talented teenager made an instant impact after a senior bow in a friendly against Queen of the South.

Charles made his league debut aged 17 at Blackburn Rovers in April 1949. Welsh international selectors had already taken note and within a year made Charles the youngest player to win full honours at 18 years and 71 days versus Ireland. Charles eventually won 38 caps scoring 15 goals and is best remembered for helping Wales reach the World Cup quarter-finals in 1958 before falling to eventual winners Brazil.

Initially Charles played at centre-half for Leeds as Major Frank Buckley rebuilt the team following the club's relegation to Division Two in 1946–47. The 1949–50 campaign was Charles's first full season in the side and saw Leeds finish fifth. United also reached the FA Cup quarter-finals for the first time in the club's history before losing to Arsenal 1–0 at Highbury.

A few months into the 1952–53 season Buckley moved Charles to centre-forward due to a lack of firepower with stunning effect. Scoring 11 goals in eight games he went on to finish the campaign top scorer with 26 goals from 28 games including three hat-tricks.

A natural leader of the line, in 1953–54 Charles set a club record 42 league goals including a record five hat-tricks. Both marks stand almost five decades on and he is still one of only two players along with Charlie Keetley to score three hat-tricks for Leeds in a season. His prowess in front of goal meant new boss Raich Carter had a dilemma because for all Charles' success in attack the defence was shipping goals.

Carter controversially moved his prize asset back into defence and Leeds ended the 1954–55 season in fourth place, missing promotion by a point. Charles wanted top-flight football and handed in a transfer request but the Leeds board turned it down although they realised they could not hold him back much longer.

In 1955–56 Carter switched Charles to centre-forward and brought the inexperienced Jack Charlton in at centre-half. By the end of the season Charles had struck 28 league goals in as many games and a late run enabled United to snatch promotion behind Sheffield Wednesday. Nine years after being relegated Leeds were back in Division 1.

Scoring on his top-flight debut in an opening day 5–1 win against Everton, Charles top scored for the fourth time in five campaigns with 39 goals including hat-tricks home and away against Sheffield Wednesday. Charles' trebles made a total of 11 hat-tricks, still the highest number by a United player.

Of historical note, in his final game for Leeds at Elland Road in April 1957 Charles scored twice in a 3–1 win against Sunderland captained by Revie. Leeds finished eighth but Charles' days at the club were over as offers flooded in. The Leeds board duly accepted a world record bid of £65,000 from Juventus and used the money to rebuild the West Stand destroyed by a fire that season.

In Italy, Charles quickly became the star attraction. During a five-year spell in Turin Charles won three championships, the Italian Cup and was elected Footballer of the Year. Nominated the 'Greatest Foreign Player' to wear the club's iconic shirt, Charles and Revie were reunited when Leeds paid a club record £53,000 in August 1962. After just avoiding relegation Revie needed to pep up his attack and Charles arrived to great acclaim by United fans. But Charles' stay was short and he returned to Italy where he played for AS Roma as United netted a profit in a £70,000 transfer two months later. During his second spell at Leeds, Charles scored three goals in 11 games but only one of his strikes at Huddersfield Town earned a point. Other Charles' goals came in defeats to Rotherham United home and away as United's poor form from the previous season continued. Charles was absent from the side when Revie blooded talented youngsters against his hometown club Swansea as the Leeds boss looked to the future. But it is historically fitting, though no games were won, that United's greatest player and export before the Revie era played alongside Charlton, Gary Sprake, Paul Reaney, Norman Hunter, Billy Bremner, Bobby Collins and Albert Johanneson versus Bury, Luton and Middlesbrough as a new era began. And it is apt that in his penultimate home game to Southampton, Charles lined up with 15-year-old debutante Peter Lorimer who would succeed him in the club's scoring charts.

During an 11-game spell United won four games but only two

when he was in the starting XI. Before hanging up his boots Charles played two seasons with Cardiff City before taking on managerial and coaching posts with Hereford, Swansea City and Merthyr Tydfil. Until his death in 2004, Charles was a regular at Elland Road. Never booked or sent off in his playing career many of those lucky enough to witness this footballing legend playing believe he is the finest player in the club's history. Nicknamed the Gentle Giant, Charles was a formidable footballer and few opponents got the better of him. The only Leeds player to hit 40 goals in a season, Charles scored 157 goals in 327 games and was top scorer on four occasions. A colossus of a footballer, King John received a CBE in 2001 and memories of him will last forever.

* * * * *

JACK CHARLTON is one of Leeds United's greatest players, winning domestic and European honours in a 23-year association with the club. A member of a remarkable footballing family, Big Jack faced younger brother Bobby when Leeds played rivals Manchester United and lined up alongside his 'kid' brother in England's World Cup triumph in 1966. And three uncles George, Jim and Jack Milburn all served Leeds with distinction.

Born in Ashington on 8 May 1935, Charlton joined Leeds as an amateur in 1950 following a recommendation from his Uncle Jim before signing professional forms in 1952. Charlton made his Leeds debut against Doncaster Rovers on the last day of the 1952–53 season but the lanky defender had to wait until United's 1955–56 campaign to receive an extended run in the first team. Raich Carter was manager and with Leeds struggling for goals, switched John Charles to centre-forward and brought the inexperienced Charlton in at centre-half.

Few pundits backed Leeds for promotion due to their inconsistency but eight wins in the last nine games snatched the runners-up spot behind Sheffield Wednesday. It was mighty close but a 4–1 victory at Hull City in the last game of the season saw Leeds over the line. Charlton's progress earned the first of six appearances for the Football League in 1957. But with Charles by now leading the Juventus attack, playing for a struggling Leeds team hindered his development. It also didn't help matters that a stubborn nature and strongly held views made for an uneasy relationship with management.

Charlton's career found new direction following the arrival of Revie and especially when the new player-boss took the helm in March '61. After scoring United's goal in a 3–1 defeat to Portsmouth when Revie made his managerial bow, Charlton filled in as an emergency centre-forward as Revie grappled with an injury crisis among his strikers. And Charlton did not disappoint, scoring two goals versus Scunthorpe United and Swansea Town at the conclusion of a tough 1960–61 season.

Charlton also demonstrated his coolness under pressure when slotting in a penalty against Scunthorpe though the match ended in defeat during an inauspicious start. A rejuvenated player, Charlton dovetailed between defence and attack in 1961–62 but still led the goal scoring charts with 12 league and cup goals alongside Billy Bremner. Donning the number nine shirt on 15 occasions in 34 league games during a tortuous campaign, relegation to Division 3 was averted with a win at Newcastle United.

Charlton had reverted to defence towards the run in following the arrival of Bobby Collins and would remain there for the remainder of his career, though it never stopped him loping up field to support the attack. The signing of Collins in March 1962 was inspirational and with youngsters Gary Sprake, Paul Reaney and Norman Hunter joining Charlton in defence in 1962–63, Leeds rapidly improved. Charlton's partnership with Hunter would last a decade with a first honour coming swiftly as United clinched the Division 2 title in 1963–64.

The promotion season also saw Bremner, Charlton and Hunter pencilled in on Revie's team sheet at 4–5–6 for the first time. It would be a combination to serve United in many campaigns. Charlton scored three goals during the season, all in draws, versus Rotherham United, Derby County and Charlton Athletic. But he was more prolific in 1964–65 as Revie's Leeds astonished rivals by finishing runners-up in the league and FA Cup. Scoring 10 goals, Charlton got the campaign off to the perfect start with a winner at Aston Villa on the opening day of the season. He was also on target in wins over Wolves, Arsenal, Sunderland and Burnley.

Despite the heartache of going close in two competitions, Charlton's form was rewarded when he made his full England international debut against Scotland. And just over a year later

Charlton formed a core partnership with skipper Bobby Moore in England's 1966 World Cup-winning team and eventually won 35 caps for his country, scoring six goals. Charlton also played in two B internationals prior to the 1970 World Cup finals.

Although assured on the field Charlton was superstitious and had already relinquished the Leeds captaincy to Collins because of his liking to leave the dressing room last. Never the most stylish of defenders, Big Jack would crane his neck to dominate in the air and used his long stride to make telescopic-like tackles, attributes that saw him dubbed 'The Giraffe'. Charlton's consistent performances brought the 1967 Footballer of the Year award. Charlton was an experienced campaigner and it helped United's cause on the battlefields of Europe though he did get into the odd skirmish, most notably in a stormy Fairs Cup affair against Valencia. Dubbed 'The Battle of Elland Road', the referee ordered both teams off the pitch to cool down after police intervened following a mass brawl when Charlton and Vidagany were sent off in a bad tempered match.

After missing out in a Fairs Cup semi-final to Real Zaragoza and final versus Dinamo Zagreb, Charlton was at his imperious best when United claimed the trophy with a sterling defensive display against Ferencvaros in September 1968. This was United's second major honour in a matter of months as the League Cup had arrived at Elland Road when Leeds landed a first domestic trophy at Wembley. And indirectly Charlton was involved with Terry Cooper's winning goal from a corner in a feisty clash against Arsenal.

In every game while opposing forwards knew they would face a stern task, opposing 'keepers also feared Charlton especially in set pieces as he caused havoc when standing on the goal line. The Twin Towers was to witness such an occasion as Arsenal 'keeper Jim Furnell was unable to handle Charlton's presence as Cooper volleyed home the winner. Charlton was at it again the following term as he scored crucial goals in early season wins over Wolves and Newcastle United. And in a historic campaign for the club the Division 1 title arrived with a supreme defensive effort to keep rivals Liverpool at bay in the penultimate game of the season. Hailed as the new champions by the Liverpool Kop, it was another memorable night for this giant of a footballer.

Edging towards the end of his career, Charlton scored the winning goal in United's Charity Shield victory over Manchester City that heralded a remarkable treble bid in 1969–70. Fixture congestion eventually took its toll as United lost out in the league title race to Everton and reached the semi-finals of the European Cup. Charlton was ever present in the FA Cup, which included an astonishing semi-final trilogy with Manchester United before Bremner sealed a Wembley place. Back at the Twin Towers, Charlton nodded Leeds into the lead against Chelsea but following a 2–2 draw Leeds' hearts would be broken in a replay at Old Trafford.

Picking themselves up United battled back to win a second Fairs Cup in 1970–71 and Charlton completed his 'domestic' set of medals when Leeds finally won the FA Cup in 1972. During a memorable campaign, Big Jack sent home trademark headers in consecutive weeks firstly in an unforgettable 7–0 romp versus Southampton before marking his 600th appearance against Coventry City with the winner and edging Leeds through an FA Cup quarter-final clash with Tottenham Hotspur.

Twelve months after helping Leeds defeat Arsenal at Wembley, time caught up with this football legend and he retired as a player at the conclusion of the 1972–73 season aged 38. With George and Jack Milburn arriving at the club in 1928 the link between the Milburn family and United had lasted 45 years. Moving seamlessly into management at Middlesbrough, Charlton won the Manager of the Year award in 1973–74 after guiding his charges to the Division Two 2.

Charlton enjoyed a successful spell at Sheffield Wednesday before a brief period at the helm of Newcastle United. Many pundits felt Charlton should have managed England but the Football Association's loss was the Republic of Ireland's gain. The international stage was perfect for his style of management and during his tenure Charlton guided the Republic to the 1988 European Championships, where they defeated England, and the 1990 World Cup quarter-finals. They also reached the 1994 World Cup finals. After failing to guide the Republic to the 1996 European Championship finals Charlton retired but was awarded the Freedom of Dublin.

In recent years Charlton has built a career as one of the most sought-after speakers at sporting dinners. A natural speaker in such circumstances, his wit and wide range of anecdotal stories from four decades in the game makes compulsive listening. Leeds supporters however will always remember Charlton for his deeds during the Revie era. A one-club player, Charlton appeared in a club record 628 league matches, scoring 95 goals. His 773 matches in all competitions is a feat matched only by Bremner. Charlton is one of only five players to make more than 500 appearances under Revie, playing 554 of his 741 games at the helm. In a career spanning over two decades Big Jack was a true legend in every sense of the word.

* * * * *

TREVOR CHERRY experienced the extremes that top-flight football offers during a decade of dedicated service at Leeds United. One of Don Revie's last notable signings, Cherry endured cup final heartache and championship celebrations before tasting relegation in a transitional period at Elland Road.

Born in Huddersfield on 23 February 1948, Cherry played for Huddersfield YMCA before leading his hometown club to the Division 2 title in 1968–69. A stalwart defender for Town, Cherry scored 10 goals in 186 games where he partnered experienced centre-half Roy Ellam in central defence. Ellam would follow Cherry to Leeds but return to his former club within two seasons. Moving to Elland Road for £100,000 during the 1972–73 close season, Cherry signed initially as a replacement for Terry Cooper who broke a leg shortly before the 1972 FA Cup final. Cherry made his debut in the opening game of the new campaign at Chelsea and quickly cemented his place in the side.

Missing three league games in his first season at the club, Cherry impressed with his coolness under pressure and willingness to work hard for the team. Cherry also had an eye for goal and struck once in the league campaign in a win over Manchester City who were flying high at the time. Leeds finished third behind champions Liverpool before returning to Wembley to defend the FA Cup. Cherry was ever present in the cup run and on his first appearance at the Twin Towers almost set up an equalising goal but Sunderland 'keeper Jim Montgomery pulled off a remarkable double save to deny Cherry and Peter Lorimer. The goalmouth incident is one of Wembley's most iconic FA Cup moments. Sunderland duly claimed a remarkable scalp as Cherry and his devastated teammates prepared to face AC Milan in the European Cup Winners Cup final.

A number of first team players were out due to injury and suspension, and rumours circulated that Revie had been offered the manager's job at Everton. It was not the best preparation. Cherry had missed one tie as United overcame Ankaragucu, Carl Zeiss Jena against whom he scored the opening goal of the second leg for his first European goal, Rapid Bucharest and Hajduk Split. Eleven days after the cup final Leeds went down to defeat in Salonika when refereeing decisions dominated the headlines. Dusting themselves down and with Revie still at the helm United embarked on a record unbeaten 29-game run that led to the title. Injured in the opening game, Cherry made 37 starts in a thrilling season that earned him the top domestic honour.

Following Revie's departure in the summer after scoring against Liverpool in the Charity Shield at Wembley, Cherry was in and out of the side under new bosses Brian Clough and Jimmy Armfield as a transition period ensued. A tough-tackling defender Cherry possessed pace, determination, a calm temperament and supported the attack well. And in 1975–76, Cherry proved his versatility. Comfortable in defence or midfield, he filled in at right-back, centre-back and midfield. This flexibility would continue throughout his Leeds career.

After Bremner's departure in 1976, Cherry was appointed captain and held the honour until his departure in 1982. A regular during a difficult period, Cherry served seven managers. Following Revie, Clough and Armfield, Cherry played under Jock Stein, Jimmy Adamson, Allan Clarke and Eddie Gray. Despite the upheaval, apart from a few months of the 1982–3 season, Cherry played for Leeds in Division 1. And during the late seventies Leeds were unlucky not to win silverware, falling at the semi-final stage of the FA Cup and League Cup. It was during the FA Cup run of 1977 that Cherry scored his most memorable goal for the club in an unforgettable fifth round encounter against Manchester City that Leeds won 1–0.

In 1978–79 Cherry scored seven goals, his most in a season. During an exciting campaign when Leeds qualified for Europe again, Cherry grabbed a goal on the opening day of the season at Arsenal in a 2–2 draw, notched the winner in an exciting 3–2 win against Ipswich and opened the scoring in a 5–1 win at home to Bolton Wanderers. Initially the only uncapped member of the first team, Cherry represented the Football League and his consistent performances brought international recognition. Winning 27 England caps, Cherry is one of two Leeds players to captain his country, versus Australia in 1980. Cherry is also one of a few England players to be sent off in a full international, his dismissal coming in a bad-tempered game against Argentina in 1977. But Cherry was unlucky having had two teeth knocked out.

United's Player of the Year in 1980–81, his last experiences at Elland Road ended in heartbreak as Leeds suffered relegation to Division 2, a far cry from when he joined in 1972. Cherry joined Bradford City as player-manager prior to becoming manager when he led The Bantams to Division 2. It is as a player that Cherry made his mark for club and country. Highly respected and an incredibly loyal footballer, Cherry scored 32 goals in 477 (8 sub) appearances at Elland Road and proved to be an exceptional signing.

* * * * *

ALLAN CLARKE was among English football's most-feared strikers in the late sixties and early seventies. Nicknamed 'Sniffer' due to his instinctive goal-poaching ability Clarke cemented his place in Leeds United folklore with the winning goal in the 1972 FA Cup final. Clarke was top draw and renowned as one of Europe's most clinical finishers. His chilling efficiency when one-on-one with a goalkeeper was extraordinary.

Born in Willenhall on 31 July 1946, Clarke, the most famous of five footballing brothers, played for Birmingham Schools and South East Staffordshire Boys before making his professional debut for Walsall at 16 where he struck 44 goals in 78 appearances. Honing his skills alongside George Cohen and Johnny Haynes at Fulham in Division 1, a strike rate of 56 goals in 99 (1 sub) games impressed Leicester City who paid a British record £150,000 for his signature in May 1968. A turbulent 1968–69 campaign saw Leicester change managers, suffer relegation and reach the FA Cup final against Manchester City. Leicester lost but Clarke won the Man of the Match award. Top-flight football was his calling and having already gained England U23 and Football League representative honours, Clarke was in the England squad that toured South America before joining the league champions in a second British record fee, £165,000. Clarke would be the final piece of Revie's great side. Linking up with Mick Jones in attack, Clarke impressed on his Leeds debut in a Charity Shield triumph over Manchester City and scored on his league debut during a 3–1 victory over Tottenham Hotspur.

Clarke and Jones formed a formidable partnership, terrorising opposing defences wherever they played. Few bettered the Clarke-Jones partnership and if that wasn't sufficient, Peter 'Hotshot' Lorimer was supporting them. The 1969–70 season brought heartache as Leeds chased a unique treble but Clarke had found his spiritual home and ended the season joint top scorer with Jones on 26 goals.

Scoring with unnerving regularity against top sides Clarke showed no mercy against minnows, hitting two on his European Cup debut against Lyn Oslo in an 10–0 rout and four during a 6–0 victory to avert any sniff of a giant-killing act in the FA Cup tie at Sutton United. Following the domestic campaign Clarke linked up with England for the World Cup finals. After playing in two B internationals in the build up Clarke was coolness personified slotting home a penalty on his full international debut against Czechoslovakia.

Carrying on his superb form in 1970–71 Clarke missed three games as United again chased honours at home and in Europe. Agony occurred in the Division 1 title race when Leeds lost an infamous clash to West Brom that effectively cost them the championship. Further heartache also saw Colchester United end FA Cup dreams with a cup shock. On the scoring front Clarke was top scorer with 23 goals and had notched his first league hat-trick when striking all four goals against Burnley. But he saved his most important United goal for the second leg of the Fairs Cup final against Juventus. Clarke's first half spontaneous strike secured victory on 'away' goals and his first major honour as a player.

United were in their pomp and served up football for the connoisseur in 1971–72. Playing breathtaking football, televised routs over Manchester United and Southampton drew rave reviews whilst Clarke was at his clinical best with crucial strikes against Liverpool and Tottenham Hotspur on Leeds' march to Wembley. For Leeds supporters, one memory stands out from the cup run, Clarke's diving header in the final against Arsenal to win the long awaited trophy. Clarke again won the Man of the Match award.

Clarke was at the peak of his career and once again led the scoring charts with 26 goals in 1972–73, three ahead of Lorimer. But the season would end in double disappointment. A Clarke hat-trick against Norwich City in a third round second replay had set Leeds on the road to Wembley again but they suffered a devastating defeat to Sunderland. United were through to another final after Clarke's goal in the opening leg at Elland Road was enough to defeat Hajduk Split in the semi-finals of the Cup Winners Cup. But his joy was tempered as he was sent off for retaliation later in the game. Suspended for the final against AC Milan, an injury hit United side suffered a controversial defeat when appalling refereeing decisions brought sympathy from all quarters of the press.

Under Revie Leeds were always resilient and determined to show they were the side to beat. They enjoyed an unbeaten record 29-game run to set up another title tilt in 1973–74. Clarke was not as prolific as in recent seasons and had to overcome a mid-season injury but true to form came good at the crucial time to finally claim a long awaited Division 1 championship medal after finishing a runner-up on three occasions. During a tense run in Clarke scored late on in the penultimate match at home to Ipswich Town to secure a 3–2 win. The result ultimately clinched the title and for good measure Clarke also struck the only goal of the final match at Queens Park Rangers.

Following Revie's departure in the close season, a tilt at the European Cup was the final challenge remaining for his former players. And during a memorable campaign Clarke scored a crucial goal against Barcelona in the semi-finals to help Leeds reach the final against Bayern Munich. But Europe's premier trophy eluded them and Clarke was at the centre of a key decision that went against Leeds when Bayern captain Franz Beckenbauer's scything tackle failed to produce what looked a cast iron penalty with the score goalless.

As Revie's legends moved on, Clarke teamed up with Joe Jordan and Duncan McKenzie. Although no longer title chasers, Leeds fell in semi-finals of the FA Cup and League Cup. Following knee surgery in 1977, Clarke's playing days at the top level were ending but not before notching his 150th Leeds goal against Middlesbrough in 1978.

An England regular in the early seventies, Clarke scored 10 goals in 19 appearances and struck in memorable encounters including when England defeated Austria 7–0 and Scotland 5–0. Clarke also scored during England's infamous World Cup exit to Poland after a 1–1 draw in 1973.

In an era when defences offered few opportunities, Clarke's speed off the mark and instantaneous touch gave him a split second to cause damage but he was also adept at harrying opponents into errors. The only mystery of Clarke's international career was that Sir Alf Ramsey never partnered him with Jones on the international stage. Clarke's finishing ability set him apart. An assassin, he could waltz around a goalkeeper with nonchalant ease, catch a defender for pace, or place a shot or header into the net with deadly accuracy. A marksman of the highest calibre, Clarke would punish mistakes by a defender.

Prior to the 1978–79 season Clarke joined Barnsley as player-manager and led them to promotion before returning to manage Leeds in September 1980. Supporters welcomed his return but in tough times Leeds suffered relegation on the final day of the 1981–82 campaign. Clarke managed Scunthorpe United before returning to Barnsley where he experienced promotion, relegation and plenty of cup giant killing acts before retiring from the game. 'Sniffer' Clarke receives a great reception on visits to Elland Road. Player of the Year in 1972–73, he was top-scorer on four occasions, is third highest goal scorer with 151 goals in 361 (5 sub) appearances but the abiding memory is his historic winner at Wembley in 1972.

* * * * *

BOBBY COLLINS is arguably Don Revie's most important and influential signing in the club's history. Hindsight is easy but 31-year old Collins' arrival at Elland Road in March 1962 for £25,000 from Everton was the catalyst to the Revie era.

Born in Glasgow on 16 February 1931, Collins made his name with Celtic at inside-forward in the 1950s where he won Scottish League, Scottish Cup and Scottish League Cup honours. It was in this latter competition that Collins helped destroy Rangers 7–1 at Hampden Park guaranteeing him a place in Celtic folklore in 1958.

Collins, dubbed the 'Wee Barra' by Celtic followers, endeared himself to players and supporters alike with his all-action game. A brilliant tactician and motivator, Collins was a superb passer of the ball and possessed a thunderous strike bamboozling many a goalkeeper with his trademark 'banana' shot. Renowned for making his presence known on the pitch, Collins was always in the thick of the action and never shirked a tackle. Collins' reputation proceeded him and, playing with or against stars of a golden era, Collins held his own against the elite. During eight years at Parkhead, where he struck 122 goals in 346 appearances, Collins played alongside Celtic legends including Bertie Auld, Charlie Tulley and Jock Stein. Collins is also one of a rare number of players to score a hat-trick of penalties in a match, the feat coming against Aberdeen in 1953.

Collins represented the Scottish League on 16 occasions and following his debut against Wales won a total of 31 Scottish caps. A star for the national team, Collins scored for Scotland against Paraguay in the 1958 World Cup finals in Sweden but the Scots failed to progress past the group stages. After winning everything in Scottish football, Collins joined Everton for £23,000 in September 1958 where he further enhanced his reputation, hitting 48 goals in 147 games for the Goodison Park club.

Collins' arrival at Elland Road was an inspirational move by Revie. Leeds sat at the bottom of Division 2 and had endured a dreadful 1961–62 campaign, winning six games by the turn of the year. In nine matches prior to Collins' arrival, United had gained one victory, a draw and seven defeats. The last, a 2–1 loss at Huddersfield Town was a week before Collins' Leeds debut and signalled the end to Revie's playing days. Leeds' fledgling boss was under no illusions that his team was in a desperate situation. A turnaround in results was required in the remaining 11 games or Revie's team would be playing in Division 3 for the first time in the club's history.

Revie had to freshen up his team. Following the capture of strikers Billy McAdams and Ian Lawson, and defender Cliff Mason, Collins would prove to be a key signature. Making an immediate impact, Collins scored the opening goal on a winning début against Swansea Town and following a number of gritty displays that yielded another victory and six draws, Leeds were on the edge of safety. Going into the final game Revie knew a win would stave off relegation and his team came through with Collins leading the way in a 3–0 win. Collins had been a revelation and inspired United's great escape with a never-say-die attitude. He also brought the best out of the experienced Jack Charlton and future stars Billy Bremner, Albert Johanneson and Willie Bell. Collins' arrival marked a major turning point in the club's history.

During the following season Revie blooded teenagers Gary Sprake,

Paul Reaney and Norman Hunter. And Revie's faith in youth paid off as Leeds finished a creditable fifth. Missing just one game, Collins, who succeeded Freddie Goodwin as captain, enjoyed a fine campaign and, with an eye for goal, notched a brace against Grimsby Town and scored in thumping wins against Plymouth Argyle 6–1 and Swansea 5–0. With Collins acting as the midfield anchor, Revie's mix of youth and experience was gathering pace.

Leeds quickly mounted a serious push for promotion in 1963–64. The arrival of Johnny Giles further strengthened the side before Alan Peacock joined the United bandwagon. In the mix all season, United grew in strength and self belief. With 10 games remaining, Collins struck his sixth and final goal of the campaign as Leeds defeated Southampton 3–1. Seven further triumphs brought home the title. United were back in Division 1 and, bizarrely, in the games in which Collins scored, Leeds won.

The 1964–65 season proved to be memorable in many ways for the club and its inspirational captain. Driving his team forward and motivating everyone around him, Leeds embarked on an amazing campaign few could have imagined at the start of the fixture list. Pushing Manchester United all the way in the league, the title was lost only on goal average. Collins missed only three games and among many highlights he grabbed nine goals, his highest return at Leeds, including a brace in comfortable wins over Blackpool and Burnley, and the only goal of a classic encounter at a foggy Old Trafford. Collins was also ever-present as Leeds embarked on an FA Cup run that took them all the way to the final. He became the first player in the club's history to lead a team out at Wembley in what was a historic moment for the club. Against Bill Shankly's Liverpool the final ended in heartache as United went down to an extra time defeat but despite the huge disappointment a golden era had dawned at Elland Road.

Collins' efforts earned him the last of his Scottish caps after an absence of five years and he also picked up the prestigious Football of the Year award. The 1965–66 campaign ended prematurely for Collins as Leeds made its European bow. After winning an opening Fairs Cup encounter against a tough tackling Torino outfit, Collins had his thighbone shattered by a horrendous challenge in the return. Collins regained fitness but would only play seven more games for Leeds. Following spells at Bury and Morton, Collins embarked on player-coach posts at Ringwood City (Melbourne), Hakoah (Australia), Wilhelmina (Australia), Oldham Athletic, prior to coaching positions at Shamrock Rovers, Leeds, Hull City and Blackpool. Assistant manager at Oldham Athletic, Collins also managed Huddersfield Town and Barnsley.

Collins will always be remembered for his playing days where he graced British football. And Leeds supporters will never forget his endeavours in scoring 26 goals in 167 appearances. In United's rich history few players have had as much impact as this amazing footballer.

* * * * *

TERRY COOPER began his playing career as an out-and-out winger before converting to a swashbuckling left-back for Leeds United. TC was a natural in the position and quickly cemented his place in the side. A world class footballer, Cooper supported the attack on overlapping runs with devastating effect. Cooper entered club folklore when he crashed home an unstoppable volley against Arsenal in the League Cup final for United's first major honour.

Born in Brotherton on 12 July 1944, Cooper was spotted playing for Brotherton School and joined Wolverhampton Wanderers' nursery team, Wath Wanderers. After trials at the Molineux club he played for Ferrybridge Amateurs, which is when he came to the attention of Leeds scouts. Joining a talented group of apprentices including Gary Sprake, Paul Reaney, Norman Hunter and Terry Hibbitt at Elland Road in May 1961, Cooper signed professional forms in July 1962 and made his first team début as a replacement for left winger Albert Johanneson towards the end of the 1963–64 campaign.

His opening games in Division 2 were a baptism of fire. Against Swansea Town, Leeds clinched promotion with a 3–0 win and on his second appearance at Charlton Athletic, United clinched the title with a 2–0 victory. It showed some faith by the United boss but in Cooper he saw great potential and in his stop-start career during the next three years, Cooper became used to coming in for crucial matches as a replacement for either Johanneson or left-back Willie Bell.

The 1964–65 Division 1 campaign saw Cooper play 21 league and cup games including three FA Cup away clashes as Leeds marched all the way to Wembley. Preferred to Johanneson due to his work rate in forward forays and helping out in defence, Cooper experienced terrific wins at Everton, Crystal Palace and most notably victory over Manchester United in a semi-final replay. The season ended in heartache as United finished runners-up in both league and cup but Cooper was at the start of his career and knew opportunities for top honours would come.

During the 1965–66 season Cooper scored his first goal for the club at Aston Villa early in the campaign and went on to notch four goals in all competitions, his best return in a season. Leeds had embarked on its inaugural Fairs Cup journey and Cooper was in the line up that faced Torino in the opening match. Cooper scored a goal against Ujpesti Dozsa as United reached the semi-finals before bowing out in a play off to Real Zaragoza.

Although a regular member of the squad a first team place eluded Cooper but once again he fulfilled various roles during another eventful season in 1966–67 when Leeds finished in the top four and battled away for cup success. Cooper played in thrilling matches including a controversial FA Cup semi-final defeat to Chelsea. And in Europe, after helping Leeds draw a tense affair on aggregate against Bologna, Billy Bremner sealed the win on the flip of a disc. Cooper also played in both legs of the Fairs Cup final defeat on aggregate to Dinamo Zagreb. The second leg against Dinamo was played at the start of the 1967–68 campaign when Cooper finally established a first team spot at left-back as the long-term replacement for Bell.

An astute and keen tackler, and possessing natural pace, TC developed a great understanding with Eddie Gray down the left flank. Cooper's experience on the wing certainly helped in the role as an overlapping full back who could set up chances for strikers with pinpoint crosses. He was also able to anticipate opponents' moves when defending as he was a former winger. Playing alongside Reaney, Jack Charlton and Hunter, Revie had a balanced defence that would become the most reliable around.

During another thrilling campaign, honours finally arrived at Elland Road. United had made it to Wembley where they faced Arsenal and in a tetchy affair, Cooper volleyed home a clinical first half strike to secure the League Cup. Within months Leeds had claimed the Fairs Cup following an aggregate win over Hungarian giants Ferencvaros with an astonishing defensive display. Cooper could not have timed his elevation to the first team better. A key member of the Division 1 title-winning team in 1968–69, his consistent form brought international recognition. Following his début in a 5–0 win against France during the season Cooper quickly became a regular in the England set up winning 20 caps for his country.

Domestically, Cooper helped Leeds defeat Manchester City in the Charity Shield before playing his part in the club's treble bid in 1969–70. There was no time to reflect on the disappointments, especially after a bitter FA Cup final defeat to Chelsea, because Cooper was flying off to the World Cup finals in Mexico. And in a tournament acknowledged as the greatest football spectacle ever, Cooper's performances in the competition especially against Brazil in the qualifying group saw him recognised as the best left-back in the world.

Carrying on his superb form into the 1970–71 season, though Leeds eventually lost out in the race for the Division 1 title to Arsenal, Cooper's displays at home and in Europe received rave reviews. And against Juventus in the Fairs Cup final, Cooper was at his imperious best enhancing his reputation as the best left-back around as Leeds claimed the trophy for a second time on away goals.

The 1971–72 campaign brought praise for United's enterprising football where televised wins over Manchester United and Southampton enthralled fans and pundits alike. The football world was seemingly at Cooper's feet but tragedy struck when he broke a leg at Stoke City a week before Leeds FA Cup semi-final win over Birmingham City. Missing United's FA Cup triumph against Arsenal at Wembley, the injury sidelined Cooper for nearly two seasons. Cooper regained fitness and played periodically during the 1973–74 and 1974–75 campaigns but was unable to recapture his previous form. With Trevor Cherry in the United first team, Cooper's career at Leeds was over after 14 seasons. Following spells at Middlesbrough in a £50,000 transfer and Bristol City in a £20,000 move, Cooper held coaching and managerial posts at Bristol Rovers, Doncaster Rovers, Bristol City, Exeter City and Birmingham City. Most recently Cooper has been assistant manager and overseas scout at Southampton. The finest left-back in the club's history, TC was a wonderfully talented footballer. Making 340 (11 sub) appearances for Leeds among his 11 goals the most memorable was his unforgettable strike at Wembley in 1968.

* * * * *

NIGEL DAVEY was one of Leeds United's unluckiest players during the Revie era. A loyal squad member on the fringes of the first team, Davey would most likely have been called up when Terry Cooper sustained a broken leg in April 1972 but United's understudy full back also broke his leg the same day in a reserve team fixture.

Born in Garforth on 20 June 1946, Davey was spotted by United scouts playing for Great Preston Juniors when he joined his home town club as an apprentice in February 1964. The Revie revolution was about to begin and Davey was in an U18 squad packed with potential. Promising youngsters included David Harvey, Peter Lorimer, Terry Hibbitt, Jimmy Greenhoff, Rod Belfitt, Mick Bates and Eddie Gray. Davey signed pro forms though he was under no illusions how tough it would be to break through especially as he had to compete with Cooper, Paul Reaney and the versatile Paul Madeley for a spot.

A hard working full back, Davey made his senior bow when he lined up against West Brom in a League Cup third round tie in October 1965. Revie was using the competition to give developing players a chance to impress. Davey duly lined up for the midweek home fixture alongside fellow youngsters including Rod Johnson, Barrie Wright and Dennis Hawkins. Two other squad members, Madeley and Belfitt, scored but on a night when United battled away after shipping four goals in the opening 25 minutes they went out of the competition.

Davey played regularly for the reserves but would have to wait two seasons for another first team chance with Reaney and Cooper occupying the full back berths. Defeat to Liverpool in the last home game of a demanding 1967–68 campaign ended any title challenge resulting in Revie calling on his reserves to complete the fixtures. Davey lined up in both full back slots in defeats at Arsenal and Burnley.

History repeated itself at the end of an exhaustive 1969–70 campaign as United chased the treble. In the final six games Revie called on his reserve squad to rest star players for the FA Cup final. Various combinations were used but the most talked about side was in a clash at Derby County. United's reserve XI lost 4–1. United received a £5,000 fine but Revie felt justified as his team had endured a crippling fixture schedule.

In 1970–71, with Reaney sidelined due to a broken leg and other first teamers picking up knocks, Davey came in for 10 games, his longest spell in the first team. To date, Davey had not been on a winning team but that statistic ended although bizarrely each league victory was against Midland opposition as United overcame Derby home and away, Coventry, Stoke City and Wolves. Davey also played in both legs of United's 'away' goals triumph over Vitoria Setubal during the European run to a second Fairs Cup title. And he lined up against Barcelona when Leeds took part in a play off for the right to retain the trophy against the first winners at the start of the 1971–72 season.

With Reaney regaining fitness, Davey slotted back in the reserves, bar a League Cup clash at West Ham, before he started his own road to recovery after a horror injury at West Brom. Domestically, Davey did not feature again but made one final appearance, as a substitute in the UEFA Cup at home to Vitoria Setubal in 1973–74. During the close season, Davey joined Rotherham United but failed to make a first team appearance. During a decade of service, full back Davey was on the fringes of the first team hoping for an opportunity to stake his claim for a regular spot. Making 20 (3 sub) appearances was scant reward for 10 years at Elland Road but Davey witnessed first hand the Revie revolution and was always ready to give his all for the club, illustrating his strength of character.

* * * * *

KEITH EDWARDS holds the record of having the shortest career in Leeds United's history. Playing 19 minutes as a second half substitute, Edwards replaced Paul Reaney against Huddersfield Town as United went down to a 'derby' defeat in September 1971.

Born in Neath on 26 September 1952, Edwards enjoyed a promising schoolboy career. A solid defender, Edwards won Welsh and Youth international honours for his country. Spotted by United's local scouting system, Edwards signed as an apprentice in October 1969. Joining the current league champions must have been an exciting time for the young defender, and like all apprentices he worked hard, but competition was tough, to say the least, at United in getting a first team opportunity.

Finally, after two seasons of hard graft and reserve team football, Edwards made the senior team sheet as a sub for a league fixture at Town's ground. Promoted two seasons earlier as Division 2 champions,

Town were led by future United star Trevor Cherry who played alongside experienced centre-half Roy Ellam in defence.

Ellam, like Edwards, would also fail to make it at Leeds in years to come. For United, this was their third game of the season at Leeds Road, having drawn with Wolves and beaten Crystal Palace after an FA order to play their opening four 'home' games away from Elland Road. United's other 'home' games were played at Hull City and Sheffield Wednesday's grounds. The ruling came after frustrated Leeds fans invaded the pitch following referee Ray Tinkler's decision to allow a Jeff Astle goal for West Brom towards the end of the previous season. United's plea for offside was ignored initiating the demonstration. United lost out by a point to Arsenal in the league. Four decades on Astle's infamous 'offside' goal is still hotly debated.

Revie had a few injury concerns to contend with leading into the West Yorkshire 'derby' clash with Town as Allan Clarke, Mick Jones and Eddie Gray were sidelined. Utilising the ever-reliable Paul Madeley in midfield, Revie selected Chris Galvin and Rod Belfitt to lead the attack with Edwards on the bench for defensive cover. Jimmy Lawson opened the scoring for Town before Jack Charlton equalised before half time. Ellam scored a second half winner in a noteworthy Huddersfield triumph. Edwards came on late in the game for Reaney but would not feature again in United's first team.

Completing his apprenticeship, Edwards returned to South Wales but was unable to impress Swansea City during a short trial and failed to make a first team appearance. Edwards later played for League of Ireland side Cork City. Of the 12 apprentices listed in the club handbook in 1969–70 only one other player made the first team. This was Jimmy Mann, who would play two games. Revie's crop of apprentices were not at the same level as those developed in his early years at Elland Road but it must also be noted that the class of '69 had a team of internationals ahead of them rather than a side fighting relegation. Despite not making it at Leeds, Edwards does have a unique place in United's history.

* * * * *

ROY ELLAM was unable to make his mark as Jack Charlton's long-term replacement during two seasons at Elland Road. Big Jack's durability and emergence of centre-half Gordon McQueen ended Ellam's chances.

Born in Huddersfield on 13 January 1943, Ellam represented South Elmsall Boys and after trials with Queens Park Rangers began his professional career at Bradford City. Ellam's consistent form in 149 games for City saw his hometown club sign him prior to the 1965–66 season and over seven seasons racked up 225 appearances, notching 10 goals.

Looking to find a successor for his stalwart defender, Revie felt Ellam could be the answer when he joined for £35,000 in August 1972. Ellam, who scored the winner for Huddersfield against United in a Division 1 encounter at Leeds Road the previous season, was immediately installed in the first team but endured a dreadful debut at Chelsea in a 4–0 defeat. Reverting to Charlton and Paul Madeley, Ellam played only a handful of games until the run in when Revie rested players before the FA Cup and European Cup Winners Cup final. Defeat in both finals was devastating for the squad but Ellam must have wondered about his future as McQueen had made astonishing progress and was preferred to Ellam for a substitute appearance in the controversial defeat in Salonika.

The 1972–73 campaign proved to be Charlton's last at Elland Road and at the start of 1973–74, McQueen was in the starting line up as they began a 29-match record breaking run. Ellam made 10 starts during the season but as a replacement for the rookie defender who was given his chance to make the number five spot his own. Playing mainly cup-ties, Ellam saw League Cup, UEFA Cup and FA Cup duty but would only feature in four league games, making three starts. For Revie, the UEFA Cup was not a top target and ended at the quarter-final stage to Vitoria Setubal. Ellam played in four of the six encounters including what would be Revie's final European match as Leeds manager against the Portuguese. He also faced Hibernian home and away, Leeds winning the tie on a penalty shoot out. On a night of stalwart defence Billy Bremner played a starring role in a sweeper role behind Ellam and Terry Yorath in the centre of defence. Towards the end of the record league run Ellam helped United defeat Arsenal 3–1 in a midweek afternoon kick off due to the electricity crisis gripping the country. And when McQueen was sidelined after helping Leeds defeat Manchester United followed by a draw with Bristol City in a fifth round clash at Ashton Gate, Ellam was recalled for three matches in a seven day spell. The weeklong period proved testing as United's cup and league dreams faltered. A shock cup defeat at Elland Road to Bristol saw the United defence wrong-footed and when Stoke City ended Leeds' record run, coming from a two-goal deficit to win 3–2, a few alarm bells starting ringing. Would United blow the title? A shaky 1–1 draw at home to Leicester City did little for confidence and was Ellam's last game in a United shirt.

McQueen returned as three defeats in five games followed but United held firm to secure a second championship. The close season brought big changes at Elland Road as Revie accepted the England manager's job and Brian Clough arrived. Ellam also moved on though it attracted less media attention as he returned to his former club Huddersfield at the end of the 1974–75 season prior to spells with Philadelphia Atoms and Washington Diplomats in the North American Soccer League. In hindsight, Ellam arrived at United at the wrong time because nobody could have predicted McQueen would make his mark so quickly. But in 19 (2 sub) appearances, Ellam always gave his best.

* * * * *

JOHN FAULKNER was a Don Revie signing to suffer great misfortune during a two-year spell with Leeds United. His arrival as a potential successor for centre-half Jack Charlton followed an impressive performance for Sutton United in an FA Cup tie against the league champions. However, his fairytale move ended before it started when he scored an own goal on his debut and suffered a serious injury in his second game for the club.

Born in Orpington, Surrey, on 10 March 1948, Faulkner was playing for Isthmian League Sutton when the non-league side drew the plumb FA Cup fourth round draw in 1970. With *Match of the Day* cameras in attendance Faulkner was the star player for Sutton in his marshalling of United centre-forward Mick Jones. It didn't alter the final result as four goals from Allan Clarke and a Peter Lorimer brace sealed a comfortable 6–0 victory at Sutton's Gander Green Lane Ground.

Revie however had been impressed by the tall centre-half's display and snapped him up in a £6,000 transfer within weeks. Faulkner's arrival at United coincided with the club chasing the treble. When the defence of the title ended, Revie used his reserve squad to rest star players for the cup final. Faulkner was given his league debut in United's penultimate home match against Burnley. Around 25,000 fans were present to see a patched up United XI including Faulkner along with youngsters Terry Yorath, Chris Galvin and Paul Peterson. Fans at the game were to witness a match that has gone down in club folklore due to two iconic goals from Eddie Gray. What has long been forgotten however was Faulkner's debut own goal for Burnley. The win would be Faulkner's only league victory in a United shirt.

Two weeks later, Faulkner lined up versus Manchester City in the penultimate game of the season also at home. But tragedy struck as he fractured a kneecap in a collision with City defender Glyn Pardoe. United lost a game of little significance 3–1. For the new signing, his dream transfer to the league champs had turned sour.

Eventually regaining fitness, Faulkner would play two more fixtures at the start of the 1971–72 season when a weakened Leeds bowed out of their Fairs Cup defence in the first round. The defeat to SK Lierse on aggregate 4–2 after winning the opening leg 2–0 was notable as it was the first time United had shipped four goals in Europe at home and were consequently eliminated from a European tournament at the opening stage. Faulkner departed for a £4,000 fee at the end of the season serving Luton Town with distinction for six seasons in over 200 games. Faulkner ended his career in America, playing for Memphis Rogues and California Surf in the North American Soccer League prior to coaching and managerial roles with Luton Town, Barton Rovers, Everton, Norwich City and Sheffield Wednesday. Looking back at Faulkner's brief four-game spell at United (like a number of players before and after) lady luck was not on his side at the crucial time.

* * * * *

PETER FITZGERALD made three of his eight appearances for Leeds United during Don Revie's opening few games in charge at the end of the 1960–61 campaign. During 11 months at Elland Road, Fitzgerald was also awarded the first of five international caps for the Republic of Ireland. And the centre-forward began his Republic career in fine form scoring two goals against Norway in the second of these fixtures.

Born in Waterford on 17 June 1937, Fitzgerald started his

professional career for his hometown club, playing in an FA of Ireland cup final before winning a League of Ireland title. Fitzgerald also played for St Patrick's Athletic and his form was rewarded with selection to the League of Ireland XI on four occasions. Following a brief spell at Sparta Rotterdam, Fitzgerald joined Leeds United after the club's relegation to Division 2 in 1959–60. One of manager Jack Taylor's final signings at the start of the 1960–61 campaign, Fitzgerald played in an opening game defeat at Liverpool when Revie was among his teammates. But in an inconsistent start, Jim McCole and Noel Peyton were the preferred striking options. Fitzgerald did replace the injured McCole in a three game spell when a Colin Grainger goal defeated Charlton Athletic sandwiched between defeats at Norwich City and Stoke City. Dropping out of the first team picture, Fitzgerald played in Taylor's last game in charge when United defeated Norwich City with an Eric Smith goal and lined up in Revie's first United XI in a 3–1 loss at Portsmouth.

Fitzgerald made two more starts alongside emergency centre-forward Jack Charlton who scored twice in a defeat to Scunthorpe United and a draw with Swansea Town. In the close season, the Republic of Ireland player linked up with Chester in 1961–62. During two tough seasons Chester gained re-election to the Football League after finishing in the bottom four on both occasions.

Fitzgerald took his football journey full circle by ending his playing days at Waterford. Crossing two manager's careers at Leeds in his brief spell Fitzgerald joined a number of players who made an unusual historical mark. Apart from making the international honours board he was in the first United XI that began the Revie era.

* * * * *

GERRY FRANCIS blazed a trail for South African footballers at Leeds United. Impressing at a trial in July 1957, Francis has the distinction of becoming the first black footballer to don a shirt for the club. In a transitional period Francis showed his class with moments of magic on the right wing but played only eight games during the Revie era.

Born in Johannesburg on 6 December 1933, Francis was a shoe repairer and played for City and Suburbian before making the long journey to England as an amateur to carve a career in professional football. Impressing at his Leeds trial as an amateur, Francis signed professional forms in July 1957. Manager Raich Carter gave Francis a first team debut at home to Birmingham City in November 1957 but it would be his sole appearance of the season.

Francis didn't make the first team again until Jack Taylor was appointed manager in May 1959. But the club was in a state of transition and three wins in the opening 11 games heralded a dreadful 1959–60 campaign. Francis came into the side after three successive defeats and scored in a 3–3 draw at home to Everton. A week later Francis struck a stunning goal at Blackpool in another 3–3 thriller. Despite moments of brilliance Francis made only 12 appearances including a winning goal against Preston North End during the Easter fixtures as United headed towards relegation.

Francis finally enjoyed an extended run in the side in Division 2 playing 35 games. In a tough 1960–61 season, Francis struck six goals including strikes in wins at Southampton, Sunderland and at home to Plymouth Argyle. Francis also scored twice for the only time in his Leeds career in a 3–0 home win against Saints. When United took part in the first League Cup tournament, Francis played in the club's first tie against Blackpool although the match was not as thrilling as the high scoring draw a season earlier when he struck a wonder goal. But historians note Francis was in supreme form in a 3–2 win at Lincoln City that began an unbeaten eight game run that included five wins in eight games.

However when Revie started a rebuilding programme Francis was not in his long-term plans although he played in Revie's opening game as manager at Portsmouth. Revie's first signing for Leeds was another South African winger to grace the club, Albert Johanneson and it is noteworthy the two wingers lined up on opposite flanks at Stoke City in Francis' last appearance of the season.

With the arrival during the close season of Derek Mayers from Preston, Francis' time at the club was ending. He did however team up one more time with Johanneson four games into the 1961–62 campaign in a 3–1 defeat at home to Rotherham United. The result five decades on is long forgotten but it is historically gratifying to visualise these two exponents of wing play occupying the wing berths for the club.

Francis joined York City in October 1961, playing 16 games, prior to ending his career at non-league Tonbridge. Francis' 50-match stint at

Elland Road was memorable albeit in a struggling team. Not until the mid-nineties would two South Africans, Lucas Radebe and Philemon Masinga, pick up the baton for the Rainbow Nation following years of apartheid and take the field at Elland Road. Their opportunity was initiated decades earlier by Francis and must not be forgotten.

* * * * *

CHRIS GALVIN was among Don Revie's elite squad in the early 1970s but failed to break into the first team. After making his debut in the European Cup, the first player under Revie to do so, Galvin deputised for Peter Lorimer, Allan Clarke, Mick Jones and Eddie Gray. Such a quartet of talent sums up the onerous task Galvin faced after signing as an apprentice in 1968.

Born in Huddersfield on 24 November 1951, Galvin's arrival at Elland Road came as Revie was guiding his side to a Division 1 title for the first time in the club's history. A tricky player, Galvin lined up in attack or on the wing and impressed in the Central League for the reserve team. During a whirlwind week, two days after his 18th birthday Galvin was called up to the England Youth squad before making his senior debut against Ferencvaros in Budapest.

The Hungarian champions were a shadow of the team that gave Leeds such a tough time at the Nep Stadium a year earlier in the Fairs Cup final. Three goals adrift from the first leg at Elland Road, and a goal behind when Galvin replaced Gray 10 minutes from time with the tie won, it was a proud moment for the teenager as Leeds ran out 3–0 winners for a 6–0 aggregate win. Of note, the crowd was just over 5,000 spectators, 70,000 less than United's previous visit to the stadium.

United were going for the treble but the team's successful run in 1969–70 brought fixture chaos. When the title defence ended Revie called up his reserves including Galvin for his league debut at Derby County. United received plenty of headlines in a 4–1 loss. Both Galvin's senior games had historical connotations and it continued with his home bow against Burnley in front of around 25,000 fans. With only Paul Madeley, Lorimer and Gray from the first team playing in the Division 1 clash, United won 2–1 with a Gray brace that has since gained iconic status at Elland Road. Playing in the final game at Ipswich Town, Galvin's debut season had been memorable but Revie's Leeds were in their pomp and he struggled for first team exposure. In 1970–71 Galvin made two substitute appearances during an FA Cup win against Swindon Town and a Fairs Cup triumph over Dynamo Dresden.

The following season brought more opportunities but Galvin's frustration was growing. Among seven appearances was a humbling aggregate loss to SK Lierse in the Fairs Cup. The away leg had started in routine fashion when Revie fielded a weakened team and Galvin scored his only goal for Leeds with a neat finish in a 2–0 win. But Revie's decision to select only four first team players for the return backfired as United played poorly and shipped four goals for a shock aggregate defeat.

In between the fixtures, Galvin deputised for Gray as United gave a battling display against Barcelona at the Nou Camp Stadium in a Fairs Cup play off match to retain the trophy. And among league starts was a win over Liverpool with Clarke sidelined. Galvin also replaced Jones' future successor Joe Jordan as United began a successful FA Cup run against Bristol Rovers.

Following a League Cup run out against Burnley and trip to Ankaragucu in the Cup Winners Cup at the start of the 1972–73 season, Galvin made one further start, in United's penultimate game of the season at Birmingham City in Division 1. Substituted by Billy McGinley, another player to struggle making an impact, this final substitution summed up Galvin's five year stay at United where he made 11 (5 substitute) appearances.

Joining Hull City, August 1973, Galvin scored 11 goals in 143 games during five seasons when he teamed up briefly with Billy Bremner at the tail end of his career. Following spells at York City and Stockport County, Galvin retired from the game having never reached his potential that looked so promising when he made his European Cup debut.

* * * * *

JOHNNY GILES was a world class playmaker in Don Revie's legendary side. One of the game's great midfield generals, Giles possessed exceptional passing ability, was a master tactician, ice-cool from the penalty spot and scored prolifically.

Born in Dublin on 6 January 1940, Giles developed at a number of local clubs, latterly Home Farm before joining Manchester United where he served his apprenticeship. An FA Cup winner in 1963, Giles joined the Revie revolution in August 1963. Giles' signing was Old Trafford boss Matt Busby's loss and among the finest signings in Leeds United's history.

Initially an outside-right at Leeds, Giles played his part throughout the race for promotion in 1963–64. Missing only two games, his goal at Newcastle United earned an important Easter victory before a strike at home to Leyton Orient put Leeds on the brink of promotion, which he helped secure a week later with another goal at Swansea Town. The Division 2 title was confirmed in the last game at Charlton Athletic.

Buoyed with confidence, United astonished onlookers in 1964–65 finishing runners-up in both the league and FA Cup. Giles had provided the cross for Billy Bremner to head United to a first Wembley final and played an influential role in a season that saw him begin a remarkable reign as penalty taker. Succeeding Willie Bell, Giles' first success from the spot came against Birmingham City in a league fixture. Giles slotted home another penalty in the return clash but the league campaign ended in heartbreak though supporters knew an exciting era had dawned.

A few weeks into the 1965–66 season Revie switched Giles to central midfield when skipper Bobby Collins suffered a horrific injury against Torino. Giles' eye for a killer pass was soon apparent and in tandem with Bremner the pair complemented each other supremely domestically and in Europe. Although not as fiery as Bremner, Giles displayed the same will-to-win as his skipper and in the heat of a battle was never phased by tough tackling opponents. Orchestrating proceedings from the centre of the park Bremner and Giles were among the most feared midfield partnership in the game.

Giles's ratio of goals from midfield was exceptional—he scored 115 in all competitions. A terrific striker of the ball, Giles hit double figures on five occasions during a season. Top scorer in 1966–67 with 18 goals, Giles scored important goals against Valencia and Kilmarnock as United made it all the way to a first Fairs Cup final before losing out to Dinamo Zagreb. And his penalty edged Leeds past Sunderland on route to an FA Cup semi-final before a controversial defeat to Chelsea.

Injury sidelined Giles during the opening stages of the 1967–68 campaign but he returned as United targeted the League Cup and Fairs Cup. Among important strikes Giles converted a spot kick in a

League Cup semi-final at Brian Clough's developing Derby County side. And after going close on a number of occasions Giles was in the United XI that finally won a major honour against Arsenal at Wembley. And he was at his clinical best in a memorable win over Rangers during Leeds' run to Fairs Cup glory though an injury prevented him from playing in the second leg of the final against Ferencvaros at the start of the following season.

After helping secure United's first league title in 1968–69, United's number 10 struck the only goal against Nottingham Forest five minutes from time to seal a record points total on a night of celebration as the Championship trophy finally arrived at Elland Road. Giles' most prolific campaign for Leeds was in 1969–70 when he scored 19 goals including a penalty haul of eight spot kicks, a figure he matched in 1970–71, one short of Jack Milburn's record nine spot kicks in 1935–36.

Dubbed the 'Penalty King' in the *Yorkshire Evening Post*, Giles came up trumps in notable pressure moments of European action. Giles held his nerve against Vitoria Setubal as United journeyed to a second Fairs Cup triumph and this time Giles played in both legs as United overcame Juventus on away goals.

The 1972–73 campaign saw Giles become only the second Leeds player to score a penalty in three consecutive league games in clashes versus Sheffield United, West Brom and Ipswich Town. In so doing Giles matched Milburn's feat of 1935–36. Giles' total of 44 penalties is more than any other Leeds player. And in an astonishing era Giles was also expert at long-range strikes as he demonstrated in a 5–0 rout against league champions Derby at Elland Road.

Sadly though he was injured when United suffered a European final defeat in the Cup Winners Cup against AC Milan. An experienced campaigner, Giles had played in a fifth FA Cup final when Sunderland stunned the footballing world before the Salonika debacle against Milan, but, like his teammates, Giles was determined to show critics that United were not a spent force in 1973–74.

And Giles made an impressive start to the league campaign scoring in the opening fixture versus Everton and notched the only goal at Norwich City as a record run ensued but injuries would limit his appearances until the run-in as Leeds claimed a second league title.

Following Revie's departure, Giles made one final appearance at

Wembley in the Charity Shield against Liverpool and played in United's European Cup campaign though the ultimate prize eluded Leeds with defeat in the final against Bayern Munich. Giles' form naturally brought international recognition, scoring on his Republic of Ireland debut against Sweden at Dalymount Park in a 3–2 win. Giles went on to captain his country, eventually winning 59 caps.

Giles began a successful spell as player-manager at West Brom guiding his players to promotion from Division 2 at the first attempt in 1975–76. Creating one of the most attractive teams in Division 1, Giles then led Shamrock Rovers to the FAI Cup prior to posts at Philadelphia Fury, Vancouver Whitecaps, the Republic of Ireland and West Brom once more. An inspiring after-dinner speaker and football analyst, this exceptionally talented footballer is eighth on the all-time United list having made 523 (4 sub) appearances. A genius in midfield, Giles is undoubtedly one of the greatest players to represent the club.

* * * * *

FREDDIE GOODWIN was Leeds United captain in Don Revie's first game as manager. A resolute central defender in the early sixties, Goodwin was clinically efficient clearing the ball from the danger zone. Injuries affected his latter seasons at the club before a horrific leg break in an FA Cup tie ended his Leeds career.

Born in Heywood on 28 June 1933, Goodwin represented Stockport and Cheshire Schools before joining Manchester United in October 1953. The Munich air disaster decimated the Busby Babes and resulted in Goodwin playing in the 1958 FA Cup final versus Bolton Wanderers. After 106 games at Old Trafford, Goodwin joined Leeds for £10,000 in March 1960. An experienced defender, Leeds boss Jack Taylor was searching for a solution to halt his team shipping goals in a desperate 1959–60 campaign.

Goodwin made his debut in a 4–3 win against Manchester City at Elland Road. The victory was welcome but United's slide continued to Division 2. The coming 12 months saw Taylor further develop a youth policy started by his predecessor Bill Lambton. Billy Bremner had made his debut just before Goodwin and was the first to impress on a regular basis. Goodwin partnered Jack Charlton in defence and succeeded Don Revie as captain in the 1960–61 season but United's form was inconsistent. With wins scarce Taylor moved Charlton to centre-forward and teamed Goodwin alongside Eric Smith. Goodwin scored his only Leeds goals against Middlesbrough during a 4–4 draw and just before Taylor's departure netted the winner at Brighton and Hove Albion in a 3 –2 triumph. When Smith scored the winning goal at Norwich City it would be Taylor's final game in charge before Revie was appointed player-manager.

Goodwin led United as they lost 3–1 at Portsmouth in Revie's first game in charge. In a tough season on and off the field only one victory, 7–0 versus Lincoln City followed. Slack defence was a major problem and it continued in 1961–62 as United battled against the drop for a second time in three seasons. Goodwin again skippered the side as Bremner and Charlton, once more used as emergency cover in attack, finished joint top scorers. With Leeds heading for the drop, Revie signed Bobby Collins to add solidity and leadership to his struggling side. And in an unbeaten 11-game run Leeds survived on the final day of a tortuous campaign with a 3–0 win at Newcastle United. It had been a close call but Goodwin had played his part, missing just one league game.

Goodwin picked up an injury at the start of 1962–63 and with Revie drafting in a number of youngsters to the side Goodwin would play only eight games. Collins also succeeded Goodwin as captain but United's former skipper played 12 games in United's promotion season of 1963– 64 when Charlton was sidelined. And Goodwin proved something of a lucky talisman as United claimed eight wins and suffered just a single loss. But his time at Elland Road was curtailed following a triple fracture after a collision with former teammate John Charles during an FA Cup third round clash at Cardiff City.

A sad footnote to Goodwin's time at Leeds was that his dozen appearances in '63–64 were insufficient to receive a promotion medal. While Goodwin went on play briefly for Scunthorpe United, his former teammates took top-flight football by storm. Goodwin took up managerial posts at Scunthorpe, New York Generals, Brighton, Birmingham City and Minnesota Kicks. At Birmingham, Goodwin led his team to an FA Cup semi-final in 1972 but his former teammates handed out a footballing lesson on the road to Wembley. Goodwin made 120 appearances for Leeds and was always respected for his endeavour in a difficult period that crossed into the Revie era.

* * * * *

COLIN GRAINGER played one season for Leeds United following his arrival from Sunderland for a record £15,000 fee. An England international, left winger Grainger arrived at Elland Road in July 1960 offering experience and attacking flair but after Don Revie took the helm his spell ended after two games due to injury.

Born in Ryehill, Wakefield on 10 June 1933, Grainger played football for schools in the South Elmsall area and got his break into the sport through a cousin, Dennis Grainger, who scored six goals in 40 appearances for Leeds when professional football resumed after World War 2. Part of a footballing family, Dennis's brother, Jack, played for Southport, Barnsley and guested for Leeds during World War 2. Another brother, Horace, played for Chesterfield.

Grainger served his apprenticeship at Wrexham and the teenager went on to play for Sheffield United and Sunderland during the 1950s. Winning the first of seven England caps in May 1956, Grainger scored twice against Brazil at Wembley in a sensational 4–2 win. The clash was the first meeting of the two countries and the debutant struck with his first touch before nodding in England's fourth in a famous win.

Grainger's arrival at Leeds was seen as a positive move but he was unable to halt Leeds' slide into mid-table mediocrity despite scoring in wins at Southampton before successive home victories against Plymouth Argyle and Charlton Athletic. It was a season when United shipped 38 goals at home and away, with goal action never in short supply. Grainger scored in a 4–4 draw at Bristol Rovers and played in a 5–4 League Cup defeat at Southampton as Leeds bowed out in its first appearance of the competition. The tournament was in its infancy and Grainger had lined up in United's goalless bow against Blackpool before scoring the third in a 3–1 replay win at Bloomfield Road.

Following Revie's appointment, Grainger was in the starting line up that lost to Portsmouth and stayed in the United XI for Revie's home managerial debut versus Sheffield United but a cartilage injury ended his playing days in West Yorkshire. A cultured footballer, Grainger represented the Football League and could also belt out a tune. Known as the 'Singing Winger' on the music circuit, Grainger went on to play for Port Vale and Doncaster Rovers after 37 appearances for Leeds including two as the Revie era began.

* * * * *

EDDIE GRAY was a majestic sight waltzing down the left wing for Leeds United. A prodigious talent, Gray was blessed with breathtaking skills making him one of the most dangerous footballers of his generation. Idolised as a player, Gray won numerous honours despite spells out through injury.

Born in Glasgow on 17 January 1948, Gray was a schoolboy international and had 30 clubs vying to sign him when he joined United as an apprentice professional. The fact that he turned down his boyhood club Celtic, like younger brother Frank a few years later, shows Don Revie's powers of persuasion. Revie's vision for the club must have impressed the youngster. A member of United's U18 squad packed with talent, Gray developed alongside David Harvey, Peter Lorimer, Terry Hibbitt, Jimmy Greenhoff and Mick Bates. United's production line was at its height and only three of a 15-man squad failed to play in the first team.

Gray turned professional in January 1965 and 12 months later scored on his league debut against Sheffield Wednesday in a 3–0 victory at Elland Road on New Years Day in 1966. And with just three starts to his name, Revie showed amazing belief when he handed Gray a European debut in a semi-final clash against Spanish giants Real Zaragoza. Showing great potential and maturity as well as natural ability, Gray played in the return leg but missed out on the play off game when United went down 3–1.

Gray was a regular in the first team on merit in 1966–67 but not in his future position on the left wing as Albert Johanneson occupied that position. Playing in the forward line and as a replacement for Johnny Giles when the midfield schemer was sidelined, Gray featured in plenty of big time games. In the FA Cup, Gray played when United bowed out to Chelsea in controversial fashion after Lorimer had a last minute equaliser ruled out. And in Europe, Gray helped Leeds overcame Valencia, Bologna and Kilmarnock on route to the final before playing in the first leg defeat against Dinamo Zagreb, the team that eventually won the trophy on aggregate.

Gray had donned the number 11 shirt on occasions before succeeding Johanneson by the end of a thrilling 1967–68 campaign as major honours finally arrived at Elland Road. Playing in every round of the League Cup run, Gray scored a vital goal as United overcame Derby County in a two-legged semi-final before picking up a first domestic honour against Arsenal at Wembley when his corner set up the winning goal by Cooper. Gray was also in fine form in Europe before another semi-final goal edged Leeds past Dundee to reach a second Fairs Cup final. Gray played in a physical opening leg against Ferencvaros but missed the return in Budapest through injury as his teammates made it a cup double.

The 1968–69 campaign would be historic as United landed the Division 1 title for the first time and Gray was in on the action after missing a number of games early in the campaign. During a record breaking season, Gray struck important goals including the winner against Everton and, important efforts over the run-in as United picked up a draw at West Brom and a home win against Leicester City in the penultimate home game of the season.

When fully fit, Gray was compared to the most celebrated footballer of his generation who played in the same position, George Best. But Gray had plenty of supporters backing his corner as he teased, tormented and bamboozled uncompromising defenders determined to stop him in his tracks. Gray scored the opening goal in the Charity Shield victory against FA Cup winners Manchester City and was in fine form at the start of the 1969–70 season securing successive away wins at Sheffield Wednesday and Coventry City but was out of action by the turn of the year.

Returning to the side Gray helped Leeds reach an FA Cup final and European Cup semi-final as United battled for an unprecedented treble. Fixture congestion ended the title defence but after being out for two months Gray played in weakened sides to improve his match fitness. Four decades on, fans still applaud his efforts in a home clash against Burnley. First team players Lorimer and Paul Madeley also played but Gray, wearing an unfamiliar number six jersey, stole the headlines when he scored both United's goals in a 2–1 win. Gray's 35-yard lob over the stranded Burnley 'keeper was top draw but his solo effort continues to make mesmeric viewing. Both stand out among his 69 goals for the club.

Goal scoring aside Gray reserved his most audacious exhibition of wing-play for the cup final. In a virtuoso performance on a horrendous surface at Wembley after it hosted the *Horse of the Year Show*, Gray ripped the Chelsea defence apart, and David Webb in particular, to deservedly win the Man of the Match award following the 2–2 draw.

A brutal replay meant Gray was unable to have the same influence at Old Trafford as Leeds went down to defeat.

The '69–70 campaign would be the last time Gray featured in 40 games under Revie due a succession of injury blows. And Fairs Cup campaigns were particularly cruel as injuries dashed hopes in two finals. After missing out on the second leg in 1968, an awkward fall in an abandoned first leg against Juventus forced Gray to miss Leeds' 1971 triumph.

Returning to fitness in 1971–72, Gray was on fire in iconic wins before *Match of the Day* cameras against Manchester United and Southampton prior to helping Leeds triumph in the FA Cup final against Arsenal. Gray played in a fourth Wembley final when Leeds suffered a shock FA Cup defeat to Sunderland but his European jinx struck again when he missed the Cup Winners Cup final debacle against AC Milan. After coming through pre-season Gray played in the opening league games of the 1973–74 season before injury ruled him out once more as United landed a second title.

Returning to fitness after Revie's departure, Gray played in the European Cup final with Jimmy Armfield at the helm. As with his club career injuries also affected Gray's international career. Having represented Scotland at Schoolboy and U23 level, a full Scottish cap followed against England in the 1969 Home International Championships but just 12 caps were spread over seven seasons. One can only wonder what the world media would have made of Scotland in the 1974 World Cup finals if there was a fit Gray, who notched three goals for his country.

As a transition period began at Elland Road, finally Gray experienced an injury-free run through the remainder of the decade. Playing for various managers, Gray again thrilled supporters and scored his only career hat-trick in a 5–1 triumph over Leicester City in March '78. The match was notable as the second occasion Eddie and Frank scored in a game together, the previous time was in a 2–1 win at Norwich City in October '76. During this period Leeds failed to win silverware but reached cup semi-finals and qualified for Europe again in 1978–79. Converting to left-back in 1980, within weeks of being voted Player of the Year in 1981–82, Gray planned for life in Division 2.

Appointed player-manager in May 1984, Gray blooded promising apprentices and results improved but it was a thankless task. And after three years at the helm his association with the club ended. Supporters were outraged, but Gray departed with dignity. Gray had witnessed the club's rise to Division 1 into one of European football's most feared teams but had also seen the club's decline to Division 2 minnows.

Varying posts ensued at Whitby Town, Middlesbrough, Rochdale, Hull City and Whitby Town before Gray returned to Elland Road as youth team coach. Guiding the class of 1997 to an FA Youth Cup, Gray also saw the reserves win a Pontins League Division 1 title for the first time in 61 years. Promoted to the first team set-up and eventually boss again, Gray endured a roller-coaster ride from Champions League contenders to Premiership relegation.

A popular radio pundit, Gray will always be remembered for his footballing skills, and rightly so, because he is arguably the most naturally gifted player to grace the club. When on song Gray was unstoppable and no defender in the world was safe. Seventh on the all-time appearances list, Gray played 561 (18 sub) games and was a sensational footballer during the Revie revolution.

* * * * *

FRANK GRAY was an elegant footballer and sublime passer of the ball for Leeds United. A Celtic follower like elder brother Eddie already at Elland Road, Gray refused overtures from his boyhood team and those of 30 other clubs to join United as an apprentice in November '71. It was a brave decision, as comparisons with Eddie would be made. But Leeds were at the height of their powers so young Frank's choice was understandable.

Born in Glasgow on 27 October 1954, Gray was a star attraction at Glasgow schools and quickly broke into the Leeds first team as a substitute against Leicester City in February 1973. Within two months he'd scored on his full debut against Crystal Palace. And with three league starts to his credit plus substitute appearances to his name including a European bow against Rapid Bucharest, astonishingly, Frank's first campaign ended with a first team spot in the European Cup Winners Cup final against AC Milan.

Injuries and suspensions hit United but in an infamous clash,

European football suffered one of its blackest nights following a shocking refereeing display. In Don Revie's final season as manager, Gray was in the first team squad but used sporadically in 1973–74, making six appearances including starts in home wins over Southampton and Manchester City as a second title arrived at Elland Road.

With the Division 1 race paramount, Gray played in all six of United's UEFA Cup matches, scoring his first European goal with a right foot strike against Stromsgodset. United bowed out to Vitoria Setubal, but European Cup battles lay ahead. And following the 44-day debacle under Brian Clough, mid-way through the 1974–75 campaign new boss Jimmy Armfield gave Gray his opportunity at left-back and Frank obliged with cultured performances against Anderlecht and Barcelona in a memorable run to the final.

A member of the side that lost to Bayern Munich at the Parc des Princes Stadium the future centred on Gray junior and the likes of fellow Scots Joe Jordan and Gordon McQueen. And in 1975–76 with McQueen and Jordan absent for long spells, Gray made his mark. A terrific reader of the game, Gray played in every league and cup game, the only squad player to do so. Bizarrely Gray's two goals came in successive games as United defeated Coventry City and drew with Derby County when his unflappable temperament made him a natural penalty taker, converting his first against the Rams.

Having represented Scotland at Schoolboy and U23 level, a full Scottish debut came against Switzerland though he would have to wait until 1978–79 to gain regular selection. As Revie's legends moved on Leeds failed to win silverware during the late seventies but reached three Cup semi-finals. During a transitional period, Frank and Eddie got on the score sheet for the first time in a 2–1 win at Norwich in October '76. The duo also found the target when Eddie bagged a hat-trick versus Leicester City in April 78.

Gray enjoyed his most prolific season in front of goal in 1978–79 when he notched 10 goals including five spot kicks to finish second equal top scorer with Ray Hankin, Graham and Currie behind John Hawley as European qualification came again. As United took up the challenge of the UEFA Cup, Cloughie tempted Gray to Nottingham Forest for a club record £500,000 in July 1979 and during a two-year spell enjoyed his most productive period as a player as Forest defended the European Cup.

But he was soon back at his spiritual home with former teammate Allan Clarke at the helm. Much had changed since Gray's departure and in a traumatic league campaign Leeds lost its top-flight status. During the close season, as Leeds pondered life in Division 2, Gray participated in the World Cup finals in all Scotland's games. And in a distinguished career for his country won 32 caps.

Gray's remaining years at Leeds would see brother Eddie at the helm. Frank added experience in defence or midfield to a young team but by 1985–86 needed a fresh challenge and helped Sunderland win promotion from Division 3 before guiding Darlington as player-coach to the GM Vauxhall Conference title prior to managerial spells at Harrogate Town, Al Manamah (Bahrain), Farnborough Town, Woking and Basingstoke Town.

The Gray dynasty continued when Frank's son Andy made his Leeds United debut. Remarkably in his fourth start, aged 18, Andy played in the 1996 League Cup final but his stay would last two seasons and he'd notch up 28 appearances. As for dad Frank, who scored 35 league and cup goals during 396 (9 sub) appearances, over 12 years at Elland Road when transition was the order of the day in Division 1 and 2, United followers witnessed a touch of class season after season.

* * * * *

JIMMY GREENHOFF came to prominence in the early stages of his footballing career at Leeds United playing his part as major honours arrived at the club. Leeds supporters only saw the formative years of Greenhoff in the mid-sixties but he made a valuable contribution to the development of Don Revie's side. The arrival of Mick Jones for a record transfer ultimately saw Greenhoff move on in the midst of a European final. An intelligent striker who scored his share of goals and also set up the ball for better placed colleagues, Greenhoff went on to be a three-time Wembley winner.

Born in Barnsley on 19 June 1946, Greenhoff represented Barnsley and Yorkshire schools before serving his apprenticeship at Elland Road. Among a number of gifted players in United's U18 squad, Greenhoff was one of the first to shine from a group that included

David Harvey, Peter Lorimer, Terry Hibbitt, Eddie Gray and Mick Bates in its ranks.

The 1962–63 campaign was one of consolidation as Revie blooded a number of talented youngsters including Gary Sprake, Paul Reaney, Norman Hunter, Rod Johnson and Lorimer. Starting out as a right-sided midfield player, Greenhoff lined up for his senior debut against Southampton in the penultimate game of the season. Though United lost 3–1 to Saints the 17-year-old remained in the line up at Swindon Town for the final match. And during a 5–0 rout Revie's side served notice that they were ready to challenge for promotion after finishing in a creditable fifth place.

With Bobby Collins guiding Revie's young charges, Greenhoff knew further opportunities would come and true to his word Revie experimented in the League Cup. Greenhoff made his cup bow in a 2–0 win over Swansea Town and when Billy Bremner was sidelined briefly during the Division 2 title run-in, helped United claim victories over Southampton and Middlesbrough.

United's first season back in Division I under Revie went better than pundits predicted and Greenhoff made his top-flight debut in a 3–2 triumph over Leicester City. Making nine league appearances, Greenhoff grabbed a first senior goal in a 3–2 win at Stoke City and repeated the effort in the return fixture. In between, the young striker set Leeds on the way to an FA Cup win over Southport in the third round but it would be his sole contribution on the road to Wembley. During a memorable season that saw Leeds as runners-up in both league and cup, Greenhoff played 11 games and was on an upward curve.

Waiting for an opportunity however was frustrating but when called upon during the latter stages of 1965–66 Greenhoff impressed in Fairs Cup semi-final clashes against Real Zaragoza during the club's first foray into Europe.

The 1966–67 campaign saw Greenhoff take advantage of an extended run in the first team with a change of role as injury sidelined United's main striker, Alan Peacock. Preferred to Rod Belfitt, Greenhoff scored 10 goals in 43 league and appearances. A gifted footballer, Greenhoff's control, distribution, composure and instinct made him a natural leading the line. Opening his goal account in a 3–1 win against Leicester City, Greenhoff was also on target in victories of the same score versus Burnley and Fulham. Arguably his best display came against Tottenham Hotspur when a Greenhoff brace earned a 3–2 win before grabbing the winner to see off defending champions Liverpool at Elland Road. The young striker played throughout domestic cup competitions that ended in a 7–0 League Cup drubbing at West Ham and in a controversial FA Cup semi-final loss to Chelsea. Greenhoff matured as a player in Europe, hitting a crucial goal against Valencia as United marched to the Fairs Cup final though Dinamo Zagreb won on aggregate.

When the 1967–68 season began there was speculation a new striker would be purchased. A record £100,000 fee duly brought Jones to the club undermining Greenhoff's position. But with Jones cup-tied and Mike O'Grady struggling with injury, Greenhoff enjoyed his longest run in the side, playing 58 games. And the campaign brought silverware in the shape of the Football League Cup while United also reached a second successive FA Cup semi-final and Fairs Cup final. Throughout a thrilling season Greenhoff was an integral part of the first team. Lining up in all League Cup and Fairs Cup ties Greenhoff finished second top scorer with 18 goals. Among strikes was a first Leeds hat-trick in a 5–0 league win over Fulham and a League Cup brace at Sunderland as Leeds pushed for a Wembley spot where Greenhoff collected his first major honour.

At the start of the 1968–69 season, Greenhoff played in the delayed Fairs Cup final first leg against Ferencvaros and opening three league fixtures but was dropped for a trip to Ipswich Town as Revie reintroduced a fit again O'Grady. Within days, Greenhoff joined Birmingham City for £70,000. Revie was building a strong squad so it was tough hanging on to all his talented players but it was still a shock to Leeds fans when this popular striker left.

Following a three-year spell at St Andrews, Greenhoff moved to Stoke City where he won a second League Cup before a £200,000 transfer took him to Manchester United. And in his third Wembley final, Greenhoff was credited with the winning goal to take the FA Cup back to Old Trafford. Greenhoff went on to play for Canadian side Toronto Blizzard prior to holding coaching and managerial posts at Crewe, Rochdale and Port Vale. Greenhoff played on four occasions for the England U23s but was somewhat unfortunate not to win a full cap. During a terrific career Greenhoff was an important squad member at Leeds, scoring 33 goals in 128 (8 sub) appearances, as they became a major force in the game.

* * * * *

GRENVILLE HAIR played in Leeds United's first team through the fifties into the early sixties. A reliable 'old school' full back, whether on the left or right flank, Hair experienced two promotions and relegation. Straddling two generations of players Hair lined up alongside John Charles in his pomp, witnessed the development of Jack Charlton, felt the impact of Bobby Collins and saw the potential United's youth policy could offer. Stylish on and off the park, Hair departed with the club on the threshold of glory.

Born in Burton upon Trent on 16 November 1931, Hair's arrival at Elland Road from Newhall United in November 1948 coincided with Major Frank Buckley starting the task of replacing players whose careers had ended during World War 2. Naturally fit, Major Buckley persuaded Hair to pursue a career in football rather than develop his prowess in athletics—a talent first shown at Burton Technical High School.

Buckley's success would be the club's gain but Hair would not make his Division 2 debut until late in the 1950–51 campaign at Leicester City with right-back Jimmy Dunn sidelined. Leeds finished in a respectable fifth place and the following term Hair replaced stalwart left-back Jim Milburn as the team improved with Charles rewriting the club's goal scoring records. Partnering Dunn in the full back berths, Hair was measured in his approach to supporting forays in attack.

By 1955–56, Raich Carter was manager and with Charles moving back into attack with the introduction of Charlton to the defensive unit, United made a promotion charge to perfection finishing runners-up behind champions Sheffield Wednesday. A determined footballer, fine passer of the ball and tough tackler, Hair could test his abilities against fifties icons Stan Matthews, Stan Mortensen and Nat Lofthouse. And an ever-present for the third time in 1956–57, Hair was not out of place in such exalted company.

Indeed, he was somewhat unlucky not to gain England selection. But having already made a tour to the West Indies with an FA representative team, Hair joined future FA tours to Nigeria and Ghana and New Zealand during the decade. Without Charles, Leeds struggled for goals and after three seasons surviving the drop under Carter, Bill Lambton and Jack Taylor, Hair experienced relegation for the first time.

Dunn had departed at the end of the 1958–59 season but United bosses realised his effectiveness with Hair in the full back slots and for six seasons between '52–53 and '57–58 the duo pulled on the number 2 and 3 shirts in 240 out of 260 league and cup matches. During United's slump to Division 2 whilst Hair displayed his usual consistency, new full back partners included James Ashall, Alf Jones and Terry Caldwell. Don Revie had been a teammate for over two seasons and on his appointment as manager asked his stalwart full back to switch to right-back to accommodate recent signing John Kilford's arrival at the club. Hair duly slotted in for a 2–1 defeat to Sheffield United and in the remaining seven games tasted one triumph, but it was sweet as United thumped Lincoln City 7–0.

Twelve months on it looked certain Hair would be playing Division 3 football. As Revie searched for consistency in defence Hair took up both full back positions as Eric Smith, Willie Bell, Jones and Cliff Mason slotted in for opposite flank defensive duties. Joining Mason among Revie's late season purchases was Collins and his arrival provided the impetus for an unbeaten run that ensured safety on the final day of the season at Newcastle United. And the run included Hair's sole league goal for the club when he opened the scoring in a priceless home win against Middlesbrough.

After years of waiting for a goal Hair doubled his tally in 1962–63 against Stoke City in an FA Cup clash before Leeds went out to Middlesbrough. In the Division 2 campaign Hair made 26 appearances and saw a renaissance as youngsters Gary Sprake, Paul Reaney and Norman Hunter made the first team on a regular basis.

However, when Revie selected his United XI for the opening encounter of the 1963–64 season versus Rotherham, Hair was omitted and must have sensed that his days at Leeds were numbered. Revie's defensive unit comprising Sprake, Reaney, Bell, Charlton and Hunter would form the backbone on which the Revie team would see promotion achieved. Hair did make 10 league and cup appearances but was no longer automatic choice with Bell's conversion to left-back.

During the close season Hair joined Wellington Town as player-manager before taking up a coaching position at Bradford City.

Appointed manager in 1968, tragically one month into the post he suffered a fatal heart attack in a training session and died aged 36. A tremendous servant to Leeds, Hair's many assets made him an indispensable member of the team in 474 appearances. Only a select number of players gave an entire career to United. Hair's loyalty was exemplary.

* * * * *

TOM HALLETT made one appearance for Leeds United during seven years at the club. Arriving at Elland Road shortly after his 15th birthday, Hallett stayed on the fringes of the first team until the 1962–63 season when he made his senior bow.

Born in Glenneath, near Swansea on 10 April 1939, Hallett impressed as a youngster and won Welsh Schoolboy honours. United had found success in its scouting policy in South Wales, most notably when spotting John Charles a few years earlier at a similar age. And tracking the progress of Hallett duly signed the promising half back as an apprentice in June 1954. Gary Sprake would also make the journey to Elland Road from the region.

Breaking through would prove tough in the late fifties as Bill Lambton and Jack Taylor succeeded Carter prior to Don Revie's appointment. In the midst of all the managerial changes and subsequent relegation, Hallett was unable to make the senior side. During an era of decline following the departure of Charles after an exceptional Leeds career, Hallett was competing for a place with a number of players including Irish international Wilbur Cush in the late fifties.

Upon Revie's elevation to the post of manager Peter McConnell got the nod. The 1962–63 campaign saw an improved performance as the results of the club's youth policy began to bring dividends. But while the likes of Sprake, Paul Reaney, Norman Hunter and Rod Johnson had been granted opportunities, Hallett was still waiting his chance. The talented quartet had made their bow and was again in the United XI when Revie named his side to travel to Ewood Park for a midweek League Cup clash against Blackburn Rovers. Hallett's opportunity had been belatedly granted for the cup clash. Since the tournament's inception in 1960–61, Revie had blooded talented youngsters for experience. Hallett at the age of 23 could not be classed in that category but his opening came with Jack Charlton being unavailable for selection. On a dismal night for the side, Blackburn ran riot, winning 4–0, but by all accounts the score would have been higher except for an inspirational performance from rookie 'keeper Sprake. Two goals adrift at the break, Blackburn sealed a comfortable win with two goals in the final three minutes, Rovers and future England centre-forward Fred Pickering scoring the final goal.

Hallett would not make another appearance for United and joined Swindon Town during the close season before returning to West Yorkshire to play close to 200 games for Bradford City. As with other players that failed to break into the United side on a regular basis, pinpointing an exact reason is tough but like those who never made it at Elland Road, Hallett has the distinction of being among a select group of 75 players to play for Revie.

* * * * *

PETER HAMPTON was the last Leeds United player to be selected by Don Revie to play in a European match. Signed by the club in September 1971, Hampton made three appearances during Revie's last two seasons at Elland Road including a UEFA Cup clash at Vitoria Setubal in December '73.

Born in Oldham on 12 September 1954, Hampton, a resolute full back, was a product of Bishop Auckland School and Durham County Schools. Initially an outside left, like Terry Cooper a decade earlier, Hampton converted to the left-back position. Biding his time, Hampton made fleeting appearances for five seasons at the club. His senior debut came at Southampton due to injuries towards the end of the 1972–73 season as Leeds edged towards two cup finals.

Trevor Cherry, adaptable in defence or midfield, slotted in at right-back while Hampton made his bow in a weakened United line up that had a number of younger players looking to impress including Joe Jordan. Leeds lost 3–1 with Norman Hunter scoring for the visitors. A week before Wembley when United faced Sunderland, Revie named Peter Lorimer and Mick Jones from his regular United XI for the penultimate game at Birmingham City. Ringing the changes, Chris Galvin, Gary Liddell, Jimmy Mann and Hampton got run-outs. Jordan scored for Leeds in a 2–1 defeat.

The following season brought disappointment for Hampton as he failed to make an appearance while United motored towards a second league title. But he did make a European bow in a 3–1 loss to Setubal, which proved to be Revie's final European game as manager. The departure of Revie and subsequent arrival of new manager Jimmy Armfield saw Hampton remain part of the first team squad.

A non-playing reserve in the European Cup final against Bayern Munich, Hampton came into the new season hoping for fresh opportunities as a transitional phase began at the club. The 1975–76 campaign would yield just one substitute appearance but Hampton made the most of his chance when he grabbed the headlines with a peach of left foot strike from outside the penalty box to seal a 2–1 win over Burnley.

When Frank Gray moved to midfield during the 1976–77 season, Armfield brought Hampton into the left-back spot. Astute, determined and a resolute tackler, Hampton joined the attack when an opportunity arose. At last he had a chance to hold down a place and during an extended run helped United reach the FA Cup semi-finals. During a memorable run, Leeds overcame Norwich City when Hampton notched the final goal in a 5–2 triumph. They then went on to play Birmingham City, Manchester City and Wolves before Manchester United ended Leeds' Wembley dreams.

It had been a great season for the young defender, who also scored against Norwich in a league win, but the following term he was sidelined until the New Year and missed out on United making a run to the League Cup semi-finals. With Gray and Cherry occupying the left-back slot, bar a brief run at the start of the 1979–80 campaign, Hampton failed to make the starting line up and moved to Stoke City during the close season.

The eighties saw Hampton make over 100 appearances for Stoke and Burnley before winding down his career at Rochdale and Carlisle United. Hampton had a frustrating spell at Elland Road but can point to two claims to fame for statisticians as Leeds won all three games in which he scored a goal during 76 (7 sub) appearances and he completed the list of players to represent the club in Europe under Revie.

* * * * *

DAVID HARVEY took seven years to break into the first team on a regular basis after making his debut but eventually became one of the club's greatest goalkeepers. Composed, determined and courageous Harvey grasped his opportunity towards the end of United's 1971–72 campaign and went on to excel for Scotland at the 1974 World Cup.

Born in Leeds on 7 February 1948, Harvey represented Leeds City Boys. His form brought him to the attention of United's scouts and he soon joined a crop of youngsters in the U18 squad that would make it all the way in the game. Of United's 15-man squad that included Mick Bates, Peter Lorimer, Terry Hibbitt, Jimmy Greenhoff, Rod Belfitt and Eddie Gray only three failed to make the first team. Harvey signed professional forms in February 1965 and at the age of 17 made his senior debut as Revie continued to launch the careers of talented players in the League Cup.

Harvey kept goal against West Brom on a night when Nigel Davey and Denis Hawkins also made first team starts. But it was a baptism of fire as the Baggies rattled in four goals inside 25 minutes. United showed character to reduce the deficit to 4–2 by full time. For the rookie 'keeper it was a tough night of action but he was at the start of a brilliant career though he'd have to contend with being Gary Sprake's understudy, playing 200 games for the reserves before getting his big chance.

Nobody could have blamed Harvey if he had decided to join another team but his dedication would pay off in a 17-year career at the club. An extremely hard trainer, Harvey put himself through punishing schedules to develop his skills and gave his all, even in defeat. Following a league debut at home to Fulham when United lost by the odd goal in 1965–66, fleeting appearances included a 7–0 drubbing at West Ham in the League Cup, before his European bow in 1967–68 versus minnows Spora Luxembourg in a 9–0 goal fest. Harvey enjoyed notable displays in the Fairs Cup adventure including a quarter-final tie at home to Rangers and semi-final leg at Dundee as Leeds reached the final to take on Ferencvaros.

Competing with Sprake for the 'keeper's jersey, Harvey displayed unbelievable patience and loyalty to wait for a chance. Revie's man-management skills were of paramount importance because a 'keeper of Harvey's calibre could have walked into other first teams but United's boss knew he needed two class goalkeepers with the team battling on all fronts. And it came to the fore as Leeds embarked on a treble bid in the 1969–70 season.

When the title defence ended Revie called on his reserves to conclude league fixtures and Harvey was in goal at Derby County when a reserve XI hogged the back page headlines following a 4–1 defeat. Harvey was also between the sticks when Gray produced two moments of magic to dismantle Burnley. Neither experience could prepare him for his last appearances of a tumultuous season dominated by fixture congestion. With Sprake picking an injury in a European Cup semi-final clash against Celtic at Hampden Park, Harvey ran out in front of a record 136,500 spectators for the fixture. Shortly afterwards he kept goal against Chelsea in an FA Cup final replay, both matches ending in a 2–1 defeat to destroy United's treble dreams.

Another brief run followed in '70–71 before the turning point of his career came following a majestic display in his third league appearance of the season at Stoke City in April '72. With an FA Cup semi-final against Birmingham City looming, Revie had a massive decision to make. Should he retain Harvey after 45 games in all competitions or bring back a fit again Sprake, a veteran of over 500 games? On the morning of the match, Harvey won the vote. Who knows what Revie's thought process was, but maybe he had finally decided that for all Sprake's natural ability he could not risk any more costly errors in high profile matches. Harvey's calm display against the Blues vindicated Revie's decision and in the final at Wembley he gave a faultless performance in United's Centenary cup win against Arsenal, finally sealing his place in first team.

As for his first campaign as United 'keeper in 1972–73, Harvey helped Leeds reach the FA Cup and European Cup Winners Cup finals. Although Leeds won neither trophy, regular football resulted in Harvey winning international recognition with his Scotland debut coming against Denmark in November 1972.

Leeds began the 1973–74 Division 1 season with an astonishing 29-game unbeaten run, and during a memorable campaign clinched the title with a game to spare. One of five United 'keepers to play in all competitions in '73–74, and four in Europe (both club records), to cap a great season Harvey played in the World Cup finals in West Germany. Though Scotland failed to get beyond the initial group stages, his sensational performances against Brazil, Yugoslavia and Zaire resulted in him winning an award for being the best goalkeeper in the tournament. Harvey would go on to win 16 caps for Scotland.

Following Revie's departure, Harvey missed a spot kick against Liverpool in a Charity Shield penalty shoot out defeat at Wembley. And after Jimmy Armfield replaced Clough as manager, a bad car crash ended his campaign prematurely. Thereafter, Harvey remained first choice bar spells out for injury when David Stewart stepped in. Leeds failed to win silverware but Harvey helped United reach two League Cup semi-finals and qualify for Europe again, his final European game coming in a 4–0 win over Maltese side Valletta.

Harvey decided to accept a new challenge in 1980 and played for Vancouver Whitecaps and Drogheda in Ireland before adding vital experience to Gray's young Leeds team in Division 2. Skipper for two seasons, Harvey helped nurture young guns like John Sheridan, Tommy Wright and Scott Sellers before severing links with the club in 1985. Following a six-match spell at Bradford City, Harvey retired from the game.

Great things come to those that wait and that was certainly the case for this modest, loyal goalkeeper. Watching from the sidelines season after season as United took on all-comers at home and abroad says much about Harvey's character. Making 445 (2 sub) appearances, Harvey won the top domestic honours in the game. A first class 'keeper, one can only speculate whether Revie might have led United to more silverware had he brought him into the first team earlier. Whatever the discussions and debate, Harvey was indeed a top notch goalkeeper.

* * * * *

DENNIS HAWKINS joined a crack squad of apprentices at Leeds United but would make four appearances for the first team. A tricky forward, Hawkins made his debut at 17 years of age but was up against stiff competition for places and only featured over a three-year period.

Born in Swansea on 22 October 1947, Hawkins was spotted by United scouts and turned professional in October 1964. Revie had a philosophy of blooding teenagers into the senior set up in League Cup ties to see how they adapted to life in the first team. And 12 months after joining the professional ranks Hawkins got his opportunity the same night 'keeper David Harvey kept goal and full back Nigel Davey lined up in defence. For the young striker it would be a tough encounter as West Brom blitzed United's makeshift outfit with four first half goals before Leeds found the net. Revie's half time pep talk saw his charges battle away and reduce the deficit to 4–2 by full time.

At age 17, there was plenty of time to develop and following the first of a handful of Welsh U23 caps, versus Scotland in November '66, Hawkins played in the final league game of 1966–67. With a top four finish secured and a Fairs Cup semi-final with Kilmarnock to negotiate days away, Revie selected a shadow side to take on Sheffield Wednesday at Elland Road. Aside from Hawkins, United included Harvey, Mick Bates, Terry Hibbitt, Rod Johnson and Jimmy Lumsden against Wednesday. Hibbitt sealed a 1–0 win for the patched up team.

United were developing each season but Revie was still trying to strengthen his forward line and the acquisition of Mick Jones spelt the end for Hawkins chances of making it at Leeds. Hawkins did make two further appearances in 1967–68, at Nottingham Forest in a league win when Jones was injured and against Sunderland in a League Cup tie as Leeds marched to a first domestic trophy. Substituted in both games, Hawkins departed four years after signing for the club.

Joining Shrewsbury Town, Hawkins played briefly in the lower leagues for Chester, Workington Town and Newport County. It is tough to evaluate Hawkins' time at Leeds, especially as he was challenging for a forward spot with Jimmy Greenhoff, Peter Lorimer and Johnson. The day United tabled a record transfer bid for Jones demonstrated the ambition Revie had set to make his team successful—unfortunately Hawkins was not part of Revie's ambitions.

* * * * *

JOHN HAWKSBY made a cracking start to his Leeds United career scoring twice in his opening two senior games. A skilful winger, Hawksby had clear potential but the teenager was not able to cement a first team spot and failed to hit another goal as Revie's Leeds battled for Division 2 survival.

Born in York on 12 June 1942, Hawksby represented England Schoolboys against Wales, Scotland and East Germany in 1959. Joining Leeds the same year, Hawksby impressed manager Jack Taylor to give him a senior debut in the third league game of the 1960–61 season.

Replacing Revie, sidelined through injury, Hawksby enjoyed a sensational debut against Rotherham United when he opened the scoring in a 2–0 win. Two days later, Hawskby repeated his goal scoring effort with the opening goal of a thrilling 4–4 draw at Bristol Rovers. A replacement for Revie again in another 4–4 thriller, this time at home to Middlesbrough, Hawksby made five more appearances in a disjointed season that saw Revie become manager.

Appearing twice for the new boss after his appointment in March '61 as a replacement for left-winger Colin Grainger, United drew at Luton Town and tasted defeat at Scunthorpe United. The arrival of South African winger Albert Johanneson saw Hawksby drop out of the first team but he quickly returned when United made a woeful start to the 1961–62 season, winning two of their opening seven fixtures. Replacing Johanneson, Hawksby played 25 matches but struggled, as did many of his teammates, to find any consistency.

In need of inspiration, Revie signed Cliff Mason to add experience to the defensive effort but the big signing was Bobby Collins. And the transfer had an instant impact on the side. One defeat in 11 games saw United survive the drop on the final day of the season. Hawksby played in seven of these crucial games before losing his place to Johanneson but returned for United's 'must-win' last game in place of inside-forward Noel Peyton. Leeds won 3–0 at Newcastle United ensuring safety.

Thereafter, Hawksby would make little impact on the first team. Following cup appearances as United bowed out of the League Cup at Manchester City and FA Cup to Everton in 1963–64, Hawksby joined Lincoln City at the beginning of the new season. Still 22 years of age, while former teammates began life in top-flight football, Hawksby helped Lincoln and hometown team York City survive relegation from the Football League before seeing out his career at non-league clubs, his longest spell at Kettering Town. Hawksby's 45-game United career failed to take off in the way he hoped as a teenager with bags of talent but he was not alone in a challenging period at Elland Road.

* * * * *

TOMMY HENDERSON was one of Don Revie's first signings after Leeds United survived relegation to Division 3 in his first full season in charge. A tricky right winger with drive, energy and the right attitude on and off the pitch, Henderson was an asset to Revie's team as it developed in Division 2.

Born in Larkhall on 25 July 1943, Lanarkshire, Henderson played for Larkhall Academy and scored against England Schoolboys playing alongside Scotland teammate Billy Bremner. Trials followed for the schoolboy pals at Arsenal and Chelsea before making the journey south to Elland Road. Henderson returned north of the border due to homesickness.

Henderson's professional career started at Hearts followed by St Mirren where he played in a Scottish Cup final against Rangers in 1962. Leeds had been monitoring his progress and were still keen on the flying Scot. Change was occurring at Elland Road under Revie who had introduced teenagers Gary Sprake, Paul Reaney and Norman Hunter into the first team giving the side a fresh look as he started to mould his own team. Henderson was in the same age bracket and made the return trip to Elland Road as a more confident footballer in a £1,500 transfer deal in November 1962.

With Bobby Collins pulling the strings in midfield, the arrival of Henderson gave Leeds pace on both wings as Albert Johanneson had emerged as a talent on the left flank. Henderson made his debut in a 1–1 draw at Grimsby Town then helped United thump Plymouth Argyle 6–1 at Elland Road. A regular throughout the remainder of the season, Henderson scored once for Leeds in a 4–1 triumph versus Charlton Athletic.

After the trauma experienced in the previous campaign, the 1962–63 league season was one of tangible progress as United pushed for promotion after play resumed following the 'big freeze' that curtailed football across the country. Indeed following a defeat at Sunderland just before Christmas '62, United's next game would not take place until March '63 when Leeds defeated Derby County 3–1. The win heralded a run of 10 wins in 15 games as Revie's side moved up the table. And Henderson played his part making plenty of scoring chances for United's attack led by centre-forward Jim Storrie. Three defeats in May ended a promotion bid as Leeds finished fifth but the message was clear to competitors that a renaissance was underway under Revie. The arrival of Johnny Giles from Manchester United in August '63 ultimately ended Henderson's spell at the club.

Making two appearances in 1963–64, Henderson scored in a 1–1 draw at Portsmouth before a goalless draw at Cardiff City. Henderson was also in the side as United pushed defending league champions Everton in an FA Cup fourth round clash that went to a replay. Over 114,000 fans watched the matches with 66,167 packed into Goodison Park for the replay. Revie's side was flying high in Division 2 on route to top-flight football and had competed with the best.

Henderson remained at the club in 1964–65 when United made its Division 1 debut under Revie appearing in two league games against Nottingham Forest and West Ham. After joining Bury during the close season Henderson went on to play at Swindon Town and Stockport County (where he won a Division 4 title) and Altrincham. Henderson made 34 appearances for Leeds during three seasons at the club. Although not a regular he adopted a winning philosophy and gave total commitment when called upon.

* * * * *

TERRY HIBBITT grabbed the headlines on his Leeds United debut when he scored with his first touch as a professional footballer. Slightly built, Hibbitt was a skilful left sided midfield player who could unlock a defence with a deft touch or pinpoint pass. Whenever called upon Hibbitt never let the team down but was unable to break into the first team on a regular basis due mainly to the form of Eddie Gray.

Born in Doncaster on 1 December 1947, Hibbitt joined United as an apprentice straight from school and signed professional forms in December 1964. A member of a crack U18 squad packed with talent, Hibbitt developed his skills alongside David Harvey, Mick Bates, Peter Lorimer, Jimmy Greenhoff, Rod Belfitt and Eddie Gray. With competition fierce for places Hibbitt had to wait for a chance which finally came at Nottingham Forest in the 1965–66 season. The match was almost called off due to torrential rain but on a tricky surface, Hibbitt replaced Paul Madeley in the first half and announced himself on the football scene by tucking home United's third goal created by Billy Bremner. Leeds went on to win 4–0 at the City Ground.

The following season Hibbitt made a handful of appearances including a European debut in intimidating circumstances, as United took on Valencia in a Fairs Cup second leg clash at the Mestella

Stadium. Hibbitt came in for Albert Johanneson and played his part in a memorable 2–0 win. When United's league challenge had ended, Revie selected a weakened side before taking on Kilmarnock in the Fairs Cup semi-finals. Hibbitt helped demonstrate the squad's strength and struck the only goal in a win against Sheffield Wednesday.

In 1967–68, United's first team took shape as Revie looked for balance on the left wing. Switching Terry Cooper to left-back Hibbitt briefly replaced Johanneson before Gray moved from forward and midfield roles to the number 11 slot. For Hibbitt it was tough, as he'd showed promise with increased appearances in the side, scoring in league wins over Southampton and Coventry City. There were also run outs as United overcame Sunderland and Stoke City on the road to League Cup success as a first major honour arrived at Elland Road. And in a thrilling season, Hibbitt featured in the Fairs Cup journey facing Spora Luxembourg and Partizan Belgrade before his most memorable moment in a Leeds shirt when he helped United lift the trophy in a supreme defensive display at the Nep Stadium against Ferencvaros.

Gray's absence at the start of the 1968–69 season brought Hibbitt a run in the first team but after helping his side make a flying start to the league campaign, winning seven of the opening 10 games, Gray's return meant reserve team football again. It must have been frustrating for Hibbitt as he'd been in great form, scoring in three of the opening games as United defeated Southampton, Queens Park Rangers and Ipswich Town. But Revie's selection of O'Grady and Gray saw Hibbitt revert to a place in the reserves or substitute bench in spite of a telling contribution on the road to a first league title success.

The 1969–70 season saw a similar pattern as United embarked on a treble bid. However, whenever called upon there were solid performances from Hibbitt including his only brace for the club as Leeds humbled Lyn Oslo 16–0 on aggregate in the European Cup for a club record score. After the league challenge faded, Hibbitt's main mini-run summed up his Elland Road career. Hibbitt played in a headline grabbing 'shadow' United XI at Derby County and was in the mix when Gray produced his two moments of magic against Burnley but knew he'd have to move on to get regular first team football.

Following three substitute appearances in the league and a final start against Sarpsborg in the Fairs Cup, Hibbitt joined Newcastle United in August 1971 for £30,000. An elegant footballer, Hibbitt enjoyed the best years of his career during two spells on Tyneside. In the first, Hibbitt provided goal scoring opportunities for Malcolm Macdonald and was a key figure as Newcastle reached the 1974 FA Cup final. Following three seasons at Birmingham City, Hibbitt returned to Newcastle and after 228 games in total retired due to injury.

A player-coach at Gateshead when they won the Northern Premier League, Hibbitt also managed Durham City. Tragically, Terry died aged 46 from cancer in 1994. Hibbitt played infrequently but left his mark for Leeds in 46 (17 sub) games. A member of the first Fairs Cup winning side and squad that lifted the league title in 1968–69, Hibbitt provided strength in depth, as United became a major force in the game.

* * * * *

ALAN HUMPHREYS kept the first clean sheet of the Don Revie era but struggled to fulfil his potential during a two-year spell at Leeds United in the early sixties. After a shaky start Humphreys was first choice goalkeeper by the time Revie became manager but would depart at the end of his first season in charge after being replaced by experienced Scottish international 'keeper Tommy Younger.

Born in Chester on 18 October 1939, Humphreys was a promising centre-half before switching positions to play in goal for Lache Youth Club. Snapped up by Shrewsbury Town at the start of the 1956–57 season Humphreys made the most of his opportunity when he eventually broke into the side. Playing 32 games for the Shropshire club, Shrewsbury gained promotion to the Third Division in 1958–59 and was well on the way to a top three finish the following season when his consistent form persuaded Jack Taylor to bring him to Elland Road in February 1960. But Humphreys, whose form had earned selection to the England U23 squad, endured a torrid start as United spiralled towards relegation in 1959–60.

It could not have been easy for the new 'keeper as he replaced veteran goalkeeper Roy Wood in goal, who in turn had replaced Ted Burgin between the sticks. Playing just three games in March '60, Fulham thumped Leeds 5–0 on his league debut before Blackpool won 4–2 in his home bow a week later. Two Revie goals and a Billy Bremner strike earned a share of the spoils in a midweek fixture against Manchester City but 12 goals conceded in three games saw Burgin restored in goal.

Relegation followed and when United continued to ship goals back in Division 2, Humphreys was brought back into the first team after just three wins from 11 games. Humphreys helped restore a semblance of stability in defence as United racked up eight wins in a 15-game spell mid-season. Bar a three-match losing streak, a flurry of goals from Jim McCole edged Taylor's beleaguered side to mid-table security. United were also playing in the League Cup for the first time and Humphreys helped Leeds claim a first victory in the competition in something of a shock result as top-fight Blackpool were dispatched in a second round replay. Humphreys missed a third round win over Chesterfield but must have wondered if a record score was on when Southampton rattled four goals past him in round four. However, United rallied to level before Reeves scored his fifth of the night to settle a thriller, 5–4, in the last minute. In a bizarre match both teams ended the match with 10 men and the match was halted twice due to floodlight failure. Inconsistency saw Taylor depart from the managerial hot seat and Revie take up the helm. Humphreys was in the line up that faced Portsmouth in his first game in charge while his last match of an eventful season saw United thump Lincoln City 7–0.

First choice when the 1961–62 season kicked off, six defeats in the opening 10 games ended Humphreys' spell in goal for the club as Revie signed veteran Stoke City 'keeper Younger. The season would see Revie play four goalkeepers with Terry Carling and teenager Gary Sprake getting run outs, a joint record at the time after similar statistics in 1924–25 and 1948–49. Shortly after Leeds survived relegation on the final day of the season, Humphreys joined Mansfield Town before ending his career at Chesterfield.

Playing in goal during the early sixties was a daunting task for United 'keepers as the team struggled for form. Humphreys made 44 appearances for the club and in a quirk of fate football threw up his successor. Strangely Stoke 'keeper Younger was in the opposing goal in April '61 when Humphreys kept the first clean sheet of Revie's tenure. Records will also show Humphreys was Revie's first selection for the 'keeper's jersey. Five decades on, it's a noteworthy accolade.

* * * * *

NORMAN HUNTER was a colossus in defence for Don Revie's legendary team and the only ever-present player in Leeds United's Division 1 and Division 2 championship seasons. A ferocious tackler, brave and totally committed, Hunter's reputation preceded him coining the endearing phrase Norman 'Bites Yer Legs'. Renowned as one of football's 'hard' men during the sixties and seventies alongside Ron Harris at Chelsea, Dave Mackay at Tottenham Hotspur and Nobby Stiles at Manchester United, Hunter was an integral part of the Revie revolution. But Hunter was far more than just a tough defender. Blessed with a sweet left peg, Hunter could ping a long pass to teammates or crash a ball home from distance.

Born in Eighton Banks, County Durham on 24 October 1943, Hunter joined the Leeds groundstaff following a trial against Bradford Park Avenue. Revie's second signing, Hunter signed pro forms shortly after the new boss became manager. With United struggling early on in the 1962–63 campaign Hunter was handed a first team debut at Swansea Town. On a landmark date for the club, Hunter along with Gary Sprake, Paul Reaney and Rod Johnson received the news of their debut an hour before kick off at the Vetch Field. The decision signalled, for many historians, the start of the Revie era. By the end of the season Hunter was a fixture in the side and in tandem with Jack Charlton became pillars of a rock solid defence. And the teenage stopper even scored his first goals for the club including a winner against Charlton Athletic in a 2–1 victory.

Among the pre-season favourites for promotion in 1963–64, Leeds' opening game versus Rotherham United saw Bremner-Charlton-Hunter line up as Revie's backbone for the first time. United clinched the title in the final game of the season. Hunter was the only ever-present during the campaign and again notched two goals, against Middlesbrough and Swindon Town.

Following the Division 2 title success, with inspirational skipper Bobby Collins driving his players on, Hunter missed one match as United went close to a remarkable double in 1964–65. And developing a superb understanding alongside Charlton, Reaney and Willie Bell, the best strikers around knew they'd be in for a tough encounter. And they were not disappointed.

In 1965–66, Hunter enjoyed his most prolific season in terms of goals, scoring five including the season's opener against Sunderland

and a brace against West Ham in a 5–0 win. Of course, goals were important but Hunter's tackling ability was his trademark and you had to feel sympathy for a forward challenging him in a 50–50 ball.

Over the years, Hunter's level of consistency was phenomenal and his value to the team immeasurable. The only Leeds player to appear in every major cup final under Revie, Hunter was in the thick of the action as United made the Fairs Cup final in 1966–67 before falling short against Dinamo Zagreb.

Twelve months later, Hunter had collected two winners medals as United landed the League Cup and Fairs Cup. The only player to play every minute of the two cup runs in '67–68 Hunter was immense as United defended with gusto to become only the fourth British team to win a European trophy and first to triumph in the Fairs Cup.

Revie by now had the best-balanced back line around with Terry Cooper replacing Bell at left-back. The combination of Reaney-Charlton-Hunter-Cooper was a sight to behold for the defensive connoisseur. Ever-present during the Division 1 title success in 1968–69, Hunter was also a regular in the side that finished league runners-up on five occasions including United's unforgettable 1969–70 treble season during an amazing era.

Hunter went on to land a second Fairs Cup success in 1970–71 against a powerful Juventus side. Player of the Year that season, Hunter finally got his hands on the FA Cup in 1972 after two losing finals. Defeat to Sunderland 12 months later would be one of the lowest moments of his career as would losing to AC Milan in the European Cup Winners Cup final when he was sent off for retaliation in the most infamous game of the Revie managerial reign. Though some of Hunter's challenges looked brutal and others were rash, Hunter never fouled with intent. And his reputation was such he achieved the ultimate accolade a player can get from peers when he received the inaugural PFA Player of the Year in 1973.

Ever present again when United landed a second league title in 1973–74, Hunter is arguably the fiercest competitor to represent the club but there was much more to his game than just being an effective defender. Blessed with great positional awareness, Hunter could slice a defence open with a raking pass, play his way out of defence with consummate ease or support the attack as he demonstrated against Southampton in '72 in front of the *Match of the Day* cameras when making a goal for Charlton in a 7–0 romp.

Hunter could also pack a thunderous shot as 'keepers found out. Yet of his 21 goals for Leeds his only strike in the FA Cup came in an infamous 3–2 defeat at Colchester United in 1971. Experiencing all Leeds' ups and downs under Revie, following his departure Hunter played in one last final when Bayern Munich ended the club's European Cup dreams. Lining up in every cup final following promotion in 1964, Hunter's consistency and fitness was extraordinary.

During his final three seasons at Leeds, Hunter formed a terrific partnership with Gordon McQueen in the centre of defence. As competitive as ever, Hunter was part of the occasional disagreement on the pitch with opponents including an iconic televised spat with Francis Lee in his Derby County days when the two players were sent off, an event which made the football headlines.

After 16 years at Elland Road, Hunter was one of the first Revie legends to depart, joining Bristol City. Following a three-year spell with Bristol, he joined Barnsley as player-coach, becoming manager when Allan Clarke left for Leeds in 1980. Finally retiring as a player, Hunter guided the Tykes to promotion prior to posts at West Brom, Rotherham, Leeds and Bradford City.

On the international scene, having won three U23s caps for England, Hunter made history on his full debut against Spain when he became the first England player to be capped as a substitute. Playing in defence or midfield, he appeared in two B internationals during the build up to the 1970 World Cup. Hunter came on against West Germany in the Leon quarter-final and went on to win 28 full caps, scoring twice. Hunter was unlucky as he competed for a place with Bobby Moore, which resulted in him winning fewer caps than his talent deserved. But, a member of the 1966 and 1970 World Cup squads, Hunter gave everything for his country. Of all his international appearances, sadly his most notable was an infamous clash against Poland in 1973. The Polish goal was a nightmare but the media reaction was harsh. Hunter also made six appearances for the Football League and played in the Common Market Celebration match in '73.

In recent years, this popular character, who is a regular at Elland Road, has become a favourite on the after-dinner circuit and is an accomplished football pundit. Playing more European ties than any other United player, Hunter made 724 (2 sub) appearances placing him fourth on the all-time list. During a sensational career, from his debut Hunter was ever present in five league campaigns playing in 475 out of 498 possible matches during the Revie era. Hunter is also one of only five players to appear in more than 500 games under Revie. Playing 11 games fewer than Bremner, Hunter appeared in 638 (1 sub) of Revie's 741 games in charge. A legend in every sense, Hunter was a fantastic servant and footballer for Revie's Leeds.

* * * * *

ALBERT JOHANNESON was Don Revie's first signing as manager of Leeds United. The first black footballer to play in an FA Cup final at Wembley, Johanneson possessed blistering pace, amazing skill on the ball and packed a terrific shot. Johanneson's impact, especially in his early years at Elland Road, was all the more remarkable because he was treated as a second class citizen in his native South Africa. And Johanneson played in England during an era when he had to overcome racist taunts from bigoted fans and opponents because he was black. A lack of confidence did hinder his effectiveness on occasions but 'The Black Flash' as United fans affectionately dubbed him was a match winner causing havoc for opposing defenders with dazzling runs on the left wing.

Born in Johannesburg on 13 March 1940, Johanneson arrived at Leeds on a three-month trial following a recommendation by a South African schoolteacher in April 1961. A star for his local 'coloured' school, Johanneson impressed new Leeds boss Revie with his natural ability and made an immediate impact on his debut against Swansea Town by creating one of Jack Charlton's goals in a 2–2 draw. On a historical footing, Johanneson lined up on the opposite flank to Gerry Francis (the club's first black player and South African footballer) at Stoke City in his second game for the club. The duo would play together once more during a 3–1 home defeat to Rotherham United four games into the 1961–62 campaign. Johanneson was out of the side by the time Francis departed for York City but Revie brought his talented winger back for the last five games of a fraught season after the arrival of Bobby Collins inspired renewed confidence and restored fighting spirit to the side. Back in the first team, Johanneson earned a draw at Walsall with his first goal of the campaign and scored the opening goal of a 3–0 win at Newcastle United in the final game to help avert relegation.

With the introduction of gifted youngsters to the side in 1962–63, Revie's mix of youth and experience blended perfectly. Johanneson benefitted and, missing just one league encounter, struck 14 goals including winners to defeat Chelsea and Newcastle at Elland Road. Johanneson also scored the final goal of the season in a 5–0 rout at Swindon Town as Leeds ended the Division 2 campaign in fifth place.

Leeds began the 1963–64 campaign confidently and headed the table for much of the season. Promotion was secured with two games to go and so was the Division 2 title in the last game at Charlton Athletic. Johanneson finished joint top league scorer with 13 goals of which nine came in triumphs including winning strikes against Plymouth Argyle and Scunthorpe United. And a peach of a goal against Newcastle secured a crucial 2–1 victory during the Easter fixtures.

Under Collins, Leeds took Division 1 by storm and astounded everyone by almost claiming the double. Johanneson celebrated his top-flight debut with the opening goal of the season in a 2–1 victory at Aston Villa. A threat when in possession, Johanneson was a marked man. His weakness was confidence, which affected some performances but when on song he could destroy any full back. Johanneson at times was a revelation, scoring terrific goals, including a brace against Everton in a 4–1 win. Strikes against Southport and Shrewsbury helped take United to a first FA Cup final but they lost to Liverpool on a day when sadly United's number 11 was unable to make an impact on Wembley's wide pitch.

Johanneson's reputation meant he had to ride horrendous challenges over the coming seasons, resulting in injuries which kept him out of the team for periods. Nevertheless, he provided memorable moments, especially in the Fairs Cup with a vital goal in a semi-final clash against Real Zaragoza and hat-tricks against DWS Amsterdam and Spora Luxembourg.

Johanneson is the only player during the Revie era to score two European hat-tricks but the emergence of Eddie Gray saw him fade from the first team. And it's ironic that in his final game for the club Gray scored two virtuoso goals against Burnley in April '70.

Johanneson joined York at the end of the 1969–70 campaign where he ended his playing career before tragedy struck. An addiction to drink took its toll and despite support from friends and former teammates, Johanneson became a recluse before his death in 1995. Almost a decade on, following years of apartheid, like Francis before him Johanneson inspired South African footballers to follow their path to Elland Road.

In Lucas Radebe and Philemon Masinga, older supporters recalled the achievements of United's former left winger who scored 67 goals in 197 (3 sub) appearances. One of the most talented wingers of his generation Johanneson was a pivotal player in United's renaissance and promotion campaign in '63–64. His two European trebles are also a mark no player equalled. But his legacy is far beyond setting up and scoring goals in the Revie era.

* * * * *

ROD JOHNSON experienced ecstasy and agony on his debut for Leeds United at Swansea Town as Don Revie ushered in a new era at the club in September 1962. One of four players to step up from a talented youth set up, Johnson opened the scoring against the Welsh side but later in the game departed injured on a stretcher. While teammates Gary Sprake, Paul Reaney and Norman Hunter went on to win major honours and full international caps, Johnson struggled to make the grade at Elland Road.

Born in Leeds on 8 January 1945, Johnson was a talented junior footballer, representing Leeds City Boys alongside Reaney, Paul Madeley and Kevin Hector, who all won full England caps. Spurned by Reading, Johnson joined the Leeds academy in March 1962 and was one of the first apprentices to graduate into the senior team. Following his Swansea bow, Johnson regained fitness and won England youth and amateur honours but after a handful of first team appearances in 1962–63 was not required as United gained promotion to Division 1 the following season.

A lack of first team opportunities must have been a concern but Revie was using the League Cup to test shadow players, especially strikers, with centre-forward Alan Peacock sidelined through injury and Don Weston slipping out of contention at the start of 1964–65. Jim Storrie was Revie's first choice forward at the time but another spot was available. Johnson duly played his first senior game since October 1962 against Huddersfield Town in a 2nd round clash but another fringe striker, Rod Belfitt, scored the winner on the night in a 3–2 win, earning him a run in the first team.

Johnson however would soon get his chance to stake a claim for the centre-forward role and struck the winner in his first game back against West Brom. Leading the line in an unbeaten eight-match run that yielded six victories, Johnson was the pick of the strikers when Leeds claimed a superb 1–0 win at title rivals Manchester United. At a foggy Old Trafford, Johnson ran experienced campaigner Bill Foulkes ragged and in the next away clash scored the only goal at Wolves in the pre-Christmas fixture.

In the midst of a purple patch as Leeds led the way in Division 1, Johnson notched United's third goal versus Southport on the road to the club's first FA Cup journey to Wembley. However, with Peacock returning from injury and Weston back in favour to bolster United's remarkable season, Johnson made one more start in a campaign that saw United finish runners-up in both league and cup. Johnson had a fair turn of pace and was adept in bringing his teammates into play with neat flicks but having made 17 starts in three seasons, the coming three campaigns would yield just eight more starts for the reserve striker.

Johnson's final Leeds goal came against Harlepools United in a League Cup clash in front of just over 11,000 fans at Elland Road in September '65, a far cry from his previous strike when he netted at Leicester City in the last game of his only senior mini-run as United began life in top-flight football. Other forwards replicated Johnson's tale as Revie looked for a cutting edge in attack. Johnson, like Belfitt and later Jimmy Greenhoff, failed to deliver the volume of goals desired by the Leeds boss. When Johnson departed having scored six goals in 25 (5 sub) appearances due to a dearth of senior games in March '68, leading the line at Elland Road was record transfer Mick Jones who would be joined by another record transfer, Allan Clarke.

Johnson went on to serve Doncaster Rovers following a £5,000 transfer, winning a Division 4 title in 1968–69 while his former teammates celebrated a first Division 1 success. Johnson later played for Rotherham United and Bradford City, scoring 47 goals in some 400 matches for lower league sides before a spell for Chicago Sting in the

North American Soccer League. Although ultimately Johnson was not quite at the level required by United's ambitious manager, for a fleeting period he enjoyed a spell in the spotlight and his golden goal at the Vetch Field is sealed in club folklore and viewed as a sign of the Revie era lifting off in earnest.

* * * * *

ALF JONES played for Leeds United across a managerial shift as Don Revie succeeded Jack Taylor in the hot seat at Elland Road. A teammate of Revie's on his senior debut at Anfield, by a bizarre irony Jones' final game for Leeds was the same day United's new manager donned a senior shirt for the last time at Huddersfield Town in March '62.

Born in Liverpool on 2 March 1937, Jones began his career at non-league Marine before signing for Leeds in April 1960. During National Service with the Royal Army Medical Corps, Jones played as an amateur for United in the North Midland's Combination League prior to turning professional on completing his military service. A versatile defender, Jones could play right or left-back, and with stalwart left-back Grenville Hair unavailable Jones pulled on the number three shirt for his league debut on the opening day of the 1960–61 season.

Following a 2–0 defeat to Liverpool, with Hair fit again, Jones ran out for his home bow against Bristol Rovers wearing the number two shirt. United drew 1–1 with Rovers and Jones kept his place at right-back as Leeds defeated Rotherham United prior to a 4–4 draw in the return fixture at Bristol. Jones would not play again until a 3–2 win at Lincoln City approaching the halfway stage in the season. The result against Lincoln started a 16-match run for Jones that began with an unbeaten spell yielding five wins in eight games followed by a worrying period of six defeats in eight games, the latter Revie's first match in charge at Portsmouth after Taylor departed the club.

Dropped from the first team in preference to John Kilford, who had been captaining the reserves, Jones would play a handful more games for United during the 1961–62 campaign, the last alongside his boss at Leeds Road in a 2–1 defeat as Revie introduced Cliff Mason and ultimately Willie Bell to the left-back position. The following seven days would see the arrival of Bobby Collins and tentative steps to

Division 2 safety before the Scot set about the task of helping re-write club history. Jones would move on to Lincoln City for a £4,000 fee playing for The Imps until 1966.

Making 29 appearances for Leeds, Jones was not a part of long-term plans but his stay, though brief, illustrated the old football pundits' cliché that indeed 'football is a funny old game'. Playing his first and last game alongside Revie is spooky but one for statos to ponder.

* * * * *

MICK JONES was Leeds United's first six-figure signing in September 1967 and spearheaded the attack for seven seasons during the Don Revie era. Signed for a club record £100,000 fee, Jones scored over a century of goals. United's boss had struggled to find a successor for veteran striker Alan Peacock but in Jones discovered the complete centre-forward.

Born in Worksop on 24 April 1945, Jones hit the local headlines after scoring 14 goals in a game for Priory Primary School. Representing Worksop and Rotherham Boys, Jones joined Sheffield United at 17 and during five seasons scored 73 goals in 167 appearances. Capped at England U23 level, then twice at full level on a summer tour of Scandinavia in 1965, Jones' transfer to Leeds offered Revie's team a new cutting edge.

Following his debut against Leicester City in a 3–2 home win, Jones scored his first Leeds goal on his European bow against Spora Luxembourg in the Fairs Cup. United's 9–0 win was a club record at the time and Jones quickly proved his undoubted potential with a fine goal against Wolves and brace in a 5–0 victory at Fulham.

Cup-tied in the League Cup when United claimed a major trophy in March '68, Jones won his first winner's memento as a player in the Fairs Cup final against Ferencvaros. Jones scrambled home the only goal of the opening leg at Elland Road then worked tirelessly as the lone striker while his teammates defended heroically at the Nep Stadium in Budapest to secure a monumental aggregate triumph.

In the 1968–69 league campaign, after scoring in the opening three games of the season, Jones ended his first full season at the club top scorer with 14 goals as Leeds clinched the Division 1 title. Notable

Jones winners came against Liverpool, Sunderland and Queens Park Rangers. And two strikes during the run-in at Arsenal and at home to Leicester City were crucial.

During the close season Allan Clarke arrived at Elland Road, which proved to be a Revie masterstroke as Jones was the perfect foil for his talents. And from their first game together in the Charity Shield win over Manchester City the Clarke-Jones partnership clicked. The duo would become renowned domestically and in Europe. With Peter Lorimer and Eddie Gray supporting on the flanks, as an attacking force no defence was safe against United. Jones used his strength to maximum effect whether shielding the ball, chasing lost causes or causing havoc in the penalty area before laying off a ball for his colleagues. Jones was also superb in the air and packed a thunderous shot.

Enjoying his most prolific season in 1969–70, Jones opened the campaign with a terrific headed winner at Manchester United and struck his first Leeds hat-trick in a club record 10–0 win against Lyn Oslo in the European Cup. By the end of a titanic campaign United's strike duo had scored 26 goals apiece as Leeds chased an unprecedented treble. But in a traumatic finale Leeds ended the season with no tangible success despite Jones grabbing the lead in both the FA Cup final and replay against Chelsea. The '69–70 season did however earn Jones a third England cap against Holland although mysteriously the best partnership in English football never played together on the international stage.

'Jonah' was now at his peak and helped Leeds to another Fairs Cup success, this time against the crack Italian side Juventus in 1970–71. Jones scored only one goal in the European adventure but what an important strike it proved to be as United overcame Dynamo Dresden on 'away goals'. Jones played in both legs of the final against 'Juve' when Leeds repeated the 'away' goal winning formulae.

Since winning the league title in '69, Leeds had finished runners-up twice and made it an unwanted treble in 1971–72 but they did have the huge consolation of winning the FA Cup. Jones was a central character in the Centenary final against Arsenal crossing the ball for Clarke's second half winner. The '71–72 campaign was memorable in many ways especially with the style of football Revie's stars were playing. And Jones contributed immeasurably not least with a noteworthy strike to sink Bill Shankly's Liverpool at Anfield on New Years Day followed by a hat-trick against Manchester United in a 5–1 victory at Elland Road. Jones became only the second Leeds player to achieve the feat against the Old Trafford side since Bobby Turnbull in December 1930.

The following season Jones and his teammates suffered double cup heartache when Sunderland and AC Milan claimed FA Cup and Cup Winners Cup victories in vastly different fashion. But the 1973–74 Division 1 campaign proved to be a season of records as a second championship crown was clinched. As in the previous title success five years earlier, Jones led the scoring charts with 14 goals. Among a number of distinguished displays, Jones struck in the opening game against Everton in a perfect start to the season and scored the only goal of a tough battle with rivals Liverpool. A clinical strike at Chelsea eclipsed the best start to a top-flight season in 24 years and his opener at Manchester United helped establish a record 29-match unbeaten run. Jones' strike at Old Trafford would prove to be his last goal for the club.

Making one start in nine games it is more than coincidental that without their target-man, United's form dipped during the title run-in. With Liverpool making a late charge, Jones donned the number nine shirt on three more occasions giving virtuoso displays of forward running as Leeds picked up vital points against his former team Sheffield United home and away, before a 3–2 win over Ipswich Town ultimately clinched the title.

Alas, Jones never played professionally again and retired in October 1975. The unsung hero of countless battles at home and in Europe there are too many games to mention when Jones demonstrated his prowess in chasing lost causes. For United supporters the abiding memory of this legendary centre-forward will always be Wembley '72. Falling awkwardly in the last minute Jones was strapped up, and with his left arm in a sling having dislocated his elbow slowly walked across the pitch to the Royal Box aided by Doc Adams. Clearly in agony, Jones then climbed Wembley's iconic steps with Norman Hunter in support to receive his medal from the Queen before departing on a stretcher while his teammates went on the traditional lap of honour. Brave as they come, Jones was Player of the Year in 1973–74 and one of 10 players to make over 300 appearances for Revie. Seventh top scorer with 111 goals in 308 (5 sub) games, Jones led the scoring charts on three occasions and was the quintessential target-man.

* * * * *

JOE JORDAN was a fearless and courageous centre-forward for Leeds United. Recommended by Bobby Collins during his brief spell at Greenock Morton, Don Revie signed the teenage striker for £15,000 in October 1970. Jordan developed rapidly as a footballer to become a renowned front runner in world football.

Born in Carluke, Lanarkshire on 15 December 1951, Jordan had trials at West Brom and played junior football for Blantyre Victoria before being spotted by Collins at Morton. Arriving at United a few months into the 1970–71 campaign, Jordan grasped his opportunity inside 12 months when he replaced Rod Belfitt in league clashes at Arsenal and at home to Liverpool in September '71. The teen sensation then scored on his full Leeds debut against Barcelona in a Fairs Cup play off for the right to retain the trophy. A weakened United lost 2–1 at the Nou Camp but a mature display saw Jordan leapfrog the more experienced Belfitt as Revie's first choice replacement.

Following a first league start in a 3–2 win over Everton at Elland Road, Jordan led the attack in a terrific triumph at Manchester United and home victory over Leicester City. A sign of the squad's continual development under Revie came at Old Trafford when Belfitt replaced Jordan from the bench in what was his last game before joining Ipswich Town.

The return to fitness of Clarke and Jones saw Jordan return to the reserves but his stock was rising. And with Jones sidelined at the beginning of the 1972–73 campaign, Jordan enjoyed extended runs domestically and in the club's European Cup Winners Cup run. Making 16 league starts and 10 substitute appearances, Jordan had been fast-tracked into the first team set up and during a memorable campaign struck nine goals including a brace against Ipswich when Belfitt ironically struck twice for the visitors. Jordan also scored home and away in victories over Norwich City on top of winning strikes against Everton and Newcastle United. In Europe, Jordan lined up in every round of the Cup Winners Cup, scoring against Ankaragucu and in both legs of an 8–1 aggregate triumph over Rapid Bucharest. With

Clarke suspended for the second leg semi-final clash at Hajduk Split, Jordan rose to the occasion in an intimidating atmosphere as United secured an aggregate win before playing in an infamous final defeat to AC Milan.

Jordan's rise had been meteoric and following his first Scotland cap as a substitute against England, he became a national hero in October '73 when scoring a stunning flying header against Czechoslovakia to book his country's place at the 1974 World Cup finals. Before departing for Germany, Jordan helped Leeds secure a second Division 1 title. Making 33 appearances in a record-breaking season Jordan scored a number of important goals including an opening strike at Chelsea as United re-wrote history for the best start to a top-flight season in 24 years. Other key goals included a late equaliser at Birmingham City, two strikes against Arsenal in a midweek afternoon fixture due to the energy crisis gripping the country and an opener at Old Trafford in the final game of United's unbeaten run. Though Scotland failed to progress beyond the group stages at the World Cup, Jordan impressed against Zaire, Brazil and Yugoslavia, scoring twice.

Following Revie's departure Jordan began the 1974–75 season in the first team. Playing against Liverpool in the Charity Shield at Wembley, Jordan led the line as Leeds reached the European Cup final. And as Revie's star players moved on, new boss Jimmy Armfield introduced Duncan McKenzie and Tony Currie alongside Jordan, Gordon McQueen and Frank Gray during the mid-seventies when Leeds were unlucky not to win silverware.

A regular for club and country Jordan was a daunting sight in full flow driving a path towards opponents. Immensely strong in the air Jordan was adept at laying off or shielding a ball for better placed teammates. A few months into the 1977–78 campaign, Jordan stunned Leeds supporters by joining arch-rivals Manchester United for a club record fee of £350,000. The move was a massive blow to Leeds fans but was a sound move for Jordan's career. After appearing in the 1978 World Cup finals where once again he scored, he enhanced his reputation during three seasons at Old Trafford where he played in the 1979 FA Cup final. In 1981, Jordan joined AC Milan for £325,000 before playing in a third World Cup. His goal scored against New Zealand made him the only Scot to score in three consecutive finals. Jordan gained 52 caps for his country, scoring 11 goals. Following a season at Verona, this cracking old-fashioned centre-forward joined Southampton for £100,000 in 1984. Jordan went on to hold managerial and coaching posts at Bristol City, Hearts, Celtic, Stoke City, Northern Ireland, Huddersfield Town and most recently Tottenham Hotspur. For all his successes Jordan played some of his best football at Elland Road. Scoring 48 goals in 183 (38 sub) appearances Jordan was top scorer in 1976–77 and the perfect replacement for Jones. Playing more games for Leeds than any of his future clubs, Leeds fans witnessed the development of a wholehearted, never-say-die striker.

* * * * *

DAVID KENNEDY played only three games for Leeds United but secured a place in club folklore when he scored a debut goal in a 'reserve' XI that went down to an infamous 4–1 defeat against Derby County amidst fixture chaos towards the climax of the 1969–70 season. The ramifications of Don Revie's decision in conceding the Division 1 title to champions-elect Everton by playing a shadow team at Brian Clough's Derby resulted in a £5,000 fine from the Football Association but Revie stood firm in resting his jaded stars. Kennedy's senior introduction will always be linked to a campaign of historical context.

Born in Sunderland on 30 November 1950, Kennedy, who played centre-half, joined Leeds as an apprentice prior to signing as a professional in May 1968. With a major honour safely tucked away in the League Cup and Fairs Cup success around the corner, Elland Road was the place to be for a teenager with ambition. But breaking into United's star-studded team would be extremely difficult. Kennedy was a promising defender and Revie was looking for a long-term replacement for the experienced Jack Charlton.

With Big Jack's normal deputy, Paul Madeley, unavailable like his teammates, the North East stopper had a chance to impress in the number five shirt. But the Baseball Ground clash came as United's treble bid of Division 1, European Cup and FA Cup faltered. Revie insisted his first XI were injured or mentally drained and they were undoubtedly the most affected top-flight club in terms of packing in games that season, but they were also victims of their own extraordinary ambitions.

When Kennedy lined up along with a host of talented fringe

players and one other debutant at Derby, left-back Paul Peterson, it ended a spell of nine high profile games in 27 days including a trilogy of FA Cup semi-final clashes against Manchester United and two European Cup quarter-final ties versus Standard Liege. Two days after playing Derby, Celtic awaited in a European Cup semi-final first leg clash. During a madcap time the Derby match ended four games in eight days and began three in a whirlwind four-day period. Alas, United bowed out of the European Cup and prepared for a cup final replay versus Chelsea when Kennedy played in another shadow XI at Ipswich Town to end the league campaign. Leeds lost 3–2 before Chelsea dashed the treble dream at Old Trafford.

United's reserve centre-half made one further start, at Norwegian side Sarpsborg, as another Fairs Cup campaign began in 1970–71. Leeds settled for a 1–0 win before crushing Sarpsborg at home for a 6–0 aggregate triumph. Kennedy would not play in the first team again and a month after United lifted the Fairs Cup against Juventus, joined Lincoln City on a free transfer. Like a number of apprentices that came to Elland Road in the late sixties, Kennedy was unable to make a sustained bid for a place in the senior team. His brief spell however will always be associated with an iconic game in the Revie era. Kennedy's input may have been just one goal in an encounter that meant little in terms of honours but it still cemented his place in United's rich history.

* * * * *

JOHN KILFORD skippered Leeds United's reserve team as the dawn of a new decade approached in 1960 but was unable to break into the senior team on a regular basis. In a transitional period at Elland Road, Kilford had a fringe role as deputy for stalwart left-backs Grenville Hair and Willie Bell.

Born in Derby on 18 November 1938, Kilford played as an amateur for Notts County, turning professional prior to the 1957–58 season. During two seasons, Kilford made 26 appearances for the Meadow Lane club before moving to United in February 1959. Kilford's arrival at Leeds came in the midst of manager Bill Lambton resigning and Jack Taylor taking the helm.

Making his debut shortly after signing in a home clash against

Portsmouth when Wilbur Cush secured a 1–1 draw, it would be his only first team game of a disjointed season. Establishing himself in the reserves throughout 1959–60 when he was appointed captain, Kilford made four senior starts, all at home, the first two coming in a win over Chelsea and a share of the spoils with Manchester United. Back-to-back appearances followed for Kilford with United facing a desperate fight for survival. Following a 4–2 defeat to Blackpool and 3–3 draw with Birmingham City when Revie scored twice, Kilford would play no further part in the club's slide to relegation.

With the club's fortunes in Division 2 stagnating, 12 months later Kilford was brought back into the first team again for Hair. United won with an Eric Smith goal but Taylor resigned 48 hours later. Seventy-two hours on, Revie was appointed Leeds manager and Kilford played in the new boss' first match at Portsmouth the following day. Kilford remained in the side until the end of the season with Hair switching to right-back in place of Alf Jones as Revie looked for defensive balance. And in his longest spell as a first team player, Leeds enjoyed one further triumph in a 7–0 rout against Lincoln City.

Unfortunately United continued to struggle for consistency the following season. Undecided on his preferred full back selections during 1961–62, Revie moved Bell from left half to left-back. But in a season when United just avoided relegation, Revie employed Jack Charlton as an emergency centre-forward with his side desperate for goals.

The striker switch necessitated Bell partnering Freddie Goodwin in defence at times with Kilford slotting in at left-back for seven league and cup games. Kilford's final appearances came during a three-day spell when United twice lost 2–1 to Rotherham United in a league and League Cup replay.

During the close season, Kilford, who made 23 appearances for Leeds, followed ex-Revie player Gerry Francis to non-league Tonbridge where he ended his playing days. Like other United players in the early stages of Revie's managerial reign, Kilford was unable to stake a regular first team spot for various reasons, not least Revie's eye for spotting a player's potential to excel in another position.

* * * * *

IAN LAWSON joined Leeds United in its fight to avoid relegation to Division 3 in 1960–61 and went on to play an important role in the club's rise to top-flight football. A tall, rangy centre-forward Lawson was a difficult target man to mark as he brought teammates into play but also scored his share of goals in United's promotion season.

Born in Onslow, County Durham on 24 March 1939, Lawson played for England's Youth team and made a spectacular start to his professional career at Burnley after joining in 1956. Drafted into the side for an FA Cup third round tie in January 1957, Lawson struck four goals for the Division 1 outfit in a 7–0 win over Chesterfield. Lawson went on to play 23 games for Burnley and his final three goals came during a thrilling title-winning campaign in 1959–60 when he made eight appearances.

Struggling to break into the first team as Burnley marched towards an FA Cup final in 1962, Lawson moved to Elland Road in a £20,000 transfer deal. Having been at a club never out of the top seven in Division 1, Lawson could not have found a bigger contrast with Leeds desperately trying to hold on to Division 2 status.

The 1961–62 campaign had seen Don Revie move Jack Charlton into the centre-forward role with some success following the departure of leading scorer John McCole. Indeed Charlton scored Leeds' goal in a 2–1 defeat against Huddersfield Town when Lawson made his debut, a match that saw Revie play his last game for the club. With Charlton sidelined for two games another recent arrival, Billy McAdams, joined Lawson in the striking roles against Swansea Town. The match was also significant as Revie's double-swoop for inside forward Bobby Collins and defender Cliff Mason joined the relegation fight. Collins and McAdams scored as Leeds picked up a first win in eight games.

Lawson struck his first Leeds goal in a 4–1 defeat at Southampton before two wins and six draws (including a last day victory at Newcastle United) secured Leeds' Division 2 status. The following campaign saw Revie purchase strikers Ian Storrie and Don Weston while introducing a number of promising junior players including rookie forward Rod Johnson. Lawson made only five starts.

But in '63–64 with United one of the pre-season favourites for promotion, Lawson featured in 24 games, scoring 11 goals as a first divisional success in 40 years was achieved. Sharing the striking responsibility with Storrie, Weston and former England international,

Alan Peacock, Lawson scored important goals throughout the season. Indeed, only one of his goals came in a defeat early in the campaign at Manchester City. During a memorable season, Lawson hit the target in consecutive away wins at Northampton Town and Scunthorpe United before notching two at Southampton in a 4–1 triumph prior to the opening goal at Grimsby Town in a 2–0 victory.

On target again as United won at Bury, Lawson scored his first 'home' goal in the league during a 1–1 draw against promotion rivals Sunderland on Boxing Day. Lawson had scored two League Cup goals early in the season and struck his first FA Cup goal since his Burnley days as Leeds pushed Division 1 champions Everton all the way during a fourth round clash in front of 48,826 fans, the biggest Elland Road crowd since the last game of United's 1955–56 promotion season. Leeds lost the fourth round replay in front of over 66,000 spectators at Goodison Park but the good times were returning.

However, a promotion campaign had to be concluded and Lawson scored opening goals in consecutive 3–1 wins over Southampton, Middlesbrough and Grimsby. Lawson did not feature in the side that ultimately clinched promotion at Swansea before wrapping up the title at Charlton Athletic but had played his part. Making three starts the following season with few first team opportunities available Lawson went on to have brief spells at Crystal Palace and Port Vale. The Revie era enjoyed many twists and turns over 13 years. A number of players would not become household names but played an important role on the journey back to Division 1. Lawson, who scored 21 goals in 51 appearances, was such a footballer and his efforts have not been forgotten especially in United's memorable Division 2 title campaign.

* * * * *

GLAN LETHEREN made only one substitute appearance for Leeds United during the Revie era but grabbed the headlines on a memorable night of European action in November 1973. The first goalkeeper in United's history to keep goal in a penalty shoot out, 17-year-old youth team 'keeper Letheren entered club folklore after a remarkable UEFA Cup game at Hibernian.

Born in Llanelli on 1 May 1956, Letheren gained Welsh youth

honours prior to joining Leeds in May 1973. A member of the United youth set up, his arrival at Elland Road came at a time when Revie's 18-man squad included 16 full internationals. First team opportunities were not on Letheren's radar as United kicked off the 1973–74 season with a second Division 1 title the primary goal. Making a blistering start in the league, Leeds were the team to catch. But the UEFA Cup campaign had seen Revie rest several first team players with niggling injuries. An aggregate win over Stromsgodset and a goalless draw against Hibernian in the second round home leg had seen United's boss call upon fringe players including Roy Ellam, Gary Liddell, Frank Gray, Sean O'Neil and Billy McGinley. Revie's resources however would be stretched to the limit for the Easter Road return.

On the 'keeper front Gary Sprake and David Harvey had already kept goal. But with Sprake joining Birmingham City, Ayr United's David Stewart had signed as back up for Harvey. Preparations for the Hibs return leg were thrown into chaos, not through the absence of Gordon McQueen, Norman Hunter, Paul Madeley or Johnny Giles, but through Harvey being unable to travel and Stewart unavailable due to UEFA regulations.

Revie had a goalkeeping crisis and travelling to Easter Road, third choice 'keeper John Shaw was set to start. At 19 years of age, he had two years on Letheren who was sat on the bench. Letheren had no experience at this level so when he ran out for his senior debut after Shaw broke two fingers, United had a task on their hands in the second half. For the United fans present it must have been a surreal sight with Letheren keeping goal in a side boasting six internationals but they were about to witness history. Hibernian had edged the first leg and first half of the return but with captain Billy Bremner relishing the challenge to shield his rookie 'keeper, Letheren kept a clean sheet. Hibs went close when Alex Cropley clipped the crossbar but United's goal was intact after extra time.

The game went to penalties and Letheren created history when he awaited the first Hibs spot kick. He then instantly added his name to the club record books when Pat Stanton, who notched a hat-trick the previous game, struck a post with his team's first effort. In an era when penalty shoot-outs had just been implemented to settle two-legged European ties both sides showed nerves of steel in the remaining spot kicks. Analysis of taking penalties was for the future as Peter Lorimer, Eddie Gray, Mick Bates and Allan Clarke slotted home to make the scores 4–4 leaving Bremner to smash home the winner for a famous 5–4 shoot out victory.

A hero for one night, Letheren, capped by Wales at U21 and U23 level, made his sole senior start the following season in the final home game as United defeated Ipswich Town 2–1. Letheren went on loan to Scunthorpe United prior to spells at Chesterfield and Swansea City. Ending his playing days in non-league football Letheren was goalkeeping coach at Swansea and Leicester City amongst other coach and scouting posts.

In terms of club history, the '73–74 campaign saw Revie bid farewell to United with a second Division 1 crown. It was also a season when five goalkeepers played for the first time in competitive games as Stewart appeared in the FA Cup. One further footnote is that the European venture is still the only time four Leeds 'keepers have played in a campaign. Sprake, Harvey and Shaw saw action but it was the youngest, Letheren, who stole the show after events unfolded in United's UEFA Cup clash two nights before Bonfire Night.

* * * * *

GARY LIDDELL made half a dozen appearances for Leeds United but left his mark by scoring the last goal in Europe of the Don Revie era. Liddell was 18 years of age when he scored United's consolation goal with a cracking strike two minutes after coming off the bench against Vitoria Setubal.

Born in Bannokburn, Stirlingshire on 27 August 1954, Liddell attended the same school as Billy Bremner and signed for United on leaving. Liddell turned professional in September '71 the month Leeds played Barcelona in a Fairs Cup play off to retain the trophy and exited the UEFA Cup with a shock defeat to Lierse SK.

A regular in the reserve side, Liddell made his senior debut in a 2–1 defeat to Birmingham City as Revie rested the first team apart from Peter Lorimer before the FA Cup final versus Sunderland in 1973. Defeat at Wembley and against AC Milan in the European Cup Winners Cup final saw United kick off the 1973–74 season determined to land a second Division 1 title. Revie rested several first team players with niggling injuries in the UEFA Cup campaign. During a 7–2 aggregate win over Stromsgodset, Liddell deputised for Lorimer in the first leg in Oslo when Allan Clarke scored the Leeds goal in a 1–1 draw. United hit the Norwegians for six in the return to set up a clash against Hibernian when it was an altogether tougher tie but a weakened United came through a penalty shoot out.

Liddell had made his League Cup debut at Ipswich Town before Leeds took on Vitoria Setubal when Revie was banned from the touchline for the first leg after being on the pitch for the Hibs penalty shoot out. Leeds edged a 1–0 win but with domestic matters paramount, Revie sent out a shadow United XI for the return leg at the Bonfim Stadium. Resting a clutch of regulars, fringe players included Roy Ellam, Jimmy Mann, Peter Hampton and Frank Gray. Liddell was named among the substitutes and, coming on after 82 minutes for Gordon McQueen, fired home a great strike. United were in the midst of a record-breaking league campaign and Liddell made a substitute appearance shortly after Leeds' unbeaten 29-match run ended at Stoke City.

Looking to get back on track, Liddell replaced Lorimer against Newcastle United in what was a disappointing home draw before the second biggest attendance of the campaign at Elland Road. The strain was beginning to show but United demonstrated resolve to exit the mini-slump and clinch another league title. Liddell made one further start, in a 1–1 draw at Sheffield United the following season with Clarke injured.

Needing a fresh challenge, Liddell went on to play for Grimsby Town, scoring 24 goals in 105 games. He then moved to Hearts and Doncaster Rovers where he teamed up with manager Billy Bremner. United's skipper had been in the United line up when Liddell played his last game for the club at Bramall Lane but was rested in Portugal when the teenage striker's goal, albeit in a weakened United XI, was his most noteworthy contribution. European football had been a major target for Revie and Liddell signed off the chapter in the 78th game. Over nine consecutive seasons, United won the Fairs Cup twice, lost two European finals and reached two further semi-finals. Winning 42 matches, drawing 22 and losing 14, no British club matched such consistency. Liddell in his UEFA Cup appearances concluded the statistics.

* * * * *

PETER LORIMER is the most prolific goal scorer in Leeds United's history. Records are set to be broken but it is doubtful 'Hot Shot' Lorimer's tally of 238 goals in all competitions will ever be challenged. Nicknamed 'Lash' by teammates due to his thunderous shot, no 'keeper was safe when Lorimer was in range but this talented footballer offered more than just a cannonball strike. Comfortable in possession, Lorimer could tuck into midfield when required, ping a ball to players in space or set up goals with precision crosses.

Born in Dundee on 14 December 1946, Lorimer was an exceptional schoolboy talent, scoring 176 goals for Stobswell School one season. Representing Dundee Schools, numerous clubs chased his signature but Don Revie worked tirelessly in getting Lorimer to join a talented crop of youngsters at Elland Road. Revie's efforts would be richly rewarded.

Joining Leeds in May '62, Lorimer was part of a prodigious U18 squad that included David Harvey, Terry Hibbitt, Jimmy Greenhoff, Eddie Gray and Mick Bates. The first to make the senior side four months later against Southampton aged 15 years 289 days, Lorimer is still United's youngest debutante. Historically, it is fitting that Lorimer's sole appearance of the season coincided with the club's previous greatest scorer John Charles' penultimate home game as he edged towards ending his Leeds career.

Winning Scottish amateur caps on a tour to Kenya, Lorimer turned professional in December '63 and following United's promotion to Division 1, Revie handed Lorimer his top-flight bow against Sheffield Wednesday nearing the end of United's 1964–65 campaign. Regular first team football ensued the following '65–66 season. Opening his club goal account in a 3–2 defeat at Tottenham Hotspur, Lorimer scored a brace in victories versus Blackburn Rovers, Northampton Town and Nottingham Forest. And shortly after his 20th birthday, Lorimer struck his first hat-trick in an FA Cup tie against Bury.

Lorimer believed in his ability and showed from an early stage he could score against any team. Playing in Europe never fazed him and after lining up in United's XI that embarked on its inaugural Fairs Cup campaign Lorimer was on fire against SC Leipzig and Valencia on route to the semi-finals. Real Zaragoza ended the run in a play off.

Top scorer with 19 goals in his first full season, injury restricted appearances in 1966–67 but Lorimer still hit the target on a regular basis though he'd taste double cup disappointment. In the FA Cup, Chelsea defeated United in the semi-finals but the match ended in controversy when the referee ruled out a Lorimer thunderbolt in the last minute. There was also Fairs Cup heartache as United lost in the final to Dinamo Zagreb.

Lorimer enjoyed his most prolific season in 1967–68, firing home 30 goals. The campaign saw Leeds win two trophies with the Scot leading the scoring charts in both competitions. United's League Cup triumph was special as finally Leeds landed a major honour. Lorimer scored a hat-trick against Luton Town in the opening round and struck versus Stoke City in the quarter finals on the road to Wembley when United accounted for Arsenal. In the Fairs Cup, Lorimer was also among the goals, hitting four, the only time in his career, against Spora Luxembourg during a club record 9–0 win. But, strikes home and away against Partizan Belgrade and Rangers proved more crucial before Leeds defeated Ferencvaros in a tense final. The league campaign saw Leeds finish fourth with Lorimer scoring winners against Burnley, West Ham and Tottenham. He also fired home in a 7–0 rout against Chelsea.

Lorimer opened United's goal account in the 1968–69 league campaign during a 3–1 win at Southampton and he'd play his part as Leeds finally clinched a Division 1 title. Sidelined for periods of the season Lorimer goals all came in victories including winning strikes versus Sheffield Wednesday and Chelsea. With Allan Clarke joining in the close season to partner Mick Jones in attack, allied to Lorimer, United had a formidable forward line. Fixture congestion denied more trophies in 1969–70 when Leeds finished runners-up in three competitions.

Though hugely disappointing, honours arrived again with the Fairs Cup in 1970–71. Lorimer top scored during the European run with five goals including vital strikes against Dynamo Dresden and Vitoria Setubal before an 'away' goals triumph over Juventus.

Lorimer finally completed his domestic collection with an FA Cup winners medal in 1972 against Arsenal in the Centenary final. On route to the final Lorimer scored twice against Bristol Rovers and netted United's second goal against Birmingham City in the semi-finals. Player of the Year in '71–72, Lorimer top scored with 29 goals including a gem of a dipping first time volley versus Manchester City, a cracker at Crystal Palace and hat-trick in Leeds' iconic 7–0 demolition of Southampton as United again finished league runners-up.

Double disappointment alas came in '72–73 as Leeds missed out in FA Cup and European Cup Winners Cup finals with the lasting memory Sunderland 'keeper Jim Montgomery's point blank save from Lorimer at Wembley. The save still defies belief decades on.

United had bounced back from heartache before and did so again in Revie's last season in charge as Leeds claimed another Division 1 crown in 1973–74. During an unbeaten 29-game run Lorimer chipped in with 12 goals including his sixth and final United hat-trick, versus Birmingham City, and match winning penalty against Manchester City although four goals in the run-in proved crucial in the final analysis as Leeds overcame a sticky spell. The relief following strikes in victories against Derby County and Sheffield United and a goal in a 3–2 victory over Ipswich Town was tangible. The Ipswich result ultimately clinched the title.

Following Revie's departure, during an exciting European Cup campaign in '74–75, Lorimer scored arguably his most crucial goal for Leeds against Barcelona to clinch a place in the final. A brilliant volley against Bayern Munich looked to have won the trophy in Paris but was ruled out as Billy Bremner had strayed offside. Alongside his disallowed free kick against Chelsea in the '67 semi-finals both efforts are still the most debated disallowed goals in United history. Leeds were no longer title contenders but went close to silverware, falling at the semi-final stages of the FA Cup and League Cup.

But after 16 seasons at Elland Road, Lorimer embarked on a five-year spell at Toronto Blizzards, Vancouver Whitecaps and York City before returning to Leeds in December '83 to aid Gray's young team languishing near the foot of Division 2. Dropping into midfield, Lorimer helped Leeds survive and on a historical footing surpassed Charles' record 153 league goals total when firing home a penalty against Oldham Athletic. Lorimer played his final game for Leeds against Grimsby Town in 1985 aged 39.

In a remarkable 24-year career, Lorimer's prowess from open play or free kicks was legendary and he even scored from halfway in a West Riding clash against Halifax Town. Lorimer's power made him a natural penalty expert but he had to wait at Leeds, as Johnny Giles was number one. Nevertheless, after scoring his first spot kick against Preston North End in October '66, Lorimer scored 32 penalties second only to Giles. Showing coolness at tense times, Lorimer struck home important spot kicks including two in a thrilling 3–2 win at Derby County in March '73.

On the international scene, Lorimer made his full Scotland debut in 1969 against Spain when bizarrely the clash came a month before his U23 debut against France. Following another U23 game, Lorimer went on to win 21 caps scoring four goals. Among memorable performances Lorimer struck a trademark volley against Zaire in the 1974 World Cup finals. An accomplished radio and newspaper pundit, Lorimer is a regular visitor to Elland Road in his club ambassadorial capacity. One of the club's greatest players, Lorimer made 677 (28 sub) appearances for the club. But for a spell away, Lorimer would have headed the appearances list and increased his goal scoring achievements. However, he is among the top 10 players in terms of games played for Revie, scoring 180 goals in 454 (13 sub) games during his tenure as boss. A world class striker, Lorimer is one of five players alongside Tom Jennings, Charles, Lee Chapman and Jermaine Beckford to score 30 goals in a season. But the overriding memory of 'Hot Shot' Lorimer is his striking ability. There was no finer sight than witnessing 'Lash' Lorimer cracking home a thunderbolt in his heyday.

* * * * *

JIMMY LUMSDEN showed admirable loyalty to Leeds United during his time at the club. Making four appearances in six years all at the back end of a season, Lumsden's final game at Derby County came against a backdrop of fixture congestion in 1969–70. With United battling in vain for an unprecedented treble, ramifications went on after Lumsden had departed although his place in a reserve line up had entered club folklore. Lumsden's debut at Hillsborough in 1967 also yielded benchmarks for statistical connoisseurs.

Born in Glasgow on 7 November 1947, Lumsden, an inside forward, played for Glasgow Schools and attended Scottish trials prior to joining

United's budding ground staff, signing professional forms in November 1964. A member of United's U18 squad Lumsden made his first team debut in the final game of the '66–67 season. Leeds had fallen at the semi-final stage of the FA Cup to Chelsea and with the league challenge over Revie selected a weakened side to face Sheffield Wednesday before a Fairs Cup semi-final against Kilmarnock.

Calling on fringe players, Lumsden, the only debutante, wore Billy Bremner's number four jersey, with Revie naming his skipper substitute. Despite only four regular first team players lining up at Hillsborough, Terry Hibbitt sealed a win over Wednesday. On a historical note, Bremner replaced Eddie Gray for his only substitute appearance in his Leeds career. United overcame Kilmarnock to reach a first European final.

Twelve months on, after Leeds had lifted the League Cup and again went out at the FA Cup semi-final stage, this time to Everton, with the title challenge over Lumsden came into the side at Burnley for the final league game as a Fairs Cup semi-final at Dundee loomed. Revie's shadow team included debutante Terry Yorath. Burnley won 3–0 before Leeds reached a second consecutive Fairs Cup final.

Not called upon throughout the 1968–69 season when United clinched a first league title, in '69–70 for a third time in four seasons Lumsden was selected to complete league fixtures. Substitute in a 3–1 home defeat to Southampton, the poor result ended United's title defence before the infamous 4–1 loss at Derby brought a £5,000 Football Association fine. Revie defended his decision insisting the first XI was injured or mentally fatigued coming at the end of nine games in 27 days including FA Cup semi-final clashes versus Manchester United and European Cup quarter-final ties with Standard Liege. Revie did have justification as the Derby game was United's third in five days.

Lumsden joined Southend United in September '70 prior to spells at Morton, St Mirren, Cork Hibernians and Clydebank. But his association with Leeds was not over. Assistant manager to former teammate Gray in the early eighties the duo served Rochdale before Lumsden assisted another United legend, Joe Jordan at Bristol City, later managing the club, prior to coaching posts at Preston and Everton.

Revie's tenure included periods when fringe players came into the first team with established stars giving them a chance to shine. Lumsden did not have such a luxury and especially so in the Baseball Ground clash when he answered his manager's call to wear Bremner's iconic jersey for a second and final time. For United statisticians, Lumsden's debut against Sheffield Wednesday will always resonate. The only Leeds player to don Bremner's jersey with the skipper on the bench is a notable fact.

* * * * *

BILLY McADAMS scored vital goals in Leeds United's titanic 1961–62 relegation battle. A brave, direct centre-forward, McAdams played as many league games as he missed during a seven-month spell in Don Revie's first season as manager, but the Northern Ireland international delivered when it mattered in the final game at Newcastle United.

Born in Belfast on 20 January 1931, McAdams played for Bainbridge Town and Glenavon before spurning a chance to join Burnley. Joining Irish League outfit Distillery, McAdams created history when he became the first Northern Ireland footballer to sign for an English club in a five-figure transfer. At Manchester City, McAdams played alongside Revie but missed successive FA Cup finals through injury. However, in the late fifties, McAdams showed his pedigree as a striker, top scoring for City with 21 goals in 30 games in 1959–60.

Notching 65 goals in 134 appearances for the Maine Road club, McAdams joined Bolton Wanderers for £15,000 and promptly struck 26 goals in 44 games. Capped by Northern Ireland, McAdams became the first player to score a hat-trick against West Germany in a 4–3 World Cup qualifier defeat. With Leeds struggling as an attacking force in '61–62, Revie had turned to Jack Charlton in October '61 as an emergency striker after the somewhat surprising departure of John McCole, leading goal scorer the previous season. And credit to United's rugged centre-half as he scored a number of goals in the role, but a leaky defence had the side in relegation trouble.

McAdams was seen as a path to safety when he arrived at Elland Road but was prone to injury. And after a seven-match run that yielded two wins and five defeats including a 3–1 loss on his debut at Charlton Athletic, McAdams would be fit for only four of the final 11 games. McAdams aside, Revie had boosted the squad with striker Ian Lawson to partner McAdams, along with defender Cliff Mason and inside forward Bobby Collins. McAdams was in the line up for Collins' debut when the two internationals scored in a 2–0 victory over

Swansea Town. But a defeat at Southampton ensued with McAdams unavailable until the final two games.

By his return Revie's triple signings had made a mark, especially Collins in leading by example. With survival in United's hands after an unbeaten seven-match run, a draw in the final home game against Bury meant a win at Newcastle would guarantee safety. And in a pulsating display at St James Park, McAdams scored United's second goal in a 3–0 win. A robust, speedy striker when fully fit, McAdams won the last of 15 international caps in a 4–0 defeat to Holland before joining Brentford for £8,000 during the close season. Winning a Division 4 title in 1962–63, McAdams ended his playing career with spells at Queens Park Rangers and Barrow. In a career that saw McAdams amass over 150 goals at six clubs, two came at a critical stage of Revie's fledgling managerial career. Revie had a hunch McAdams would deliver. In '55, McAdams had missed a cup final against Newcastle when Revie was Footballer of the Year. Luckily for the Leeds boss, McAdams was fit to produce the goods on Tyneside among 13 United appearances and justify Revie's faith in a former teammate.

* * * * *

JOHN McCOLE is the only Leeds United player to score four goals in a League Cup tie. McCole achieved the feat in a 4–1 victory over Brentford before the lowest crowd at Elland Road in the competition in September 1961. On a night of records McCole's opening strike was his fourth in four consecutive ties, an accolade still intact five decades on.

Born in Glasgow on 18 September 1936, McCole started out at Vale of Leven and Falkirk before joining Bradford City where he struck 32 goals in 1958–59. McCole's prolific scoring resulted in Leeds manager Jack Taylor signing him for £10,000. Following his debut in a defeat at West Brom in September '59, McCole partnered Don Revie when both scored in a 3–2 home defeat to Newcastle United.

Taylor had discovered a striker who could plunder goals and McCole hit 12 by the New Year but United's dismal form meant they'd only contribute to two victories versus Arsenal and Tottenham Hotspur. The Tottenham result was a surprise because United had been soundly beaten by the North London team 48 hours earlier on Boxing Day but it had a brief impact as Leeds followed up with victories over West Ham and Chelsea when United's hitman was again on the score sheet. Alas four victories in the final 15 games resulted in relegation to Division 2. McCole had done his utmost in a struggling team, top scoring with 22 goals in 33 league appearances, but these were hard times at Elland Road.

Leeds had a mixed start in 1960–61 when McCole was in the goals during wins over Rotherham United and Southampton. And United's leading marksman was on target in 4–4 thrillers against Bristol Rovers and Middlesbrough. Inconsistency was a major issue despite McCole's best efforts. McCole hit five goals in an unbeaten eight-match run that yielded five wins including consecutive victories over Rotherham, Southampton and Huddersfield Town in the New Year period. But five defeats in the following seven games saw Revie take the helm. McCole was injured for a number of Revie's first games in charge as United continued to struggle but hit two goals in a 7–0 win over Lincoln City and both Leeds goals in a draw with Scunthorpe United. Leeds ended the season mid-table.

McCole headed the scoring charts for a second season with 23 league and cup goals. The campaign saw United take part in the inaugural League Cup competition when McCole scored in each round as Leeds defeated Blackpool and Chesterfield before a nine-goal thriller at Southampton that Saints edged 5–4. In Revie's first full season at the helm United opened with two wins before six defeats in 11 games forced him to consider offers for his talented striker.

But prior to rejoining Bradford City in October '61 before spells at Rotherham United, Shelbourne, Newport County and Cork Hibernians, McCole left behind a goal scoring legacy while Revie was on a scouting trip in Scotland. Only 4,517 spectators witnessed McCole's four-goal blast against Brentford. Scoring two goals in each half McCole's haul included a header, a clinical strike and two poacher's goals. And McCole should have made it five after being scythed down for a penalty but Derek Mayers fired wide. McCole's quadruple effort has yet to be matched let alone surpassed.

An archetypal centre-forward, McCole scored 53 goals in 85 games in his two years at Leeds but was more than just a prolific goal scorer. Adept at bringing colleagues into play, McCole looked for openings even it meant getting a whack for his efforts. United's misfortune was having McCole during a low point in its history. A brave, strapping centre-forward McCole's goals-to-game ratio was impressive throughout his career. It is lamentable that so few supporters, as well as Revie, saw first hand his League Cup escapades but his effort is recorded. One of only three players in the Revie era alongside Peter Lorimer and Allan Clarke to hit four goals in a game, McCole was a supreme sharpshooter.

* * * * *

PETER McCONNELL broke into Leeds United's first team during a transitional period. A fully committed player McConnell was popular with supporters for his attitude and willingness to battle. An attacking half back who also played inside forward, McConnell had a wholehearted approach to football but failed to make a lasting impression after Don Revie took the helm.

Born in Reddish on 3 March 1937, McConnell represented Stockport and Cheshire Schools before being snapped up by Leeds manager Major Frank Buckley. McConnell signed professional forms in March 1954 when a new boss, Raich Carter, was in charge but would not make his senior debut until a 4–3 defeat to Bolton Wanderers in December 1954 a couple of weeks into Bill Lambton's brief tenure as manager. The match coincided with Revie's eighth game at the club and McConnell went on to play in the final five games of the season when centre-forward Alan Shackleton settled clashes with Blackburn Rovers, Nottingham Forest and West Ham.

The following campaign was one of frustration for McConnell. Jack Taylor had succeeded Lambton and caretaker boss Bob Roxburgh but young McConnell spent most of the campaign in the reserves. Struggling to make an impact in Division 2 during the 1960–61 season Taylor eventually brought McConnell back into the first team as United lost at Luton Town prior to a welcome home win against Norwich City. Changes were afoot at Elland Road as chairman Harry Reynolds announced a few days later that Revie would be succeeding Taylor.

Revie kept faith with McConnell during an inauspicious nine-game run to the end of the season when he scored his first goal for the club in a 7–0 romp against Lincoln City. Revie's first victory was welcome but a lot of hard work lay ahead. McConnell was given a run in the side and

117

enjoyed a mini-scoring spree in October '61 scoring in four out of five fixtures. At the time United was struggling for goals to such an extent that Revie moved Jack Charlton to centre-forward in order to pep up the attack. McConnell's goals were welcome starting with the winner in a League Cup triumph over Huddersfield Town. Further strikes came in 1–1 draws against Plymouth Argyle and Southampton but his goal at Swansea Town proved to be a consolation. McConnell remained in the side until the final third of the season when a home defeat against Plymouth signalled his last game under Revie. With reinforcements including Billy McAdams, Ian Lawson and Bobby Collins arriving at Elland Road, United eventually reached safety.

Revie offered McConnell the chance to join Carlisle United where former United trainer Ivor Powell was manager. Accepting the challenge, McConnell played over 300 games at Carlisle and won a Division 3 title before a spell at Bradford City and lastly Scarborough. Although he didn't play a bigger role in the Revie revolution McConnell, who scored five goals in 53 games, was there at the start when a stunned group of players in the home dressing room first heard Revie was the new boss.

* * * * *

BILLY McGINLEY made two substitute appearances for Leeds United in the Don Revie era. Spanning 64 minutes in Division 1 and UEFA Cup clashes McGinley was among Revie's last intake of junior players at Elland Road.

Born in Dumfries on 12 November 1954, McGinley was a star in the Scotland Schoolboy forward line before joining United's ground staff, turning professional in January 1972. At the time United was in its pomp having gone from a team battling to stay in Division 2 to one of the most feared sides in British and European football. Just turned 18 years of age, signing for United was a great achievement for McGinley but breaking into the first team would be an enormous challenge. Playing in midfield, McGinley established himself in the Central League side but would have to wait until the penultimate game of the 1972–73 season for his first senior appearance.

With Revie resting his entire first team, bar Peter Lorimer, the week before the FA Cup final versus Sunderland at Wembley, McGinley was handed the substitute jersey in a shadow XI that included reserve players

Frank Gray, Gary Liddell and Jimmy Mann. Just before half time at St Andrews, McGinley got the call to strip off for his first team debut as a replacement for injured centre-half Roy Ellam. Revie reshuffled his side and United battled away but lost 2–1.

The following season, Revie used a number of fringe players in UEFA Cup matches with the Division 1 campaign the top priority. United drew 1–1 in a opening round first leg at Stromsgodset and in a reasonably strong line up including seven full internationals for the Elland Road return, McGinley was named among the subs. During an imperious performance, Leeds showed no mercy to the Norwegian side rattling in three goals before half time. With Leeds coasting by 5–1, McGinley replaced two-goal hero Allan Clarke on 76 minutes for his home debut. United added a sixth goal from Mick Jones in a convincing victory.

McGinley did not feature again during the '73–74 season and following Revie's departure to take up the England post McGinley joined Huddersfield Town where he had more first team opportunities prior to a spell at Crewe Alexandra. Amongst McGinley's Central League teammates only Gray, Peter Hampton and Byron Stevenson would enjoy extended spells at Elland Road. Of some historical consolation, McGinley featured in the fifth highest European win of the Revie era.

* * * * *

GORDON McQUEEN ended Don Revie's protracted search for a successor to Jack Charlton. Replacing Charlton had been an ongoing issue due to his unwavering presence in the heart of Leeds United's defence but McQueen developed swiftly after his debut in a rip-roaring encounter at Derby County in March '73. Impressing throughout United's 1973–74 title winning season the young centre-back matured into a commanding central defender.

Born in Kilbirnie, Ayrshire on 26 June 1952, McQueen played on the wing at school and also in goal like his father, Tom, who had spells at Hibernian, Berwick Rangers and East Fife. McQueen though was a natural centre-half despite failing to impress Liverpool and Rangers at trails. Starting out at St Mirren in 1970, Leeds scouts spotted McQueen's raw potential. Revie had experimented with John Faulkner and Roy Ellam to succeed Charlton but neither made the transition whereas United's boss recognised McQueen's aptitude and after a

£30,000 transfer in September 1972, the Scot progressed rapidly. Following his debut at the Baseball Ground in a thrilling 3–2 win McQueen made five starts during the 1972–73 campaign before a substitute appearance against AC Milan in the European Cup Winners Cup final.

Leeds started the '73–74 season determined to prove doubting pundits wrong after being written off as Division 1 candidates. With Charlton retired, McQueen began the campaign in the first team. Forming a great understanding with Norman Hunter in central defence, and with plenty of experience around in Paul Reaney, Paul Madeley and an emerging Trevor Cherry, McQueen settled into the side seamlessly during a club-record 29 game unbeaten run. Growing in stature with each match McQueen made 36 league appearances and played his part as Leeds clinched the title. At the end of the season, McQueen won his first Scotland cap and made the provisional squad for the World Cup finals in Germany.

Following Revie's departure, McQueen played in the Charity Shield against Liverpool at Wembley and was an assured presence in defence during a tough 1974–75 campaign culminating in United reaching the European Cup final. Notching his first Leeds goal during a league encounter against Sheffield United in a 5–1 victory, McQueen scored crucial European goals against Anderlecht and Ujpesti Dozsa on route to Paris but missed the final following his sending off against Barcelona in the semis.

Bar a spell out due to an Achilles tendon injury in the mid-seventies McQueen held central defence together alongside Hunter, Madeley and Cherry at varying times as a revamped Leeds side came close to honours during a transitional period. A dominating presence in the air, McQueen was also a majestic sight in full flow breaking from defence to set up attacks. Comfortable on the ball, a solid tackler and determined, McQueen was a formidable opponent. The popular Scot also caused havoc at set pieces. McQueen finished second top scorer with eight goals in '76–77 notching winners against West Brom and Birmingham City. And a late two-goal burst snatched victory against Middlesbrough sending Elland Road into raptures.

McQueen had also helped Leeds reach the FA Cup semi-finals before falling to rivals Manchester United in an exciting season. When he followed Joe Jordan for a British record transfer fee of £495,000 to

Old Trafford in February '78 after 172 appearances for the Yorkshire club it understandably angered Leeds supporters. The move benefitted McQueen's career despite spells out through injuries. McQueen scored in a classic FA Cup final against Arsenal in 1979 before collecting a winner's medal against Brighton four years later. McQueen made 228 appearances for Manchester United and ended his playing days as player-coach at Seiko FC (Hong Kong) before managing Airdrie prior to coaching posts at St Mirren and Middlesbrough.

On the international stage, McQueen was a regular for Scotland in his pomp. His most memorable game came at Wembley in the '77 Home Internationals when he headed a powerful goal in an iconic 2–1 win for the Scots. The match was also notable as the Tartan Army destroyed Wembley's goal posts during extensive celebrations at full time. Alas injuries sidelined McQueen from appearing in the '78 and '82 World Cup finals, which would have capped his Scottish career that saw him win 30 caps, scoring four goals. McQueen, a popular TV pundit with Sky Sports, enjoyed productive careers on both sides of the Pennines with Leeds followers witnessing the start. Player of the Year at Leeds in 1974–75 and 1976–77, McQueen was a gifted centre-half who performed a tremendous role at the tail end of the Revie era.

* * * *

PAUL MADELEY is the most versatile footballer in Leeds United's history. Selected by Don Revie in every outfield position, Madeley wore jerseys numbered two to 11 in a remarkable career. Not regarded as simply a fullback, centre-half, midfielder or forward Madeley could play anywhere and did. Dubbed 'Mr Versatile' due to his astonishing flexibility and Leeds' 'Rolls Royce' because of the way he glided around a football field, Madeley was a unique player and essential to the success achieved under Revie.

Born in Leeds on 20 September 1944, Madeley represented England Schools prior to joining United as an apprentice in 1961. Turning professional in May '62, Madeley quickly followed his Middleton Parkside teammate Paul Reaney, together with talented youngsters including Gary Sprake and Norman Hunter, to be fast-tracked into the first team. Initially seen as a centre-half Madeley made his debut against Manchester City in January '64 as a replacement for the injured Jack Charlton and a back up to Freddie Goodwin. Leeds won 1–0 and three more league appearances followed in '63–64 before Charlton returned.

Madeley scored his first goal for the club with a long-range strike at Leicester City when left-back Willie Bell was sidelined for a period in September '65. Shortly afterwards he made his Fairs Cup debut in United's first European campaign against tough-tackling Italians Torino. Revie recognised Madeley's flexibility and the '66–67 campaign proved exceptional as he wore every outfield shirt except number 11, a fact rectified within 12 months.

Absent through injury in the Fairs Cup final against Dinamo Zagreb, Madeley was just as versatile in '67–68 covering in defence, midfield and attack during League Cup and Fairs Cup triumphs. Playing centre-forward was not Madeley's preferred role and Mick Jones' arrival in September '67 meant less striking roles. But Madeley wore the number nine jersey for the League Cup final in March '68 with United's record signing cup-tied at Wembley. Madeley was involved in pressing the Arsenal defence leading to Terry Cooper firing home the winner and also struck a crucial 'away' goal at Dundee in a Fairs Cup semi-final with Jones injured before lining up in midfield against Ferencvaros when United lifted the trophy for the first time in Budapest.

Following this European victory, Madeley switched to other team duties in 1968–69 although he filled in for forward Peter Lorimer when unavailable in United's Division 1 title success. And Madeley strikes, though rare, proved crucial in a draw at Leicester City in addition to wins at Coventry and at home to Newcastle United on Boxing Day '68 during an unforgettable campaign culminating in a memorable night at Anfield when the championship was secured. Thereafter, with sharpshooter Allan Clarke joining for a British transfer to partner Jones in attack, Madeley concluded his remaining years under Revie and beyond across defence and midfield depending on requirements.

But Madeley was not averse to chipping in with a 'special' goal to settle games and none more so than in '70–71. Indeed, teammates dubbed him 'Goal-a-Game' Madeley after strikes versus Blackpool, Stoke City and Wolves in consecutive league games. However, Madeley's most important goal in an illustrious career came against Juventus in the first leg of the Fairs Cup final in Turin when Leeds went on to win the trophy on 'away' goals. Madeley's 20-yard drive, United's first goal in Italy, made the score 1–1 to take the sting out of 'Juve' before Mick Bates cracked home a second equalising 'away' goal. Both efforts aligned to a Clarke strike in the return leg secured a second Leeds' win.

An FA Cup winner in the Centenary final of 1972 when he played left-back after Cooper tragically broke a leg shortly before Wembley, following the double disappointment of losing FA Cup and European Cup Winners Cup finals in '72–73, United began the 1973–74 season determined to prove critics wrong and challenge for another Division 1 crown. Madeley began the campaign at left-back and when a goal was required pulled out another 'special'. With Leeds looking to make an early marker after pre-season jibes, Madeley notched the winner in United's opening away game at Arsenal in a 2–1 victory. Within a few weeks Madeley had moved to midfield with Eddie Gray picking up a long-term injury. Aside from Gray, Johnny Giles was soon injured but linking up with Billy Bremner and a combination of Bates then Terry Yorath, United enjoyed a record 29-match unbeaten run to set up a second title. During the noteworthy run, Madeley moved up from holding duties to fire home another Boxing Day goal and secure a 1–0 win at Newcastle silencing the Geordie faithful. Madeley duly collected his second championship medal a few months later but it would signal the end of Revie's time at the club as he took on the England job. As new managers arrived at Elland Road in the late seventies, the coming seasons would see Madeley play alongside Gordon McQueen, Trevor Cherry and Paul Hart in central defence.

Although not title contenders, anymore Leeds finished fifth in 1975–76 and 1978–79 and reached FA Cup and League Cup semi-finals. The latter campaign saw Madeley's final goal of 34 in all competitions securing a 4–0 win against Southampton in November '78. Madeley was involved in all the ups and downs of a glorious era and holds a unique accolade of playing in four domestic cup finals at Wembley in different positions. After lining up against Arsenal at centre-forward in the League Cup, in a trio of FA Cup finals Madeley played right-back against Chelsea, left-back versus Arsenal and centre-half when Sunderland stunned the football world.

To cap his remarkable versatility Madeley played outside left in the Charity Shield win over Manchester City and midfield in Fairs Cup triumphs over Ferencvaros and Juventus before an infamous defeat to AC Milan in the European Cup Winners Cup. And following Revie's departure he faced Bayern Munich at centre-half in the European Cup final. On the international stage Madeley hit the national headlines when he dropped out of Sir Alf Ramsey's 28-man squad for the 1970 World Cup finals. Ramsey understood Madeley's reasons and awarded him a full debut in 1971. And as with Leeds, Madeley represented his country in various positions across defence and midfield in winning 24 caps.

Player of the Year at Leeds in 1975–76, Madeley was a class act in various positions. A ball-winner and playmaker, Madeley had great positional awareness, strength and was superb in the air. Playing as a defensive midfielder demonstrated his abilities best. Madeley's long stride enabled him to eat up ground quickly before playing a sweeping pass or making a deft flick to teammates, and his tackles were crisp and immaculately timed. In an amazing career, Madeley will always be known for his versatility but it does have an ironic twist. Revie's team in its pomp was recognised by football pundits who eulogised about his international XI comprising Sprake, Reaney, Cooper, Bremner, Charlton, Hunter, Lorimer, Clarke, Jones, Giles and Gray. Likewise, supporters of rival clubs realised the power of Leeds United as this famous XI team was made up of household names. It is bizarre that this line up is actually a 'One-Match' XI that fails to mention Madeley although in some ways it is understandable as his teammates had set positions. However it is apt to note this XI did play a senior game versus Mansfield Town in an FA Cup clash in January '70. Despite not having a dedicated role Madeley was always selected whether for tactical reasons, injury or a suspension to a key player. And if everyone was fit Madeley still played as record books testify. Being able to slot into a variety of positions at a moment's notice without affecting the balance of the side was vital for Revie, as a star player was always absent for one reason or another. Revie was fully aware he had at his disposal a world class footballer. Madeley is fifth on the all-time United list with 712 (13 sub) appearances and among the top 10 players selected by Revie as he appeared in 447 games during his tenure at Elland Road. Madeley was quite simply priceless in the Revie era.

* * * * *

JIMMY MANN played a handful of games for Leeds United in the Don Revie era. An energetic player, Mann played in the forward line or midfield and featured in matches that remain of historical significance.

Born in Goole on 15 December 1952, Mann represented Yorkshire Schools prior to joining United as an apprentice and signed professional forms at 17 years of age. A regular in the Central League side, Mann had to wait until the 1971–72 season for a three-match run in the first team, playing in three competitions in a six-day period.

United started the campaign having to play its opening four home games away from Elland Road following an FA order after an infamous Division 1 clash the previous season when referee Ray Tinkler allowed a goal by West Brom striker Jeff Astle. Leeds' appeals for offside were ignored prompting a demonstration by a number of home fans. Four decades on Astle's 'offside' goal is still the most debated goal at the stadium. After playing their 'home' fixtures at Huddersfield Town, Hull City and Sheffield Wednesday's grounds, United were back on home territory. Revie named Mann substitute against Derby County for a League Cup first round replay when a Peter Lorimer brace sent Leeds through. Mann made his senior debut as a sub for skipper Billy Bremner.

Forty-eight hours later Mann played in a weakened Leeds side humbled by SK Lierse in the Fairs Cup. Ahead 2–0 from the opening leg, United were expected to cruise through but with Leeds 3–0 adrift at half time Norman Hunter and Gary Sprake substituted Mann and 'keeper John Shaw. A 4–2 aggregate defeat produced shockwaves. Out of Europe for the first time in an opening round, it was also the first time United had shipped four goals at home.

For Mann, there would be one further home outing against West Ham in a Division 1 clash with Allan Clarke and Bremner injured. And facing England skipper Bobby Moore in top form was some top-flight bow. Chris Galvin substituted Mann in a 0–0 draw. Mann would not feature again until donning the number 10 shirt in a shadow team for the penultimate game of 1972–73. With Revie resting his first team, apart from Lorimer, prior to United's FA Cup final versus Sunderland, Mann battled away in a 2–1 defeat.

Of note, Lorimer is the only player in Revie's first team to feature in all Mann's games as he also played in a shadow XI at Vitoria Setubal in the UEFA Cup. In what proved to be Revie's 78th and final European game in charge Leeds lost 3–1. Over nine seasons, United had won the Fairs Cup twice and lost two European finals. Winning 42 matches, drawing 22 and losing 14, no other British club was as consistent.

Joining Bristol City on a free transfer at the end of the season Mann scored 31 goals in 231 games, winning promotion to Division 1 in 1975–76. Impressing for Bristol on visits to Elland Road, Mann also played for Barnsley, Scunthorpe United and Doncaster Rovers. As with other fringe players Mann gave his all for United when called upon and it is notable his endeavours came in well-remembered games decades after his spell at the club.

* * * * *

CLIFF MASON was an unsung hero during the latter stages of Leeds United's relegation battle in 1961–62. An experienced left-back, Mason arrived at Elland Road with 11 games to go and was charged with helping United tighten up in defence. Bobby Collins' role is well documented in a tough debut season for manager Don Revie but the new boss' decision to bring Mason to the club was also astute.

Born in York on 27 November 1929, Mason failed to play for his hometown club but following spells at Sunderland and Darlington, went on to captain Sheffield United in Division 1 during a six-year career at Bramall Lane. With only 11 goals scored in as many games in '61–62 Leeds centre-half Jack Charlton moved with some success to centre-forward but sloppy defending had seen United lose 17 of 31 games and 11 by the odd goal. In response, Ian Lawson was signed by Revie to partner pre-Christmas signing Billy McAdams alongside Mason and Collins entering the final third of the league campaign. Mason and Collins duly lined up for home debuts against Swansea Town. Winning 2–0 a heavy defeat followed at Southampton but any reservations Revie had disappeared following a 2–1 victory over Luton Town courtesy of two Billy Bremner strikes. The win heralded an unbeaten eight-match run including six draws. And in 10 games only eight goals had been conceded by a re-jigged back four of Grenville Hair, Eric Smith, Charlton and Mason. Also, in United's Dell defeat 16-year-old rookie 'keeper Gary

Sprake had been flown down as a late replacement for Tommy Younger when he was taken ill. With one game remaining victory at Newcastle United would guarantee safety and in a powerful display Leeds assured survival with a 3–0 triumph.

Mason's cool demeanour especially in anticipating danger was valuable during the early months of the '62–63 season when Revie bloodied the first of his talented youngsters in Sprake, Paul Reaney and Norman Hunter into the first team set up. But approaching the festive fixtures, Mason's 33-match spell at Elland Road ended. Departing before the end of the season Mason had brief spells for Scunthorpe United and Chesterfield.

The Revie era contains many unbeaten runs along with consecutive victories that were hailed, and rightly so, in terms of historical significance. But periods when survival battles were fought are sometimes forgotten. And United's escapades in '61–62 were such a time. No trophies were at stake but the exhilaration felt by Revie and his team in the St James Park away dressing room in April '62 was special as they'd completed the 'great escape'. Collins led the way to safety in terms of being a driving force but Mason was also inspirational when United needed to dig deep at an important juncture in the club's history.

* * * * *

DEREK MAYERS was Don Revie's only signing prior to the start of his first full season in charge at Elland Road. Alas the 1961–62 campaign would prove to be a tough baptism for the rookie manager and his right winger from Preston North End. Mayers has the unusual distinction of being the only Revie player to score in consecutive games but never play for the club again.

Born in Liverpool on 24 January 1935, Mayers played for Everton before making his name at Preston when they finished runners-up to Division 1 champions Wolves in 1957–58. Mayers scored 25 goals in over 100 appearances for Preston and joined Leeds after the Deepdale club suffered relegation to Division 2 three years later. A new era had begun under Revie and although funds were tight United kicked off the '61–62 campaign with a 1–0 win at Charlton Athletic.

Goal scorer Billy Bremner had moved infield to inside right the previous season to accommodate Gerry Francis at outside right. Mayers succeeded the South African winger whilst Francis' countryman, Albert Johanneson, had broken through on the left wing. Bremner and Mayers were both on target in a 3–1 win at Brighton as United made it two wins from two games but a 5–0 defeat against Mayers' hometown club Liverpool heralded a dreadful run of form as United slipped down the table. Mayers flitted in and out of the side but opened the scoring in a 3–1 win at Middlesbrough and was on target in a 3–3 draw at Derby County as the winter months kicked in. To date Mayers' goals had come in away fixtures and the trend continued with a fourth goal of the season in a 2–1 defeat at Scunthorpe United when he slotted in a penalty. Another Mayers strike in a 3–2 home loss to Plymouth Argyle when Jack Charlton also scored summed up United's inability to keep clean sheets with just six achieved in 30 games.

Dropped for a derby at Huddersfield Town when Revie played his last game for the club, Revie's major predicament was playing central defender Charlton at centre-forward. Initially solved by the acquisition of Billy McAdams, Revie also signed striker Ian Lawson along with full back Cliff Mason and inside forward Bobby Collins to help stem the goals. The trio of new faces ended Mayers' run in the side with Bremner reverting to outside right and Charlton finally returning to defensive duties. An unbeaten nine-match run saw United safe in the final game at Newcastle United. The close season saw Mayers move on to Bury after 24 matches and later play for Wrexham. Timing is crucial in football and in Mayers' case he was at United during a turbulent time when decisions took place with an eye on the 'bigger picture'. As with other Revie signings Mayers left a note for historians with his successive strikes versus Scunthorpe and Plymouth before departing for new challenges.

* * * * *

MIKE O'GRADY enjoyed his finest season for Leeds United when they won the Division 1 championship in 1968–69. When fully fit O'Grady was one of the most dangerous wingers around whether flying past opponents on the outside or cutting inside before unleashing a strike at goal and helped secure two major honours.

Born in Leeds on 11 October 1942, O'Grady starred for Leeds City Boys and Yorkshire Schools but slipped through Leeds' scouting system. Huddersfield Town meanwhile tracked his progress and

Mike Addy

Mick Bates

Rod Belfitt

Willie Bell

Billy Bremner

Bobby Cameron

Terry Carling

Terry Casey

John Charles

Jack Charlton

Trevor Cherry

Allan Clarke

Bobby Collins

Terry Cooper

Nigel Davey

Keith Edwards

Roy Ellam

John Faulkner

Peter Fitzgerald

Gerry Francis

Chris Galvin

Johnny Giles

Freddie Goodwin

Colin Grainger

Eddie Gray

Frank Gray

Jimmy Greenhoff

Grenville Hair

Tom Hallett

Peter Hampton

David Harvey

Dennis Hawkins

John Hawksby

Tommy Henderson

Terry Hibbitt

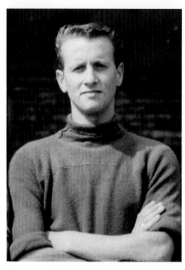

Alan Humphreys

Norman Hunter

Albert Johanneson

Rod Johnson

Alf Jones

Mick Jones   Joe Jordan

David Kennedy

John Kilford   Ian Lawson

Glan Letheren

Gary Liddell

Peter Lorimer

Jimmy Lumsden

Billy McAdams

John McCole

Peter McConnell

Billy McGinley

Gordon McQueen

Paul Madeley

Jimmy Mann

Cliff Mason

Derek Mayers

Mike O'Grady

Jimmy 'Sean' O'Neil

Alan Peacock

Paul Peterson

Noel Peyton

Paul Reaney

John Shaw

Bobby Sibbald

Eric Smith

Gary Sprake

David Stewart

Jim Storrie

Don Weston

Brian Williamson

Barrie Wright

Terry Yorath

Tommy Younger

Don Revie

snapped him up in October '59. O'Grady won the first of three England U23 caps after just 16 games. A full cap followed against Northern Ireland when he scored twice before bizarrely being dropped. O'Grady, who also represented the Football League on three occasions, scored 26 goals in 160 appearances for Town during six seasons at Leeds Road.

Revie signed O'Grady for £30,000 in October '65 and he made his debut in a 6–1 win against Northampton Town. Hitting the winner at Stoke City in his second game, O'Grady enjoyed a fine '65–66 campaign as United finished runners-up to champions Liverpool. Quick, determined, elusive and possessing a terrific shot O'Grady was a handful when running at opponents but never got fazed if he lost possession. O'Grady quickly made an impact in Europe following his bow at SC Leipzig when he set up Peter Lorimer for the opening goal in a 2–1 victory. O'Grady also played in an infamous Fairs Cup clash dubbed 'The Battle of Elland Road' against Valencia when a 1–1 score belied a stormy night of action that saw three players dismissed including Jack Charlton. Both teams departed to cool down and in the return leg O'Grady snatched a late winner in a memorable triumph at the Mestella Stadium.

Eliminated by Real Zaragoza in the semi-finals, United hoped to go one better in '66–67. A nasty injury restricted O'Grady's appearances in a season that included a record 7–0 defeat at West Ham in the League Cup.

United duly reached the Fairs Cup final and O'Grady was fit to play in both legs against Dinamo Zagreb at the start of '67–68. Defeated 2–0 on aggregate, another injury sustained shortly after the second leg wrecked his season. Months of hard work yielded two appearances shortly after United lifted the League Cup and O'Grady's persistence paid off at the start of the '68–69 season when he celebrated a first major honour in another delayed Fairs Cup final, this time versus Ferencvaros, in what was his first European outing since facing Dinamo.

O'Grady made a scoring comeback in the league as United racked up a fourth successive win with a 3–2 triumph at Ipswich Town. And O'Grady again showed Leeds fans on a sustained basis what he was capable of when free from injuries. With the emergence of Eddie Gray on the left wing and O'Grady raiding from the right, the duo wreaked havoc to defences around the country, creating opportunities galore for Lorimer and record signing Mick Jones. In a landmark campaign O'Grady chipped in with eight goals including United's second in a home triumph versus Arsenal and terrific solo winner against Manchester United in a 2–1 win. O'Grady featured in every round of the Fairs Cup defence and was particularly dangerous against Napoli. A bruising second leg saw Leeds progress on the toss of a disc before an injury-hit United fell to Ujpesti Dozsa in the fourth round.

The pursuit of a league title was the key objective and O'Grady continued to make his mark scoring in wins against Coventry City and at Stoke when he notched a brace in a 5–1 away win during a seven match winning streak. One of United's most valuable players during the season O'Grady enjoyed the highlight of his Leeds career when celebrating the title success against Liverpool at Anfield. To cap a remarkable campaign O'Grady won his second England cap against France when again he scored before being dropped as Alf Ramsey decided to adopt a wingless strategy as in the '66 World Cup. Not many footballers have scored three times in two games at international level before being dropped but then football is a 'funny old game'.

During the close season Revie strengthened his squad further with the purchase of Allan Clarke for a British record fee. O'Grady played in opening league games against Tottenham Hotspur and Arsenal before Revie selected Lorimer and Gray on the wings. The decision was tough on O'Grady who had just enjoyed his finest season at the club. After scoring a 35-second goal in a record-breaking 10–0 European Cup win against Lyn Oslo O'Grady played against Chelsea three days later before joining Wolves for £80,000. O'Grady's departure was a surprise to many United fans and sadly further injuries at Wolves, Birmingham City and Rotherham United saw his retirement at the end of 1973–74. Leeds supporters have not forgotten O'Grady's efforts in 120 (1 sub) appearances. A match-winning winger during United's early trophy successes of the late sixties, O'Grady set games alight with dazzling skills.

* * * * *

JIMMY 'SEAN' O'NEIL made three substitute appearances for Leeds United totalling 90 minutes of first team action as the Don Revie era drew to a close in 1973–74. United's pursuit of a second Division 1 title gave O'Neil his opportunity after years of patience.

Born in Belfast on 24 February 1952, O'Neil joined United from school before signing professional forms in May '67. O'Neil developed in the Central League side but Paul Reaney and Paul Madeley's expertise at right-back resulted in few first team openings. And compounding O'Neil's quandary, Nigel Davey and Trevor Cherry were also ahead in terms of selection in his latter years at Elland Road.

O'Neil's senior debut came in a UEFA Cup first round second leg clash against Stromsgodset following a 1–1 draw in Norway. Among the substitutes in a home match, United were expected to win comfortably in September '73, two Allan Clarke goals and a Mick Jones strike settled the tie by half time. With Leeds 5–1 ahead, O'Neil replaced Reaney 10 minutes from time. Jones completed the scoring in a thumping 6–1 win.

Frank Gray and Gary Liddell were fringe players included for a League Cup clash at Ipswich Town a week later. O'Neil was again selected as substitute and replaced Reaney at half time. In what would be his longest run out in a Leeds jersey, Brian Hamilton settled the tie at Portman Road with a late goal for a 2–0 victory. But there were few tears shed at Elland Road with aspirations focused on a second league title.

O'Neil's final appearance for United came a month later in the home leg of a UEFA Cup second round tie against Hibernian when he replaced Gray against Hibernian on 55 minutes. Leeds were a shade fortunate to draw the clash 0–0 before prevailing in a shoot-out at Easter Road when junior 'keeper, 17-year-old Glan Letheren, wrote himself into club folklore.

For O'Neil, the realisation he would not break into United's first team was clear. After Leeds clinched the Division 1 title, O'Neil joined Chesterfield where he'd become a legend over 12 seasons, playing over 350 games. Though O'Neil failed to make it at Elland Road he did pull on the famous white jersey adopted by Revie when he took the helm 13 years earlier.

* * * * *

ALAN PEACOCK provided the cutting edge to Leeds United's 1963–64 promotion campaign. Don Revie lacked a quality centre-forward and Peacock was his top target. Revie's hunch was proved right as his new striker, a prolific goal scorer in his prime, struck eight goals in 14 matches at a crucial stage of the title winning campaign helping Leeds win the title and promotion.

Born in Middlesbrough on 29 October 1937, Peacock won England youth honours and after serving his apprenticeship at his hometown club signed as a professional in November 1954. Tall, brave and strong in the air, Peacock partnered Brian Clough in attack and was a match for any centre-half in his heyday, scoring 126 league goals in 218 appearances for the Teeside club. Peacock also won four England caps during this period.

Revie's team began the Division 2 campaign in fine fashion and by Christmas sat top of the table but a mixed run of results after New Year ensued as they batted for the title with Sunderland and Preston. With skipper Bobby Collins pulling the midfield strings and Jack Charlton marshalling United's defence, Peacock added experience to the attack alongside Ian Lawson and Don Weston. And Peacock made his mark immediately following a club-record £55,000 transfer in February '64 with a debut goal at Norwich City. Settling in over the next few games Peacock was on target in consecutive 3–1 wins against former club Middlesbrough and Grimsby Town. Eight victories in the final 10 games brought a return to top-flight football. Peacock sealed promotion with a brace at Swansea Town, when Johnny Giles also hit the target in a 3–0 victory, before another double in the final game at Charlton Athletic sealed the title.

Peacock's input to the campaign had been brief but a major boost to the club's success. Leeds looked clinical and the move gave Peacock a new challenge although an ongoing knee injury meant he wouldn't feature until the second half of the 1964–65 campaign. Peacock returned to partner Jim Storrie with the team pushing for the Division 1 title and FA Cup. Fit again, Peacock's class proved important in a bruising FA Cup quarter-final clash at Crystal Palace, scoring twice in a 3–0 triumph. Leeds then overcame Manchester United to reach the club's first FA Cup final but ultimately both trophies eluded Revie's side. Peacock's form brought two further

England caps and he was tipped for a place in Alf Ramsey's '66 World Cup squad.

The 1965–66 campaign was one that would capture the nation's attention but first there was a league campaign to fulfil and Peacock enjoyed a fine start scoring in three of the opening four fixtures including goals during a 'double' over Aston Villa. Following a brace at Leicester City in a thrilling 3–3 draw Peacock showed his goal scoring knack in victories over Northampton Town, Stoke City, Sheffield Wednesday and West Brom. Leeds were demonstrating that the previous season's performance was not a one-off in top-flight football under Revie. And Peacock was in form especially with his teammates playing to his strength of aerial dominance. When United's inaugural Fairs Cup adventure kicked off against Torino, Peacock provided a trademark header for the winning goal. But an injury sustained at Sunderland after New Year wrecked his season and World Cup ambitions.

Making nine starts in 1966–67, Peacock scored his only League Cup goal for Leeds in a win over Newcastle United after returning to first team action following three knee operations. An Easter double over Sheffield United took his Leeds tally to 30 goals in all competitions. Peacock's final appearance for Leeds came in the last game of the league campaign against United's rivals Sheffield Wednesday when Terry Hibbitt scored the only goal in a 1–0 victory. Joining Plymouth on a free transfer in October '67, within six months Peacock retired from the sport he had served with distinction due to his persistent knee injury. Football often throws up ironic twists so it is perhaps apt that after scoring his final goals in a Leeds jersey against Sheffield United, a few weeks into the '67–68 season Revie signed Blades top striker Mick Jones for a record fee of £100,000 signalling the end to Peacock's Leeds career after 65 games. Peacock was a fantastic target man and scored his share of goals but also made opportunities for teammates with a deft flick or cushioned header and was an excellent team player. During his time at Leeds, Peacock's endeavours helped United achieve Division 1 status and he is undoubtedly one of Revie's most perceptive signings.

* * * * *

PAUL PETERSON made four appearances in 'shadow' Leeds United teams during one of the most renowned seasons in the club's history. The 1969–70 campaign ended in heartache when a treble bid to land the Division 1, European Cup and FA Cup floundered as fixture chaos ensued. As star players rested up before high prolife clashes, Peterson helped Leeds complete a chaotic fixture list.

Born in Luton on 22 December 1949, Peterson joined Leeds from school and signed professional forms on his 20th birthday. At the time United were flying high in the league and on course for an unprecedented achievement. Peterson, a promising left-back, had signed for the league champions and played in the reserves hoping for a chance to impress. His opportunity came along with another debutante, centre-half David Kennedy, as Revie's fringe players faced Brian Clough's Derby County at the Baseball Ground. United lost 4–1 in a match that grabbed plenty of back-page headlines.

Don Revie had decided to concede the title to Everton but playing his shadow XI brought a £5,000 fine from the Football Association. Revie insisted his jaded stars were injured or mentally fatigued and they did gain sympathy in sections of the media because no other club that season had such a schedule of fixtures. On a historical footing, the Derby clash concluded nine high profile games in 27 days including three FA Cup semi-final clashes versus Manchester United and two European Cup quarter-final ties versus Standard Liege. Two days after playing Derby, Leeds faced Celtic in a European Cup semi-final first leg clash. During a crazy period, the Derby clash ended four games in eight days and heralded three in four days.

Peterson was retained in three further semi-shadow line-ups including one in a 2–1 victory over Burnley on his home debut when Eddie Gray scored two wondrous goals to cap an unforgettable individual display. After replacing John Faulkner, who sustained a serious injury against Manchester City in the penultimate game of the season in a 3–1 defeat, Peterson pulled on the famous white shirt of Leeds for a last time at Ipswich Town as United finished the league season also in defeat.

While the first team squad bounced back with trophy success in 1970–71, Peterson joined Swindon Town the same month United triumphed in the Fairs Cup against Juventus. Like many apprentices at Elland Road in the late sixties, Peterson discovered just how hard it was to make the senior team. But in a brief spell, Peterson remains linked to a momentous period of the Revie era.

* * * * *

NOEL PEYTON battled away for Leeds United during a transitional period at the club. Relishing a challenge, Peyton was blessed with a turn of pace and played with a never-say-die spirit for a number of managers in a turbulent time on and off the field.

Born in Dublin on 4 December 1935, Peyton, a hard working inside forward, began his career at Shamrock Rovers in 1953, winning championship and FAI Cup winner's medals. Peyton also gained his first Republic of Ireland cap in a famous win against West Germany. Leeds manager Raich Carter was impressed with Peyton's application when he played for the League of Ireland against the Football League at Elland Road and duly signed him three months later in a £5,000 transfer in January 1958.

Following his Leeds debut in a 2–0 win at Bolton Wanderers, Peyton scored in a 3–2 defeat to Wolves. Inconsistency was an issue but after Peyton sealed a 2–0 win over Arsenal prior to the Easter fixtures, United did enough to survive a tough season. Bill Lambton succeeded Carter as manager in the close season but another tough campaign ensued although Lambton did sign Don Revie from Sunderland for a £12,000 fee. Peyton lost his place to Chris Crowe for much of the campaign with his only goal earning a 2–2 draw at Newcastle United in the penultimate away game when Revie also scored for Leeds. Striker Alan Shackleton had joined mid-season and promptly led the '58–59 scoring charts.

John McCole took up the scoring reigns in 1959–60 after Jack Taylor succeeded Lambton as manager. Peyton competed with Crowe and Jack Overfield for a place in the side. In 20 league appearances, Peyton again found a liking against Arsenal, scoring twice in a 3–2 triumph before hitting the target in wins over Chelsea, when Billy Bremner made his debut, and a 4–3 thriller versus Manchester City. But a season of woe saw United relegated.

Adjusting to life in Division 2, Peyton continued to play with zest and enthusiasm in '60–61. And he enjoyed rare moments of joy with league goals coming in goal-frenzied games, notching United's third goal in a 4–4 thriller at Bristol Rovers, opening the scoring at Sunderland in a 3–2 victory prior to hitting the winner in a 3–2 triumph at Lincoln City. But 48 hours on from the Lincoln triumph, Peyton was out of the first team after scoring the first goal in an extraordinary League Cup clash as United came back from 4–0 behind at Southampton to equalise before losing in the last minute 5–4.

Defeat ended United' first League Cup run but the match was recorded as the longest in English history as the floodlights failed for 32 minutes with the match finishing at 10.10pm. Bizarre records aside, United's form was poor. Freddie Goodwin, signed prior to relegation, succeeded Revie as captain. But with nine games of a traumatic season to go Revie was appointed player-manager and Peyton was back in the first team. An inauspicious start brought a 7–0 triumph over Lincoln but it was the only win of the run in. Peyton scored one of the goals but big challenges lay ahead.

Leeds began the 1961–62 campaign in fine style, winning the opening two encounters including a 3–1 win at Brighton when Peyton opened the scoring but a 5–0 drubbing at Liverpool heralded woeful form. In adversity, Peyton was a mainstay of the side, scoring in wins against Stoke City and Walsall before striking in a hard fought draw at Derby County. With relegation a distinct possibility Revie signed a number of players including Bobby Collins and his instinct paid off with a late run to survive on the final day of the season at Newcastle. Peyton missed the final two games but played his part in seven matches following Collins' arrival that brought two wins and five draws illustrating the desire required to survive.

With the introduction of numerous youngsters the following season, Peyton made only eight appearances as the Revie revolution began in earnest. A determined footballer, Peyton, who made five more appearances for Ireland whilst at Leeds, went on to briefly play for York City following a £4,000 transfer in July '63. Just under half of Peyton's 117 games for United came following Revie's appointment. His role in the Revie team was important, especially in a fraught '61–62 campaign when Revie needed players who would battle the full 90 minutes of a game. Peyton scored 20 goals for Leeds but more importantly for United, when Revie called on players to stand up and be counted, this diminutive inside forward was in the thick of the action.

* * * * *

PAUL REANEY was one of Leeds United's most consistent stars under Don Revie. 'Speedy' Reaney was a committed right-back as Leeds went from Division 2 strugglers to the team to beat every season. Winning every major honour in the Revie era, Reaney was a strong tackler and superb man-marker. Speed was Reaney's major asset but also stamina and positional awareness in nullifying the effectiveness of top wingers of the era including Manchester United's George Best, Liverpool's Peter Thompson, Chelsea's Charlie Cooke and Everton's Johnny Morrissey.

Born in London on 22 October 1944, Reaney's family moved to Leeds when he was baby. A fine sprinter and junior footballer, Reaney joined the Leeds ground staff in October 1961. Inside a year Reaney, Gary Sprake and Norman Hunter were thrust into the first team at Swansea Town as Revie began the process of introducing his talented youngsters.

A key member of the team that won the Division 2 title in 1963–64, Reaney was part of a defensive backbone alongside Jack Charlton, Hunter and Willie Bell that enabled Revie to develop a side capable of challenging for honours. Runners-up in the first two seasons of top-flight football in Division 1 to Manchester United and Liverpool, Bill Shankly's team also defeated Leeds led by inspirational captain Bobby Collins in the '65 FA Cup final.

An injury to Collins saw Billy Bremner take over as skipper in '66–67 and forge a dynamic partnership with Johnny Giles in midfield. With more youngsters coming through including Peter Lorimer, Paul Madeley, Eddie Gray and Terry Cooper, Leeds continued to go close. And during an exciting period, Leeds lost to Dinamo Zagreb in the Fairs Cup final when Reaney played as an 'auxiliary' winger in the second leg. Top honours had to come and duly arrived following Cooper's conversion to left-back taking over Bell's slot in the back four. Revie had a formidable defensive unit and with the signing of centre-forward Mick Jones, a cutting edge was developing.

Playing every game of United's League Cup, Fairs Cup and Division

1 title successes of the late sixties, Reaney was an integral part of the first team as United celebrated a hat-trick of trophies. The first trophy came at Wembley after victory over Arsenal, followed by another at the Nep Stadium after a staunch defensive display versus Ferencvaros and finally came a trophy at Anfield when another defensive master class against Liverpool clinched the title.

The 1968–69 campaign was memorable in many ways, not least because of the number of records United created including just two defeats and a record haul of 67 points. The season also saw Reaney's sixth goal for Leeds in the opening league fixture at Elland Road during a 4–1 win against Queens Park Rangers. And a Reaney goal was noteworthy because Leeds had never lost when their number 2 popped up with a Reaney 'special'. Since scoring his first against Stoke City in a 3–1 FA Cup victory in March '63, further goals had come in a 3–3 draw at Birmingham City in '64–65, a 6–0 win over Bury and a 1–1 draw at Old Trafford in '65–66, and a 3–1 win against Manchester United in '66–67.

Incredibly consistent and naturally fit, Reaney had missed only eight league games since his debut leading up to the 1970 FA Cup final against Chelsea. But after helping Leeds win the Charity Shield at the start of the 1969–70 campaign and battle all the way towards an unprecedented treble, Reaney's season ended in a flash when he suffered a broken leg at West Ham nine days before Wembley. The injury also wrecked Reaney's chances of playing in the World Cup finals in Mexico. Reaney's misfortune was a devastating blow having represented the Football League on three occasions, gained England U23 caps and two full caps versus Bulgaria and Portugal. But working hard, Reaney was back in first team action within months and added a third England cap to his collection after playing Malta. But, it would be his final England call up, which was a poor return for a player of his calibre.

Following the heartache of missing out on the treble, United won the Fairs Cup again in 1970–71 in a campaign that also saw Leeds crash out of the FA Cup to Colchester United and finish a fourth time Division 1 runners-up. But defeating Juventus on aggregate courtesy of 'away' goals was a tremendous achievement and encapsulated six seasons of endeavour by Leeds. Reaney had competed against the cream of wingers in European football and rarely been outfoxed by skilful opponents. United was now in its pomp and turned on the style in 1971–72. Whether battling to victories or scoring for fun, Leeds could take on any team around.

Allan Clarke had joined United's international line up partnering Jones in attack. And the front two were indebted to many a pinpoint cross from both flanks. As Cooper and Gray had a wonderful understanding on the left wing, Reaney and Lorimer had also developed a great relationship down the right. With his pace, strength and endurance Reaney caused havoc for opposing defences overlapping Lorimer before putting in teasing crosses for United's strike force to convert.

One of the most reliable right-backs in his generation, of all Reaney's attributes, goal line clearances became his trademark. It was an uncanny skill but repeatedly Reaney came up trumps appearing from nowhere to stop a certain goal. Reaney's sense of space and danger was invaluable and arguably his most important intervention came during the Centenary FA Cup final triumph over Arsenal in May '72 when in a pivotal moment of the match Reaney cleared a goalbound shot from Alan Ball off the line. Clarke's winner in the second half completed a domestic hat-trick for Reaney after losing in a cup final and two semi-finals in the sixties.

The '72–73 campaign saw a Reaney 'special' in a triumph at Coventry City but the season yielded more heartache with cup final losses to Sunderland and AC Milan in the European Cup Winners Cup final. United's FA Cup loss was hard to take, but the manner of Milan's victory when Reaney led Leeds in the absence of Bremner, through suspension, in Salonika was especially galling as the referee received a UEFA ban following his disgraceful officiating.

As ever though, United reacted in adversity and during another record-breaking season when they enjoyed an unbeaten 29-match run, Leeds claimed a second league title in Revie's last season in charge. Following Revie's departure, Reaney played in United's European Cup final defeat in '75 and saw further semi-final action in both the FA Cup and League Cup. And Reaney continued to be a lucky talisman in front of goal as strikes against Norwich City in league and FA Cup encounters meant Leeds had a record of seven wins and two draws after a Reaney 'special'. Reaney ended his playing days at Bradford City and New South Wales side Newcastle United where he was voted

Australian Player of the Year. Making 736 (11 sub) appearances over 18 seasons for United, just Bremner and Charlton played more games than Reaney, who is an all-time great at Elland Road. And only Bremner and Hunter played in more games during the Revie era itself with Reaney lining up on 582 (10 sub) occasions. A generation of high quality wingers knew they'd be in for a battle when facing this steadfast footballer. Bestie noted his most difficult games were against Reaney and there can be no finer tribute.

* * * * *

JOHN SHAW made two European appearances for Leeds United during the Don Revie era. United's games in the Fairs Cup and UEFA Cup are firmly ensconced in club folklore following events that unfolded on two extraordinary nights of action when teenager Shaw was substituted in both matches at half time.

Born in Stirling on 4 February 1954, Shaw joined the United ground staff before turning professional in February 1971. When Leeds were drawn to face Norwegian side SK Lierse in the Fairs Cup first round in 1971–72, the Flemish team were not expected to give the cup holders many problems. And a shadow United XI ran out comfortable 2–0 first leg winners with goals from Chris Galvin and Peter Lorimer. A week on from the Lierse win, Leeds lost a Fairs Cup play off against Barcelona at the Nou Camp Stadium for the right to retain the trophy.

Though disappointing, there was a packed fixture list to complete. In that regard, Revie selected 17 year old Shaw to play in goal for his senior debut in the return leg with Lierse at Elland Road. United started with five full internationals including Paul Reaney, Terry Cooper, Paul Madeley and Lorimer in the side so should have had more than enough experience to see off Lierse. Instead, the rank outsiders found themselves 3–0 ahead in six astonishing minutes just past the half hour point. In a lacklustre performance by Leeds, Shaw had been unlucky as Lierse profited from a deflected shot and a defensive slip up before the shell-shocked rookie 'keeper missed a cross for a tap in. Substituted at half time by first choice Gary Sprake, Lierse compounded United's misery with a fourth late on for a 4–0 win. The result was barely believable. On a humbling night for the club, United were out of Europe for the first time in an opening round and had also shipped four home goals for the first time in European competition.

By Shaw's final appearance in Revie's last season in charge, David Harvey was first choice 'keeper. United kicked off the 1973–74 season aiming for a second Division 1 title. In the UEFA Cup, Leeds coasted past Stromsgodset to set up a second round clash with Hibernian. Following a goalless draw, United prepared for the return leg at Easter Road. On the goalkeeping front Sprake and Harvey had already kept goal. But with Sprake joining Birmingham City, Ayr United's David Stewart had signed as Harvey's back up. Preparations for the return leg were frenzied with Harvey rested and Stewart unavailable due to UEFA regulations. Revie called up third choice 'keeper Shaw while 17 year old youth goalie Glan Letheren sat on the bench. Revie also rested Gordon McQueen, Norman Hunter and Madeley with Johnny Giles the only long-term casualty. On a night of massive frustration for Shaw, the 19 year old 'keeper was unable to play in the second half after breaking two fingers in his right hand. The rest is history as Letheren came on and skipper Billy Bremner marshalled his team to a 0–0 draw before crashing home the winning spot kick for United's first penalty shoot out triumph.

At the end of an eventful season when Leeds clinched a second league title, Shaw joined Bristol City, serving them with distinction in 295 games. Returning with City to Elland Road, Shaw showed his talent on a number of occasions before playing 109 games for Exeter City. In a season when Revie selected five goalkeepers for the first time in the club's history and four for European action, in another first, Shaw had crafted his place in United's story.

* * * * *

BOBBY SIBBALD made two appearances for Leeds United in the 1960s. For the rookie right-back his patience was finally rewarded after waiting on the fringes of United's powerful first team squad. Like other reserves in the Don Revie era, regular first team football would have to be achieved elsewhere. But Sibbald did play in a strong United XI and eventually faced many of the world's great players of United's heyday when he was among a growing number of British footballers to play in the burgeoning North American Soccer League in the late seventies.

Born in Hebbern, County Durham on 25 January 1948, Sibbald

joined the United ground staff before signing as a professional in January 1965. Sibbald made the Central League side but with first team regulars Paul Reaney, Paul Madeley and reserve Nigel Davey selected at right-back, opportunities were thin on the ground. Sibbald's senior debut came when he was named as substitute for a trip to Everton as Leeds were mounting another title challenge in February '67.

The clash with the FA Cup holders saw three of England's World Cup '66 stars on parade with Ray Wilson and Alan Ball playing for the hosts and Jack Charlton in United's side. United went down 2–0 at Goodison Park with Sibbald replacing Terry Cooper who had yet to convert from left wing to left-back where he'd become world class.

Sibbald pulled on a United jersey for the last time in the final home game of the '67–68 season as Revie rested players following an exhaustive fixture list with an impending Fairs Cup semi-final clash at Dundee four days away. The season had seen Leeds lift the League Cup and European honours would soon follow. The Division 1 challenge was already over when United's shadow team including two first team regulars went down 3–0 at Turf Moor for a fourth consecutive defeat, the only time Revie experienced such a run as manager, but there were extenuating circumstances.

Sibbald joined York City in February '69, making 79 appearances before playing well over 200 games for Southport prior to a stint at Los Angeles where teammates included Johan Cruyff and George Best. Many other stars of world football joined the NASL razzamatazz as they wound down careers including Pele, Eusebio, Franz Beckenbauer, Carlos Alberto and Giorgio Chinaglia. From a frustrating start in the mid-sixties at Elland Road, Sibbald made the most of his career. During the mid to late sixties during the Revie era, too many players came into their prime to make an impact but on a winter's afternoon in the aftermath of England's victorious '66 win Sibbald joined the battle for Division 1 points.

* * * * *

ERIC SMITH added steel to Leeds United's relegation battle during the early stages of the Don Revie era. A disciplined, tough tackling right half, Smith recovered from a serious injury in his second game for the club to bolster the side in Revie's first season in charge. Tragically, Smith suffered a double fracture of his leg shortly after Revie began introducing his crop of young players in September '62. This would ultimately end Smith's Leeds career.

Born in Glasgow on 29 July 1934, Smith played for Glasgow Benburb before joining Celtic in 1953. Following his debut in the 1954–55 season Smith played in the 1956 Scottish Cup final defeat to Hearts among nearly 100 appearances for the Hoops. Capped by Scotland versus Portugal and Holland in 1959, Leeds manager Jack Taylor signed Smith for £10,000 in June '60 to boost United's defensive side in the game.

Smith made his Division 2 debut in a 2–0 defeat to Liverpool on the opening day of the 1960–61 season before breaking a leg on his home bow against Bristol Rovers, a match United drew 1–1. As Leeds struggled for results, Smith battled back to fitness and returned on New Years Eve in a 3–1 win at Rotherham United. The win came in the midst of an unbeaten eight-match run that brought five victories but five defeats in the next seven games ended Taylor's tenure at Elland Road. Leeds actually won Taylor's final game in charge when Smith scored the only goal at Norwich City but within days Revie was installed as player-manager.

Unavailable for Revie's first game in charge at Portsmouth, Smith played in the final eight games of the season that brought one victory, a 7–0 triumph over Lincoln City. United finished clear of relegation but it had been a tough debut season for the Scottish international. A gregarious, jovial character in the dressing room Smith began the 1961–62 campaign at right-back when Billy Bremner got the season off to a flyer with goals in consecutive victories against Charlton Athletic and Brighton and Hove Albion. But a fraught season soon ensued as United battled relegation. Revie needed strong personalities in his struggling side and Smith was a key player both off the field and in the heat of a battle whether in defence or a defensive midfield role. In a season where wins were a rare commodity, Smith knocked in a welcome winner in a home clash with Sunderland just after the New Year. By this juncture of the season, Revie had brought the first of a number of fresh faces into the team with the signing of striker Billy McAdams. And entering March '61 with relegation a distinct threat, experienced campaigners Bobby Collins and Cliff Mason joined the survival bid. Playing every game of a memorable late dash to safety, Smith was a resolute character not afraid of making his point to colleagues showing anything less than total commitment to the cause as United staved off relegation on the final day of the season at Newcastle United.

In only the second game after Revie introduced future stars in Gary Sprake, Paul Reaney and Norman Hunter during the early stages of the '62–63 season, Smith suffered a horrific double leg break during a 2–0 home win over Chelsea when Revie's first signing Albert Johanneson struck both goals. Smith had made 69 appearances and would not play for United again, joining Morton in June '64 as Leeds prepared for top-flight football. Smith coached and managed the Greenock club before posts at Cypriot side Pezoporikos Larnaca, Hamilton Academicals and United Arab Emirates outfits Sharjah FC, Al Nasr and Al Shaab. Smith, who died in 1991, also worked briefly with Revie in the UAE. Before the glory years that were to come under Revie's watch, building a team capable of survival was the initial objective. Smith played with gusto for Leeds and Revie had a player who set the right example on and off the pitch.

* * * * *

GARY SPRAKE made a dramatic entry to senior football at the age of 16 for Leeds United. A late replacement for veteran 'keeper Tommy Younger against Southampton in March '62 the rookie goalkeeper flew down to the South Coast and just made a delayed kick off. United lost 4–1 but Sprake was soon Don Revie's first choice 'keeper. Winning numerous honours domestically and in Europe, Sprake was unbeatable on his day.

Born in Winch Wen, near Swansea, on 3 April 1945, Sprake grew up close to legendary Welsh goalkeeper Jack Kelsey. Capped at schoolboy level Sprake joined Leeds' band of youngsters being groomed for stardom at Elland Road. With Younger and reserve 'keeper Alan Humphreys unavailable Sprake made his senior debut at the Dell and turned professional two months later.

After surviving relegation in 1960–61, United's sluggish start to the new campaign prompted Revie to introduce Sprake along with debutants Paul Reaney and Norman Hunter at Swansea Town in

September '62. The trio alongside Jack Charlton and Willie Bell formed the backbone of a solid defence enabling Revie to develop a winning side.

A key member of United's Division 2 title team in 1963–64, Sprake capped a memorable season when he became the youngest Welsh 'keeper at 18 years of age. The first of 37 full caps Sprake also won five U23 caps for his country over an 11-year period.

Led by inspirational skipper Bobby Collins, Sprake enjoyed a terrific first season in top-flight football as Leeds finished runners-up in the league and FA Cup in '64–65. Missing just 11 league games by the end of the decade Leeds went close to major honours before winning the League Cup in 1967–68.

Terry Cooper, who scored the winning goal at Wembley, completed Revie's back four in front of Sprake. The quartet of Reaney-Charlton-Hunter-Cooper was a formidable defensive unit and aligned to Sprake, who was one of the best British 'keepers around during the late sixties, Leeds were the most consistent team in English football. And Sprake needed to be on his game as David Harvey was an outstanding deputy. Blessed with natural ability, Sprake was a terrific shot-stopper and won many games for Leeds. Sprake enjoyed his finest hour for United against Hungarian giants Ferencvaros in the hostile atmosphere of the Nep Stadium, Budapest in the Fairs Cup final second leg. Holding a one-goal advantage from the first leg at Elland Road, Sprake pulled off a string of world class saves as Leeds clinched the trophy for the first time.

Ever-present when Leeds won the Division 1 championship with a record number of points in 1968–69, Sprake kept goal in a period when on top of winning three trophies United were Division 1 runners-up twice, FA Cup and Fairs Cup finalists, and reached three cup semi-finals.

Sprake was a model of consistency but also made a few 'howlers'. Sprake's most embarrassing gaffe came at Liverpool in December '67 when he swung the ball into his own net attempting to clear upfield. Anfield's ever-alert stadium announcer at half time played singer Des O'Connor's hit song 'Careless Hands'! Sprake had also been at fault against Everton during a key moment of an FA Cup semi-final later in the season but arguably his worst error came in United's faltering treble bid in 1969–70 against Chelsea in the FA Cup final when he failed to hold a long range effort from Peter Houseman approaching half-time at Wembley. Sprake's woes continued the following season at Crystal Palace and against Division 4 Colchester United when United crashed out of the FA Cup. But the campaign ended on a high as United claimed a second Fairs Cup against Juventus on 'away' goals.

However, the watershed of Sprake's career came in 1971–72. Leeds played irresistible football at times, notably turning on the style against Manchester United and Southampton in the second half of the season. Sprake was first choice throughout the campaign up to a 3–1 win at home to Huddersfield Town. Sidelined from a league clash at Stoke City a week before United's FA Cup semi-final clash against Birmingham City, Harvey stepped in, as he had done on many occasions before, and put in a faultless display in a 3–0 victory. Pondering whether to retain Harvey or reinstate Sprake, Revie selected the Scottish 'keeper to face Birmingham. Leeds cruised through to Wembley where Sprake was a non-playing reserve as Leeds won the Cup.

Making just two more senior starts, Sprake's last game for Leeds was in a UEFA Cup tie at Stromsgodset. Sprake would shortly join Birmingham City before retiring due to a back injury in December '75. Of note, Sprake's final game against the Norwegians helped set a new mark that still stands at United as he was one of five 'keepers, along with his successor Harvey, David Stewart, John Shaw and Glan Letheren to play in a campaign, demoting a benchmark he had equalled in his '61–62 debut season when Younger, Humphreys and Terry Carling also played.

During Sprake's career at Leeds, he undoubtedly enjoyed far more good games than bad ones. Although Sprake occasionally lost his temper he could pull off stunning reflex saves, was assured in claiming crosses and brave when studs were flying about or if he had to dive at a forward's feet. But his Achilles heel was lapses of concentration. Should Revie have switched Harvey for Sprake earlier in United's pursuit of honours? It's a debate that will continue whenever followers of the club discuss the era but record books state Sprake played in goal for Leeds more than any other 'keeper in the club's history. One of only five players to line up in over 500 games during the Revie era alongside Billy Bremner, Hunter, Reaney and Charlton, Sprake is ninth on the all-time list with 505 (2 sub) appearances.

During his trophy-laden career, aside his big match display against Ferencvaros, Sprake enjoyed notable Fairs Cup semi-final performances against Dundee and Liverpool on route to winning the Fairs Cup twice. Sprake also pulled off stunning saves versus Manchester United in FA Cup replays in '64–65 in '69–70 on the last stop before Wembley. It must also be noted that in '68–69 when Leeds set numerous Football League standards, Sprake played in every game as United shipped 26 goals of which nine were at home (both records) suffered only two defeats (a record) and were unbeaten at home (matching a club record) as in '63–64 when he missed only one game. Revie assembled a superb defence of which Sprake undoubtedly played his part.

* * * * *

DAVID STEWART was Don Revie's last signing to play for Leeds United's first team in his time at the helm. During the 1973–74 campaign Stewart's four appearances in goal were all at Elland Road and the Scot was an assured presence as deputy to first choice 'keeper David Harvey.

Born in Glasgow on 11 March 1947, Stewart developed his goalkeeping skills at a number of local teams, winning the Scottish Junior Cup at Kilsyth Rangers prior to joining Ayr United before the start of the '67–68 campaign. During six seasons at Ayr, Stewart impressed Scottish selectors who picked him for the U23 side. And his consistent displays were rewarded when he joined United in a £30,000 transfer with the departure of Gary Sprake to Birmingham City in October '73.

When Stewart arrived at Elland Road, Leeds were heading the way in the Division 1 title race. Stewart had to bide his time for a first team opportunity as Harvey did with Sprake. But a senior start soon arrived when Harvey was sidelined for an FA Cup replay against Wolves in January '74. The match was brought forward to a 1.30pm kick off with the country in the midst of a three-day week due to an energy crisis. Leeds won 1–0 and Stewart received praise after coming in as a late replacement when Harvey failed a fitness test. Unwittingly Stewart also completed a piece of club history against Wolves as he became the fifth goalkeeper selected by Revie during the campaign, eclipsing three previous seasons when four goalkeepers had kept goal.

During a memorable league campaign, Leeds put together a record breaking 29-match unbeaten run from the start of the season that ended at Stoke City, which in turn came a few days after United surprisingly crashed out of the FA Cup to Bristol City. The mini wobble generated plenty of headlines speculating that the pressure was getting to Leeds as they prepared for a league game at home to Leicester City.

With Harvey failing a fitness test, Stewart was called up for his Division 1 debut. Leeds drew 1–1 against Leicester after letting in a late equaliser in an uninspiring performance. Newcastle United were the next visitors to Elland Road when Stewart deputised in another 1–1 draw. Again Leeds let a lead slip but United were indebted to Stewart for a reflex stop from a Malcolm MacDonald header. Stewart's final appearance of the season came against Manchester City. This time Leeds dominated the home fixture but had to settle for a disputed penalty, slotted home by Peter Lorimer. Stewart's three-match run coincided with one win in six league and cup games. Three successive defeats followed spelling danger but Revie's team found resolve with Liverpool waiting to pounce and enjoyed an unbeaten run to seal a second league title.

Following Revie's departure during the close season, Stewart enjoyed further spells of first team action in a transitional period under four managers. After Brain Clough's 44-day reign, Jimmy Armfield was at the helm as Leeds embarked on a European Cup run. Stewart came into the side for the last third of the season when Harvey was injured in a car crash, making his European debut at a fog-bound Elland Road against Anderlecht. United won 3–0 before the second leg when he made a number of fine saves. Through to the semi-finals, Leeds faced Barcelona and Stewart enjoyed his finest game for United in a second leg clash at the Nou Camp, especially late on when Barcelona threw everything at the Leeds defence who held out for a 1–1 draw to reach the final. Amid controversy on and off the pitch, Bayern Munich ended United's bid for the trophy.

Stewart would not feature again until the last third of the 1976–77 campaign when Leeds lost to Manchester United in the FA Cup semi-finals. And he shared the 'keeping duties with Harvey the following season as Leeds reached the League Cup semi-finals. Stewart's consistent form earned him a Scotland call up in a friendly with East

Germany. The Scots lost 1–0 but Stewart, in his only appearance for his country, was superb, making a string of saves and stopping a penalty. Following Jock Stein's 44-day tenure at Leeds, Stewart joined West Brom for £70,000 a month after Jimmy Adamson took the helm at United in October '78 before a spell at Swansea City, succeeding Glan Letheren in never appearing for the Baggies. During Stewart's five-year Leeds career when he played in 74 games, supporters became used to his poised performances in goal. Calm, brave, a dominating presence and possessing great reflexes, Revie's final purchase proved to be a shrewd investment.

* * * * *

JIM STORRIE was an astute signing by Don Revie after Leeds United avoided relegation in his first season as manager. A strong, fearless centre-forward Storrie had a never-say-die attitude leading the attack and scored his share of goals in the early sixties.

Born in Kirkintilloch, Lanarkshire on 31 March 1940, Storrie was a prolific goal scorer for Airdrie prior to a £15,650 transfer to Elland Road in June '62. After the shenanigans in '61–62 when Jack Charlton played as an emergency striker Revie strengthened his attack firstly by acquiring Storrie then with the record £53,000 purchase of Leeds legend John Charles from Juventus for a second spell at the club.

United fans travelled to Stoke in large numbers to welcome back Charles but Storrie grabbed the headlines in a 2–0 win on the opening day of the '62–63 season. Storrie, Charles and Albert Johanneson scored in the first home game versus Rotherham United but Leeds went down to a 4–3 defeat. A mixed start saw Revie introduce youngsters to the first team including Gary Sprake, Paul Reaney, Norman Hunter, Rod Johnson and Peter Lorimer. Charles and other veteran players departed as a new era dawned with Bobby Collins charged to gel Revie's side together. Storrie led the line supported by Johanneson and mid-season signing Don Weston during an exciting campaign as Revie's team knitted together. Storrie struck hat-tricks against Plymouth Argyle and Cardiff City. And United's sharpshooter struck twice against Walsall and Luton Town before a 5–0 win at Swindon in the final fixture served notice that fifth-placed Leeds could challenge for promotion. Top scoring with 27 league and cup goals Storrie also hit the target in the FA

Cup and League Cup. Only five players have exceeded Storrie's feat in the club's history and for a debut season it was an incredible effort. Of note, Tom Jennings, John Charles, Peter Lorimer, Lee Chapman and Jermaine Beckford accumulated more goals in one campaign.

United were amongst the favourites for promotion in '63–64 but nine games into the season Storrie was sidelined after goals in home wins against Bury and Portsmouth. A niggling injury resulted in Storrie making 15 starts in the title winning campaign. Recovering in the close season, Storrie was not fazed by top-flight football. Playing alongside Weston in addition to youngsters Rod Belfitt and Rod Johnson before Peacock's return, Storrie finished top scorer with 19 goals slotting home braces in wins against Wolves, Fulham and Stoke City.

Revie's team stunned pundits by challenging for the title with Manchester United and in a thrilling campaign lost out to Matt Busby's team on goal average. United also reached the FA Cup final for the first time in the club's history when Storrie scored against Everton and Crystal Palace on the road to Wembley. In the final Storrie was carrying an injury as a lacklustre Leeds lost to Liverpool.

In '65–66 after missing the opening months of the season due to injury, Storrie returned to the team in a 6–1 rout against Northampton Town. And Storrie proved something of a lucky talisman, as Leeds never lost when he hit the back of the net. Among Storrie's goals was the winner at Blackburn Rovers in a 3–2 win and brace against Arsenal in a 3–0 victory before the lowest gate ever recorded at Highbury, just 4,554. Storrie also scored his only goal in Europe during a 4–1 win against Ujpest Dozsa. Runners-up to Division 1 champions Liverpool, Leeds also reached the Fairs Cup semi-finals. Storrie finished the campaign second top scorer with 15 goals behind Lorimer.

But the form of emerging forwards including Lorimer, Jimmy Greenhoff and Eddie Gray saw Storrie make a handful of appearances in '66–67. Storrie donned United's all-white strip for a last time in a Boxing Day clash versus Newcastle United and scored in a 5–0 triumph in front of a packed house at Elland Road. There was no better way to sign off his United career before joining Aberdeen in February '67 where he helped the Dons reach the Scottish Cup final against Celtic. Storrie later had spells at

Rotherham United, Portsmouth and Aldershot. St Mirren player-coach and Airdrie coach, Storrie was also Waterlooville and St Johnstone player-manager. Storrie played an important role at United. Scoring 67 goals in 153 (3 sub) appearances, Storrie was top scorer twice. Revie's intuitive investment was a bargain, as United became a force in Division 1.

* * * * *

DON WESTON is the only Leeds United player signed by Don Revie to score a hat-trick on his first team debut. Weston's effort in a 3–1 victory at Stoke City approaching the festive games in December '62 came in a season curtailed by the 'big freeze' that shut down football for two months. An experienced centre-forward Weston finished joint top scorer in United's 1963–64 Division 2 title campaign.

Born in New Houghton on 6 March 1936, Weston played for the 31st Training Regiment Royal Artillery in North Wales during his national service. Beginning his career at Wrexham in June '59, Weston scored 40 goals in 84 appearances for the Welsh club. Weston played briefly for Birmingham City after a £15,000 move before Rotherham United signed him in a £10,000 transfer. Weston played against Aston Villa in the first League Cup final and scored Rotherham's winning goal when they knocked Leeds out of the competition the following season.

In 1962–63, Revie promoted youngsters into the first team and strengthened his attack with the purchase of Jim Storrie although signing John Charles did not work out. Weston arrived at Elland Road after scoring 21 goals in 76 appearances for the Millers and made the perfect start at Stoke. Following atrocious weather Weston scored again in the next home game when Leeds defeated Derby County 3–1 in March '62. Ten victories followed in a 15-match spell as United moved up the table. Weston struck in wins over Charlton Athletic and Luton Town as a promotion bid built up momentum however three defeats ended hopes of catching the leading pack.

Progress had been made and Weston got the '63–64 campaign off to the perfect start with the only goal against former team

Rotherham on the opening day of the season. And in a promotion battle with Sunderland and Preston, Storrie's absence through injury meant Weston and Albert Johanneson provided the bulk of goals with skipper Bobby Collins and Johnny Giles chipping in with important efforts. Enjoying a rich vein of form Weston scored in early season wins against Portsmouth, Norwich City, Northampton Town, Huddersfield Town and Grimsby Town.

Another Weston goal against Manchester City kept Leeds top of the table in the New Year before a dip in form prompted Revie to sign Alan Peacock to boost the attack. And the new strike-force of Peacock and Weston scored a goal apiece in a 2–2 draw at Norwich. An injury kept Weston out for a spell but he was fit again for the last five fixtures. Weston duly helped take Leeds to the brink of promotion with strikes in 2–1 triumphs over Newcastle United and Leyton Orient. And United sealed promotion at Swansea Town before wrapping up the title at Charlton Athletic.

Leading the scoring charts alongside Johanneson with 13 league goals, all Weston's goals contributed to points in a first title success in 40 years. Weston made 15 appearances in United's debut Division 1 season under Revie in 1964–65, memorably scoring in a 4–2 victory against defending champions Liverpool in the first home game of what would prove to be an astonishing season. Weston also hit the winner in a 2–1 triumph at Arsenal and as Leeds embarked on the road to Wembley, struck a brilliant winning goal in a fourth round replay at Everton. In a thrilling campaign Leeds missed out on the title to Manchester United by goal average and Liverpool won the FA Cup in extra time. Making four starts in '65–66, Weston ended his playing days at Huddersfield and Chester.

Weston, who died in 2007, scored 26 goals in 78 games for Leeds. It also seems fitting that after his dream debut at the Victoria Ground, Weston's final goals for Leeds came in another 3–1 win over Stoke in April '65. During an important period in United's development under the new boss, Weston was one of Revie's most influential signings that began a renaissance at Elland Road.

* * * * *

BRIAN WILLIAMSON played eight games over a five-year period for Leeds United in the early sixties. Understudy to teenage 'keeper Gary Sprake, Williamson deputised in all three domestic competitions until another teenage 'keeper David Harvey took up the standby duties.

Born in Blyth on 6 October 1939, Williamson began his career at Seaton Delaval before a two-year spell at Gateshead until they lost Football League status in July '60 when he joined Crewe Alexandra. Williamson arrived at Elland Road as Revie had begun to build a team around promising youngsters in December '62. Apart from Sprake other gifted teenagers to earn first team breaks included Norman Hunter, Rod Johnson, Peter Lorimer, Paul Reaney and Barrie Wright in a landmark 1962–63 season. Not all would make it long term but Revie's intent regarding his youth policy was clear.

With Sprake sidelined for a three-match spell at the end of March '63, Williamson kept a clean sheet on his debut against Grimsby Town in a 3–0 victory when Billy Bremner and Bobby Collins scored. Bremner, who'd succeed Collins as skipper, scored the only goal in a midweek win against Scunthorpe United when Williamson kept another clean sheet before tasting defeat at Plymouth Argyle.

Leeds had flirted with promotion but were serious contenders in 1963–64. United led the table when Williamson made his only first team appearance of the campaign in a 2–2 draw at Swindon Town just after New Year. Johnny Giles and Hunter scored for Leeds. Following promotion Revie rested first team players in the League Cup and gave promising players first team exposure. Williamson deputised for Sprake against Huddersfield Town and Aston Villa when Terry Cooper and Paul Madeley were among future stars to get run outs. And credit to Revie's makeshift team because they knocked Huddersfield out before exiting to the first winners of the trophy in round three.

Leeds challenged for the Division 1 title and Williamson was called up for his top-flight debut when Sprake failed to recover from a leg injury. Johnson scored the only goal against West Brom and Williamson received plaudits following saves from Jeff Astle and Bobby Hope. After finishing runners-up in the league and FA Cup, Williamson's final appearance came in an FA Cup clash when Lorimer struck a hat-trick against Bury in a 6–0 triumph in January '65.

With Harvey ready to step up as understudy, Williamson joined Nottingham Forest where he made 19 starts as deputy to Peter

Grummitt. Following a loan spell at Leicester City, Williamson ended his playing days at Fulham. Williamson's loyalty was never underestimated by coaching staff and players at Elland Road. Always prepared, whenever called upon he stepped in and gave solid performances. Leeds won five games in which he played. Williamson also kept four clean sheets. It is also worth noting United's FA Cup win over Bury was only equalled once in the Revie era against non-league Sutton United. Fringe players were key to the Revie philosophy and Williamson took on the role admirably.

* * * * *

BARRIE WRIGHT captained Leeds United's Central League team packed with promising players at the beginning of the Revie era. An outstanding prospect at left-back Wright skippered England Schools and won Youth honours but was unable to carve out a regular first team place at Elland Road.

Born in Bradford on 6 November 1945, Wright joined United's ground staff and turned professional in November '62. A member of United's gifted U18 squad with David Harvey, Peter Lorimer, Terry Hibbitt, Jimmy Greenhoff, Rod Belfitt, Rod Johnson and Eddie Gray, when Leeds made a poor start to the 1962–63 campaign, first team opportunities quickly arrived. Don Revie was looking to build a team around youngsters backed by experienced professionals including Bobby Collins, Jack Charlton and Willie Bell. In a watershed season Revie gave senior debuts to Paul Reaney, Norman Hunter, Johnson and Lorimer before Wright was handed an opportunity with veteran full back Grenville Hair injured.

Wright's promotion to first team football could hardly have gone better as Leeds defeated Preston North End 4–1 at home before recording an Easter double over Charlton Athletic, 2–1 at The Valley and 4–1 at Elland Road. For some weeks there was talk of promotion but results tailed off with Leeds finishing fifth.

United started out among the favourites for promotion in 1963–64. But while former reserve teammates including Gary Sprake, Reaney and Hunter were becoming established first team players, Wright had to settle for two starts due to Bell successfully converting to the left-back position. In fact, Wright deputised for both full backs, Reaney in a 2–0 win at Leyton Orient and Bell in a draw against Cardiff City.

Back in top-flight football, Revie continued to blood promising teenagers particularly in the League Cup including Terry Cooper, Paul Madeley, Greenhoff and Belfitt. For Wright it must have been a frustrating time as he faced Huddersfield Town and Aston Villa but he had to keep battling away. Wright's eighth and last first team game again came in the League Cup as a shadow side boasting just two senior players lost 4–2 to eventual cup winners West Brom in October '65. Weakened by injuries and international call-ups Leeds played three debutants Harvey, Dennis Hawkins and another full back, Nigel Davey. Four goals adrift in 25 minutes Leeds battled back but of the rookie players that night only Harvey became a first team regular. Wright went on loan to New York Generals before the end of United's 1965–66 campaign prior to spells at Brighton and Hove Albion, Hartlepool, Bradford Park Avenue, Gainsborough Trinity and Thackley. Wright quit full time football at the age of 25. For talented apprentices during the Revie era, breaking through was incredibly difficult due to the pool of players at his disposal. Wright lamentably illustrated that point.

* * * * *

TERRY YORATH developed into a resolute ball-winning midfield player during the Revie era. A versatile footballer, Yorath started out as a defender before playing an important role in Leeds United's second Division 1 title success.

Born in Cardiff on 27 March 1950, Yorath was a talented scrum half at rugby union and had trials for Cardiff Schools before fortuitously getting his break into football when Cardiff Boys were a player short against Rhondda Valley in a trial match. Impressing selectors, Yorath represented Welsh Schools. Spurning a chance to play for Bristol Rovers, Bristol City and his hometown club, Cardiff City, Yorath followed in the footsteps of John Charles and Gary Sprake in joining United who both were also spotted by Leeds' local scout Jack Pickard.

Signing professional forms in April '67, Yorath made his first team debut in the final league game of the 1967–68 season in a weakened side that lost to Burnley with Revie resting players before a Fairs Cup semi-final at Dundee. Yorath was a regular for the reserves in the Central League when he won the first of seven Welsh U23 caps and a full cap versus Italy in Rome prior to his European debut for Leeds in the Fairs Cup against Ujpesti Dozsa in March '69.

A handful of sub appearances followed before Yorath enjoyed a seven match run in the side at the end of an extraordinary treble campaign as Revie rested his first XI. Yorath was in United's defence in an infamous 4–1 loss at Derby before a noteworthy 2–1 win against Burnley when Eddie Gray struck two wonder goals. Occasional appearances ensued and Yorath scored his first goal for Leeds in a 5–1 victory versus Newcastle United in September '71. Like other reserve players at United during this period, Yorath showed great loyalty but unlike them he was in an unusual situation of being a regular on the international stage. More than capable of being in first teams elsewhere in Division 1, Yorath's dedication was commendable and demonstrated Revie's man-management skills.

Yorath's perseverance was rewarded when he came into United's midfield alongside Billy Bremner and Johnny Giles following an injury to Gray approaching the festive fixtures in 1972–73. Alongside Revie's star players Yorath was far from out of place as a winning streak ensued. Among a number of notable performances, United were superb in a memorable 3–0 win in front of the *Match of the Day* cameras against Manchester City. Making 23 starts in 35 games during the campaign on four fronts, Yorath demonstrated his flexibility with outstanding displays in central defence alongside Norman Hunter after substituting Jack Charlton in Leeds' FA Cup semi-final win over Wolves before United's European Cup Winners Cup semi-final clashes against Hajduk Split. Yorath replaced Gray at Wembley against Sunderland in a shock defeat before partnering Hunter in a traumatic loss to AC Milan in Salonika.

Having been on the fringes of United's first team Yorath broke through the following season as Leeds responded in stoic fashion to the disappointment of losing two cup finals. Written off by pundits, United embarked on an unbeaten 29-match run. Yorath came into the side in the midst of an astonishing period of form initially for the unlucky Gray then Giles and Mick Bates. Playing on the left side of midfield alongside Bremner and Paul Madeley, Yorath impressed during a thrilling campaign to sign off the Revie era in style. Scoring twice during the season, Yorath's audacious lob opened the scoring in a 3–0 win against Ipswich Town at Portman Road. Yorath also headed the only goal in a home win versus Norwich City as Leeds powered to the league title in a campaign that also saw the emergence of centre-half Gordon McQueen and centre-forward Joe Jordan.

After Brain Clough's shambolic 44-day spell Yorath filled in across midfield in 1974–75 under new boss Jimmy Armfield as a new era dawned at Elland Road. Yorath played throughout the European Cup run before Bayern Munich shattered United's hopes. In what appeared a breakthrough campaign for Yorath, he also chipped in with six goals scoring his only European goal for Leeds versus Ujpesti Dozsa during a 5–1 aggregate triumph and terrific strike against Stoke City in a 3–1 home win.

Armfield continued the process of replacing Revie's legends in 1975–76 and Yorath was handed Giles' number 10 shirt. Playing the majority of the campaign, alas Yorath became a scapegoat for a section of frustrated home supporters in what was a transitional phase. For Yorath, it heralded a sad end to his Leeds career after showing steadfast loyalty whether in midfield, defence or on occasion as an auxiliary striker. Yorath joined Coventry City for £125,000 in August '76 before spells at Tottenham Hotspur, where his industry gave the mercurial Glen Hoddle time to express his skills, Vancouver Whitecaps, Bradford City and Swansea City.

On the international stage Yorath led Wales in 42 of his 59 games for his country. And in his first managerial job went agonisingly close to taking Wales to the 1998 European Championships prior to posts at Bradford City, Swansea City, Cardiff City, Sheffield Wednesday and Huddersfield Town. An assiduous footballer, Yorath made 165 (31 sub) appearances for Leeds, scoring 12 goals. Always displaying steel when required, Yorath showed total commitment whenever he took the field. Without players of his ability and character Revie's Leeds would not have become the force they were. Stepping into a world class team at short notice, Yorath took to the task with gusto and no shortage of skill. Eventually Yorath enjoyed a run in the side and delivered the goods particularly in '73–74.

* * * * *

TOMMY YOUNGER was a shrewd signing by Don Revie on and off the field. Possessing vast experience, Younger helped Leeds United escape relegation in Revie's first season in charge and the development of understudy Gary Sprake.

Born in Edinburgh on 10 April 1930, Younger was based in Germany with BAOR during his National Service and flew home each weekend to play for Hibernian where he won Scottish League titles in 1950–51 and 1951–52. A top 'keeper of his era, Younger represented the Scottish League and won the first of 24 Scotland caps at Hibs. Younger joined Liverpool for £9,000 in 1956 and whilst at Anfield led his country in the World Cup finals two years later. Among Younger's teammates was Celtic star and future Leeds teammate Bobby Collins. Appointed Falkirk player-manager prior to the 1959–60 season, Younger joined Stoke City in March '60 before announcing his retirement due to a slipped disc.

Revie persuaded Younger to come out of retirement in September '61 with United experiencing a woeful time in his first full season in charge. Alan Humphreys and Terry Carling had kept goal during six defeats in the opening 10 games of the 1961–61 season. Leeds lost to Preston on Younger's debut but in a turbulent few months the veteran 'keeper worked hard to get fit and his jovial manner off the field benefited the dressing room. Younger also made time to hone the talents of Sprake in extra sessions designed to toughen up the rookie 'keeper who would face roughhouse centre-forwards.

While United continued to struggle on the field into the New Year, Younger's agility improved. His bravery had never deserted him and the arrival of experienced pros Bobby Collins and Cliff Mason in March '61 ultimately helped to turn United's season around. Leeds lost only one of the last 11 matches. Younger was ill in the build up to a game at Southampton and Sprake was flown down to The Dell as a late replacement in a 4–1 defeat. Playing in 10 games of the run-in, Younger shipped four goals during four wins and six draws as United survived with a 3–0 win at Newcastle United on the final day of the season.

Seven games into the 1961–62 season, Sprake became United's number one 'keeper. Younger retired after a distinguished career in October '62 and went on to scout for Leeds prior to coaching

Toronto City and working in public relations at Hibernian. Younger was president of the Scottish Football Association when he died in 1984. Revie's first season at Elland Road had many twists and turns and the signing of Collins had a major impact but Younger also played an important role amongst his 42 appearances in providing a calming influence in tense games and helping the progression of his successor. Amongst Revie's early signings, Younger was a wise decision.

FIFTY MEMORABLE MATCHES

Don Revie built a world class squad that was the team to beat domestically and in Europe. Leeds United played sublime football but could also battle in intimidating circumstances. They were Division 1 champions and Inter-Cities Fairs Cup winners twice, victorious in the FA Cup, League Cup and Charity Shield. During a decade of consistency Leeds never finished out of the top four in top-flight football after becoming Division 2 champions in 1963–64.

Revie's boys overcame cup shocks and outrageous refereeing injustices to become a major force in the game. Division 1 runners-up five times, FA Cup finalists three times, Fairs Cup and European Cup Winners Cup finalists; United followers witnessed the greatest period in the club's history. Taking on the might and minnows of English, British and European sides this eclectic chronology of unforgettable clashes summaries the 'ups and downs' Revie's boys experienced in an astonishing period from 1961–74.

PORTSMOUTH 3 LEEDS UNITED 1
Football League Division 2 (at Fratton Park, Portsmouth)
Saturday, 18 March 1961
Leeds United: Humphreys, Jones, Kilford, Cameron, Goodwin, McConnell, Francis, Fitzgerald, Charlton, Bremner, Grainger. Att: 16,230
A new era dawns for Leeds United as Revie takes charge for the first time. Playing out of position at centre-forward, Charlton scores for United in the first-half but the new Leeds player-boss endures a disappointing baptism in the 'hot seat' as United crash to a 3–1 defeat.

LEEDS UNITED 7 LINCOLN CITY 0
Football League Division 2 (at Elland Road, Leeds)
Saturday, 22 April 1961
Leeds United: Humphreys, Hair, Kilford, Smith, Charlton, Bell, Bremner, McConnell, McCole, Peyton, Johanneson. Att: 8,432
Revie oversees his first win as player-boss in a 7–0 rout against Lincoln City at Elland Road. With three draws and three defeats recorded in the six games to date, United strike top gear to record the biggest league or cup win since an 8–3 victory versus Leicester City in October 1938. McCole (2), Bell, Peyton, McConnell, Bremner and Drysdale (og) score the Leeds goals in a welcome triumph.

NEWCASTLE UNITED 0 LEEDS UNITED 3
Football League Division 2 (at St James Park, Newcastle)
Saturday, 28 April 1962
Leeds United: Younger, Hair, Mason, Goodwin, Charlton, Smith, Bremner, Collins, McAdams, Hawksby, Johanneson. Att: 21,708
Only victory in the final game assures Division 2 safety in Revie's debut season as boss and United achieve it courtesy of first half goals by Johanneson, McAdams and Keith (og). The arrival of Collins in March '62 is the catalyst to a successful relegation battle as Leeds collect 14 points in the final 11 games (four wins, six draws, one defeat) during a tense run in.

SWANSEA TOWN 0 LEEDS UNITED 2
Football League Division 2 (at Vetch Field, Swansea)
Saturday, 8 September 1962
Leeds United: Sprake, Reaney, Mason, Smith, Charlton, Hunter, Peyton, Bremner, Johnson, Collins, Johanneson. Att: 17,696
A poor start to the 1962–63 season sees Revie blood a trio of future stars. Sprake makes his second appearance in goal while defenders Reaney and Hunter along with centre-forward Johnson are handed first team debuts. Johnson and Bremner score the goals in a great win while the defensive rock of Leeds' back line begins to form. United enjoy a fine season finishing fifth as Revie builds a team capable of mounting a promotion charge.

SWANSEA TOWN 0 LEEDS UNITED 3
Football League Division 2 (at Vetch Field, Swansea)
Saturday, 11 April 1964
Leeds United: Sprake, Reaney, Bell, Bremner, Charlton, Hunter, Giles, Weston, Peacock, Collins, Cooper. Att: 14,321
Promotion is achieved and United reclaim top-flight status after four seasons. The early season signing of Giles and acquisition of Peacock in February '64 proves vital in the promotion campaign. Peacock (2) and Giles are on target in the first half at Swansea. And backed by 3,000 travelling supporters, Leeds go up in style.

CHARLTON ATHLETIC 0 LEEDS UNITED 2
Football League Division 2 (at The Valley, Charlton)
Saturday, 25 April 1964
Leeds United: Sprake, Reaney, Bell, Bremner, Charlton, Hunter, Giles, Weston, Peacock, Collins, Cooper. Att: 21,323
After failing to tie up the title at home to Plymouth Argyle in a disappointing 1–1 draw, 'Classy Champs' is the headline in the *Sunday Express* as United claim a clinical win at Home Park. Peacock again is the hero, scoring twice to seal only the second divisional title in the club's history 40 years after the first success. The triumph heralds the Revie era.

ASTON VILLA 1 LEEDS UNITED 2
Football League Division 1 (at Villa Park, Birmingham)
Saturday, 22 August 1964
Leeds United: Sprake, Reaney, Bell, Bremner, Charlton, Hunter, Giles, Weston, Storrie, Collins, Johanneson. Att: 28,000
United make their top-flight bow at Villa Park under Revie and recover from going a goal behind inside four minutes to record a hard fought victory. Collins is inspirational while a cool finish by Johanneson and neat header by Charlton provide the goals to clinch victory. Revie gives Sprake, Reaney, Bell, Hunter, Weston, Storrie and Johanneson Division 1 debuts as Leeds make an immediate impact.

LEEDS UNITED 4 LIVERPOOL 2
Football League Division 1 (at Elland Road, Leeds)
Wednesday, 26 August 1964
Leeds United: Sprake, Reaney, Bell, Bremner, Charlton, Hunter, Giles, Weston, Storrie, Collins, Johanneson. Att: 36,005

Facing the defending league champions in a first home clash appears a daunting prospect for Revie's Division 1 newcomers but United show tremendous spirit in a famous win against Bill Shankly's champions. A Yeats own goal plus goals by Weston, Bremner and Giles put Leeds 4–1 ahead before Liverpool grab a consolation goal. On a night when United put in a magnificent performance, chairman Harry Reynolds is a proud man.

EVERTON 0 LEEDS UNITED 1
Football League Division 1 (at Goodison Park, Liverpool)
Saturday, 7 November 1964
Leeds United: Sprake, Reaney, Bell, Bremner, Charlton, Hunter, Giles, Storrie, Belfitt, Collins, Johanneson. Att: 43,605
A blood and thunder encounter sees Everton reduced to 10 men when Brown is dismissed on four minutes after a foul on Giles. A seething atmosphere on the field is matched on the terraces resulting in missiles being thrown onto the pitch. Bell gives Leeds the lead but on 39 minutes with the ball yards away he clashes with Temple and as both players receive treatment, referee Stokes takes the unprecedented step of taking both sides off the pitch to cool down. The match resumes but United prove they can battle at the top level.

MANCHESTER UNITED 0 LEEDS UNITED 1
FA Cup semi final replay (at City Ground, Nottingham)
Wednesday, 31 March 1965
Leeds United: Sprake, Reaney, Bell, Bremner, Charlton, Hunter, Giles, Storrie, Peacock, Collins, Cooper. Att: 46,300
'Wembley Here We Come!' Following a 0–0 draw at Hillsborough in the first semi-final Revie guides Leeds to an FA Cup final for the first time in the club's history. On an unforgettable night Bremner nods home the winner two minutes from the end of extra time in a thrilling encounter. Magnificent defence is a prime reason for United's success as they astonish every pundit outside Yorkshire who tipped Busby's team to win. Revie played a masterstroke late on by switching Giles from right-wing to right half and it pays dividends as he sets up the winning goal with a precise free kick.

LEEDS UNITED 1 LIVERPOOL 2 (after extra time)
FA Cup final (at Wembley Stadium, London)
Saturday, 1 May 1965
Leeds United: Sprake, Reaney, Bell, Bremner, Charlton, Hunter, Giles, Storrie, Peacock, Collins, Johanneson. Att: 100,000
Five days after missing out on the Division 1 crown, Leeds experience extra-time heartache against Liverpool. On a soggy pitch, both teams find it hard going and only a series of fine saves by Sprake keep United in the game. Goalless at 90 minutes, Hunt heads Liverpool in front from broken-collarbone victim Byrne's cross before Leeds strike back when Bremner fires past Lawrence but St John heads home the winner from close range with nine minutes remaining. Being runners-up in league and cup is tough to take but what a debut top-flight season.

LEEDS UNITED 2 TORINO 1
Inter-Cities Fairs Cup first round first leg (at Elland Road, Leeds)
Wednesday, 29 September 1965
Leeds United: Sprake, Reaney, Madeley, Bremner, Charlton, Hunter, Peacock, Collins, Cooper, Lorimer, Giles. Att: 33,852
Revie takes his team into European competition for the first time and attempts to outfox Torino by naming Peacock (7), Cooper (9), Lorimer (10) and Giles (11) in shirt numbers they don't normally wear. Taking the game to the tough tackling Italians, Leeds open a 2–0 lead through Bremner and Peacock but let in a late goal. United draw the second leg 0–0 but suffer a major blow when Collins has his thigh bone shattered by a horrific challenge. Leeds win on aggregate 2–1.

VALENCIA 0 LEEDS UNITED 1 (Leeds win on aggregate 2–1)
Inter-Cities Fairs Cup third round second leg (at Mestalla Stadium, Valencia)
Wednesday, 16 February 1966
Leeds United: Sprake, Reaney, Bell, Bremner, Charlton, Hunter, Storrie, Lorimer, Madeley, Giles, O'Grady. Att: 45,000
Bremner leads Leeds out at the Mestalla Stadium as underdogs against the Spanish giants following a brutal clash dubbed 'The Battle of Elland Road' when a 1–1 draw includes a mass brawl. The incident sees a player from both sides including Charlton sent off before a second Valencia player is also dismissed. Leeds put on a brilliant display to win

the return when Madeley sets O'Grady away to score a superb counter attack winner. Leeds impress in their inaugural European adventure before losing to Real Zaragoza in a semi-final play off.

LEEDS UNITED 1 BOLOGNA 0 (Leeds win on toss of disc after aggregate score 1–1)
Inter-Cities Fairs Cup fourth round second leg (at Elland Road, Leeds)
Wednesday, 19 April 1967
Leeds United: Sprake, Reaney, Madeley, Bremner, Bell, Hunter, Giles, Belfitt, Greenhoff, E Gray, Cooper. Att: 42,126
On a night of unbearable tension Leeds turn around a 1–0 deficit from the opening leg. Giles levels the scores on aggregate with a sweetly taken penalty before Bremner sends United into the semi-finals by choosing correctly on the toss of a disc. This is the first time Leeds win a game in this manner.

CHELSEA 1 LEEDS UNITED 0
FA Cup semi final (at Villa Park, Birmingham)
Saturday, 29 April 1967
Leeds United: Sprake, Reaney, Bell, Bremner, Madeley, Hunter, Giles, Belfitt (Lorimer), Greenhoff, E Gray, Cooper. Att: 62,378
A match renowned for Lorimer's last minute 'equaliser' that is chalked off. And United felt aggrieved when Cooper had a goal ruled out on 83 minutes by referee Ken Burns. Striker Hateley (worth £100,000) scores for Chelsea in the first half but the match is remembered for substitute Lorimer's thunderbolt after Giles touched the ball to him. While United celebrate Burns ruled the goal out, as he was 'not ready'.

LEEDS UNITED 0 DINAMO ZAGREB 0 (Dinamo Zagreb win on aggregate 2–0)
Inter-Cities Fairs Cup final second leg (at Elland Road, Leeds)
Wednesday, 6 September 1967
Leeds United: Sprake, Bell, Cooper, Bremner, Charlton, Hunter, Reaney, Belfitt, Greenhoff, Giles, O'Grady. Att: 35,604
A Belfitt hat-trick accounts for Kilmarnock in the semi-finals but Zagreb claim a 2–0 first leg win in the final. With Peacock out through injury, Greenhoff leads the line while Reaney plays on the right wing. Despite peppering the Zagreb defence, Leeds fail to score. Within two weeks Jones arrives for a club record £100,000 fee as Revie continues to strengthen his side.

LEEDS UNITED 7 CHELSEA 0
Football League Division 1 (at Elland Road, Leeds)
Saturday, 7 October 1967
Leeds United: Sprake, Reaney, Madeley, Bremner, Charlton, Hunter, Greenhoff, Lorimer, Jones, E Gray, Johanneson (Hibbitt). Att: 40,460
Chelsea arrive at Elland Road in turmoil after the departure 24 hours earlier of manager Tommy Docherty and United take full advantage as they tear the Blues to shreds in a brilliant display. Johanneson opens the floodgates followed by Greenhoff, Charlton and Lorimer before half time. Goals by Gray and Hinton (own goal) are added to by Bremner, who set up four goals, when he makes it 7–0 with a superbly executed overhead kick. This is the first time in Football League history seven different players score for the same side in a match.

LIVERPOOL 2 LEEDS UNITED 0
Football League Division 1 (at Anfield, Liverpool)
Saturday, 9 December 1967
Leeds United: Sprake, Reaney, Cooper, Bremner, Charlton, Hunter, Greenhoff, Lorimer, Madeley, Belfitt, E Gray. Att: 39,675
A match that goes down in club folklore due to a bizarre goal when Sprake accidently throws the ball into his own net while trying to play the ball to Cooper just before half time. Leeds were already a goal down due to a defensive mix up on a terrible surface with the country gripped by snow. During the interval Liverpool's DJ sums up Sprake's gaffe when he plays Des O'Connor's hit record 'Careless Hands' to the delight of home fans.

ARSENAL 0 LEEDS UNITED 1
Football League Cup final (at Wembley Stadium, London)
Saturday, 2 March 1968
Leeds United: Sprake, Reaney, Cooper, Bremner, Charlton, Hunter, Greenhoff, Lorimer, Madeley, Giles, E Gray (Belfitt). Att: 97,887
For three successive nights before the final, left-back Cooper dreamt he would score the winning goal against Arsenal. And after 17 minutes of a dour battle Cooper thumps home a left footed volley after Graham headed out Gray's in-swinging corner. Leeds dictate the game with Charlton, Hunter and Reaney outstanding in defence, Bremner and Giles run midfield while Greenhoff and Lorimer threaten on occasion. Defence wins the day as United land Revie his first major honour as a manager.

EVERTON 1 LEEDS UNITED 0
FA Cup semi final (at Old Trafford, Manchester)
Saturday, 27 April 1968
Leeds United: Sprake, Reaney, Cooper, Bremner, Charlton, Hunter, Lorimer, Madeley, Jones, Giles, E Gray. Att: 63,000
For the second year running United suffer FA Cup semi-final heartache as Everton claim victory after a Sprake error just before half time. With the match goalless Leeds' 'keeper makes a hash of a clearance and Charlton stops a goalbound shot by Husband. Morrissey tucks away the penalty. In a game of few chances the closest United come is a Cooper strike that hits the bar and a Lorimer special that West brilliantly keeps out. Defeat denies United a chance of becoming the first club to reach two domestic Wembley finals in a season.

FERENCVAROS 0 LEEDS UNITED 0 (Leeds win on aggregate 1–0)
Fairs Cup final second leg (at Nep Stadium, Budapest)
Wednesday, 11 September 1968
Leeds United: Sprake, Reaney, Cooper, Bremner, Charlton, Hunter, O'Grady, Lorimer, Jones, Madeley, Hibbitt (Bates). Att: 75,000
In the first leg during the middle of the annual summer holidays Jones scrambles home the only goal for a slender lead at Elland Road. Defending deep, Ferencvaros hold out and are only denied a breakaway goal by a superb Sprake save from Rakosi. The Hungarians are buoyant at full time. But in front of a partisan crowd, United enjoy their finest hour in Europe on a night of unrelenting tension. Sprake puts in his best display between the posts with a string of world class saves while United defend heroically to pull off a 0–0 draw at a capacity Nep Stadium to claim their first European trophy by the narrowest of margins. Revie comments afterwards that his heart almost stopped beating in the final minutes. 'Every minute as the final whistle grew nearer seemed like an hour,' he says after the gripping finale.

LEEDS UNITED 3 STANDARD LIEGE 2 (Leeds win on aggregate 3–2)
Fairs Cup first round second leg (at Elland Road, Leeds)
Wednesday, 23 October 1968
Leeds United: Sprake, Reaney, Cooper (Bates), Bremner, Charlton, Hunter, O'Grady, Lorimer, Jones, Madeley, Hibbitt (E Gray). Att: 24,178
Following a 0–0 draw in Liege the return fixture looks straightforward but after donning a blue strip when both teams line up in all-white, United come back from 2–0 down for the only time in European competition under Revie. In a thrilling comeback Charlton scores a minute after Liege go two up on 51 minutes. Lorimer fires home a twice-taken free kick before Bremner, playing as an extra striker, forces the ball home from a corner a minute from time for a fantastic win.

STOKE CITY 1 LEEDS UNITED 5
Football League Division 1 (at Victoria Ground, Stoke)
Saturday, 8 March 1969
Leeds United: Sprake, Reaney, Cooper, Bremner, Charlton, Hunter, O'Grady, Madeley, Jones, Giles, E Gray. Att: 24,327
United make a tremendous start to the league campaign, winning 10 of the opening 13 matches. Following a 5–1 drubbing at Burnley, Leeds respond with an unbeaten 28-match run and go one better against The Clarets with a 6–1 triumph approaching Christmas '68. United's superb form includes seven successive wins culminating in a 5–1 rout at the Victoria Ground when Bremner (2), O'Grady (2) and Jones score in a scintillating away display.

LIVERPOOL 0 LEEDS UNITED 0
Football League Division 1 (at Anfield, Liverpool)
Monday, 28 April 1969
Leeds United: Sprake, Reaney, Cooper, Bremner, Charlton, Hunter, O'Grady, Madeley, Jones, Giles, E Gray. Att: 53,750
On the proudest night in the club's history a 0–0 draw at Anfield clinches the Division 1 league championship for the first time. Finishing ahead of the Merseysiders, a sterling defensive display enables Revie's conquering team to claim the point required for the title. And in a moment etched into club folklore Liverpool's Kop shows true sportsmanship by chanting 'Champions, Champions' as Bremner leads the players towards them at full time.

LEEDS UNITED 2 MANCHESTER CITY 1
Charity Shield (at Elland Road, Leeds)
Saturday, 2 August 1969
Leeds United: Sprake, Reaney, Cooper, Bremner, Charlton, Hunter, Madeley, Clarke, Jones (Lorimer), Giles, E Gray. Att: 39,835
Leeds win the traditional curtain raiser to the season thanks to goals by Gray and Charlton. Bell scores a late consolation goal for the FA Cup winners. The victory sets United on the way to a memorable campaign and the match is notable for the debut of British record £165,000 signing, Clarke, who makes an impressive debut.

LEEDS UNITED 10 LYN OSLO 0
European Cup first round first leg (at Elland Road, Leeds)
Wednesday, 17 September 1969
Leeds United: Sprake, Reaney, Cooper, Bremner, Charlton, Hunter, Madeley, Clarke, Jones, Giles (Bates), O'Grady. Att: 25,979
Leeds make a sensational start to the European Cup campaign against a team of part-timers. One-way traffic from the kick off, transfer-listed O'Grady opens the scoring on 35 seconds. Goals from Jones, a smart header and a superbly executed hook shot, Clarke and Giles end a brilliant first-half. And after the break, the tide continues towards the Oslo goal. Clarke, Giles, Jones with a hat-trick and two Bremner strikes round off a tremendous victory to equal a British club record in Europe. Leeds win the second leg 6–0 for an aggregate 16–0 win.

CHELSEA 2 LEEDS UNITED 5
Football League Division 1 (at Stamford Bridge, London)
Saturday, 10 January 1970
Leeds United: Sprake, Reaney, Cooper, Bremner, Charlton, Hunter, Lorimer, Clarke (Bates), Jones, Giles, Madeley. Att: 57,221
United turn on the style at Stamford Bridge with a five star performance in front of the *Match of Day* cameras. Chelsea go 2–1 up but have no answer to an awesome display as Clarke, Cooper with a beauty, Giles from the penalty spot, Lorimer and Jones put the Blues to the sword. The performance draws rave reviews as Leeds chase an unprecedented league, European Cup and FA Cup treble.

MANCHESTER UNITED 0 LEEDS UNITED 1
FA Cup semi final second replay (at Burnden Park, Bolton)
Thursday, 26 March 1970
Leeds United: Sprake, Reaney, Cooper, Bremner, Charlton, Madeley, Lorimer, Clarke, Jones, Giles, E Gray. Att: 56,000
Bremner provides the knock out blow after eight minutes to settle a titanic battle with their great rivals over a trilogy of tension filled games. The first two clashes had ended 0–0. Leeds skipper was named Footballer of the Year in an outstanding season and was superb as United reached Wembley. The clash came in the midst of fixture congestion undermining United's treble bid.

DERBY COUNTY 4 LEEDS UNITED 1
Football League Division 1 (at Baseball Ground, Derby)
Monday, 30 March 1970
Leeds United: Harvey, Davey, Peterson, Lumsden, Kennedy, Yorath, Galvin, Bates, Belfitt, Hibbitt, Johanneson. Att: 41,011
A capacity crowd watches on as Revie's shadow team runs out at the Baseball Ground signalling the end of the league challenge. Kennedy scores Leeds' consolation goal. Leeds receive a £5,000 fine from the Football Association but Revie insists his stars are injured or mentally fatigued. Sympathy comes from sections of the media as no other club that season had such a schedule of fixtures. The Derby clash concludes nine high profile games in 27 days including three FA Cup semi-finals versus Manchester United and two European Cup quarter-final ties versus Standard Liege. The Derby clash ends four games in eight days and heralds three in four days including a European Cup semi-final first leg clash with Celtic.

LEEDS UNITED 2 BURNLEY 1
Football League Division 1 (at Elland Road, Leeds)
Saturday, 4 April 1970
Leeds United: Harvey, Yorath, Peterson, Madeley, Faulkner, E Gray, Lorimer, Bates, Johanneson, Galvin, Hibbitt. Att: 24,691
United's clash with Burnley ends a crazy schedule of four games in eight days but Revie's weakened team pull off a memorable win with Gray scoring two of the greatest goals witnessed at Elland Road. Arguably the most naturally gifted player to pull on the white shirt of Leeds United, Gray scores his first with an outrageous 35-yard lob before waltzing past

the entire Burnley defence inside the penalty area to score an astonishing solo goal.

CHELSEA 2 LEEDS UNITED 2
FA Cup final (at Wembley Stadium, London)
Saturday, 11 April 1970
Leeds United: Sprake, Madeley, Cooper, Bremner, Charlton, Hunter, Lorimer, Clarke, Jones, Giles, E Gray. Att: 100,000
In a classic cup final played on a heavily sanded pitch due to the *Horse of the Year Show*, United and Chelsea share a four-goal thriller. Gray torments Webb on the left wing to claim the Man of the Match award but Leeds twice lose the lead. A Charlton header eludes two defenders on the line for the opening goal before a soft goal by Houseman levels the scores when Sprake fails to stop a daisy-cutter. Gray strikes the crossbar before a Clarke header hits the post but Jones fires home the rebound six minutes from time. But with United fans singing 'We've Won The Cup!' Chelsea equalise on 86 minutes when Hutchinson heads a Hollins free kick past a stranded Sprake. Neither team scores in extra time resulting in the first replay since the FA Cup moved to Wembley in 1923.

CELTIC 2 LEEDS UNITED 1 (Celtic win on aggregate 3–1)
European Cup semi-final second leg (at Hampden Park, Glasgow)
Wednesday, 15 April 1970
Leeds United: Sprake (Harvey), Madeley, Cooper, Bremner, Charlton, Hunter, Lorimer (Bates), Clarke, Jones, Giles, E Gray. Att: 136,505
Due to an unprecedented demand for tickets the match is switched to Hampden Park to accommodate a record European clash. A goal up from the first leg Celtic attack from the kick off in a match dubbed 'The Battle of Britain' but Bremner silences home fans with a stunning 25-yard strike to level the aggregate scores. But after Hughes strikes just after half time, Leeds lose Sprake to an injury and Harvey picks the ball out of the net within two minutes as Murdoch seals a 3–1 aggregate victory. United's energy sapping cup final four days earlier takes its toll as the second leg of the treble bid ends.

CHELSEA 2 LEEDS UNITED 1
FA Cup final replay (at Old Trafford, Manchester)
Wednesday, 29 April 1970
Leeds United: Harvey, Madeley, Cooper, Bremner, Charlton, Hunter, Lorimer, Clarke, Jones, Giles, E Gray. Att: 62,078
A season promising so much ends in heartbreak as Chelsea come from a goal down to claim victory in extra time. During a brutal encounter both teams are guilty of over-zealous tackling but all seems on track for United when Jones opens the scoring in the first half of the Old Trafford replay. However headers by Osgood on 78 minutes and Webb in extra time ends United's treble bid in the 64th game of a momentous season.

COLCHESTER UNITED 3 LEEDS UNITED 2
FA Cup fifth round (at Layer Road, Colchester)
Saturday, 13 February 1971
Leeds United: Sprake, Reaney, Cooper, Bates, Charlton, Hunter, Lorimer, Clarke, Jones, Giles, Madeley. Att: 16,000
United experiences the biggest giant-killing result of the Revie era. Bremner is sidelined through injury but pundits give the Division 4 outfit no chance against the Division 1 leaders however a capacity crowd at Layer Road is ecstatic as defensive mix ups see Colchester take a 3–0 lead following goals by Crawford (2) and Simmons. Stung into action Hunter and Giles pull goals back before a point blank save by Smith from Jones ensures the greatest upset in FA Cup history stunning English football.

LIVERPOOL 0 LEEDS UNITED 1
Inter-Cities Fairs Cup semi final first leg (at Anfield, Liverpool)
Wednesday, 14 February 1971
Leeds United: Sprake, Reaney (Davey), Cooper, Bremner, Charlton, Hunter, Bates, Clarke, Jones, Giles, Madeley. At: 52,877
Bremner returns to first team action after three months out through injury and playing as an extra striker alongside Clarke and Jones heads home the only goal of the tie on 67 minutes. The winner comes after Evans misses a sitter for Liverpool, who fails to penetrate United's rearguard. Revie's gamble on his skipper pays off with a vital 'away' goal. A 0–0 draw in the second leg at Elland Road takes United through on aggregate 1–0. In a third Fairs Cup final United will take on Italian giants Juventus.

LEEDS UNITED 1 WEST BROM 2
Football League Division 1 (at Elland Road, Leeds)
Saturday, 17 April 1971
Leeds United: Sprake, Reaney, Cooper, Bremner, Charlton, Hunter, Bates (Davey), Clarke, Jones, Giles, E Gray. Att: 36,812
On track for a second league title Revie watches in horror as United suffer the most infamous home defeat of his tenure. A goal behind, United chase the game when Brown intercepts a Hunter pass before breaking across halfway with Suggett standing yards offside but referee Ray Tinkler ignores a linesman flagging offside. Leeds players and Suggett stop but Tinkler waves play on and Brown squares for Astle also looking suspiciously offside to score. Stunned United fans invade the pitch while Revie and his players protest in vain. Revie looking at the heavens is a haunting site. Tinkler requires a police escort at full time and the loss enables Arsenal to pinch the title by a point. Tinkler never referees at Elland Road again.

JUVENTUS 2 LEEDS UNITED 2
Inter-Cities Fairs Cup final first leg (at Comunale Stadium, Turin)
Friday, 28 May 1971
Leeds United: Sprake, Reaney, Cooper, Bremner, Charlton, Hunter, Lorimer, Clarke, Jones (Bates), Giles, Madeley. Att: 45,000
Torrential rain washes out the opening leg after 51 minutes with the score at 0–0. Gray suffers a dislocated shoulder during the time played and misses the replayed game 48 hours later. United show resilience to record a tremendous 2–2 draw at the Comunale Stadium. Bettega scores the opener before Madeley blasts home United's first goal on Italian soil from 35 yards before half time. Capello fires in a 20-yarder past Sprake to edge Juventus ahead for a second time only for Leeds substitute Bates to notch a priceless second 'away' goal ahead of the return fixture. Four days later Revie names the same team for the second leg at Elland Road. On a sultry summer evening United lift the Fairs Cup for the second time in three years in an entertaining clash. Sweeping forward from the kick off Clarke scores an early goal only for £444,000 striker Anastasi to equalise on 17 minutes. Both sides show plenty of skill with Cooper particularly impressive overlapping on the left flank. In a tense last 10 minutes Charlton and Hunter keep the crack Italian outfit quiet. Leeds win on away goals after an aggregate score of 3–3.

BARCELONA 2 LEEDS UNITED 1
Inter-Cities Fairs Cup play off (at Nou Camp Stadium, Barcelona, for possession of trophy)
Wednesday, 22 September 1971
Leeds United: Sprake, Reaney, Davey, Bremner, Charlton, Hunter, Lorimer, Jordan, Belfitt, Giles, Galvin. Att: 35,000
With the UEFA Cup replacing the Fairs Cup, United take on Barcelona for the right to retain the trophy. Cooper, Clarke, Jones, Gray and Madeley are sidelined but Revie's patched up team battle away at the Nou Camp Stadium. Jordan levels Duenas' early second half strike but the Barcelona sharpshooter nets the winner six minutes from time.

LEEDS UNITED 2 LIVERPOOL 0
FA Cup fourth round replay (at Elland Road, Leeds)
Wednesday, 9 February, 1972
Leeds United: Sprake, Reaney (Jordan), Cooper, Bremner, Charlton, Hunter, Lorimer, Clarke, Madeley, Giles, E Gray. Att: 45,821
The dream of winning the FA Cup burns brightly after a terrific midweek encounter switched to an early kick off with the country in the grip of an energy crisis. Two 'Sniffer' Clarke goals, one in each half, the first a cool chip over Clemence in goal before a solo run and typical clinical finish, settles an enthralling contest between the top two sides of the era.

LEEDS UNITED 5 MANCHESTER UNITED 1
Football League Division 1 (at Elland Road, Leeds)
Saturday, 19 February 1972
Leeds United: Sprake, Madeley, Cooper, Bremner, Charlton, Hunter, Lorimer, Clarke, Jones, Giles, E Gray. Att: 45,399
United rip their great rivals from the late sixties apart in a scintillating second half display before a capacity crowd. Revie's side are in their pomp and receive rapturous praise in the media for a top class performance. Gray is on fire while Jones is the hero with a hat-trick. Clarke and Lorimer also find the target against dishevelled opposition. One Sunday newspaper cartoonist quips that Pele has gone to Leeds for a coaching session! And the coming weeks will see United turn on the style with breathtaking football as Bremner and co chase the double.

LEEDS UNITED 7 SOUTHAMPTON 0
Football League Division 1 (at Elland Road, Leeds)
Saturday, 4 March 1972
Leeds United: Sprake, Reaney, Madeley, Bremner, Charlton, Hunter, Lorimer, Clarke, Jones, Giles, E Gray. Att: 34,275
In an iconic display captured on *Match of The Day*, Leeds crush Southampton. Two up before half time through Clarke and a Lorimer special, an imperious United run riot in the second half. Clarke jinks through for number three before Lorimer fires home prior to completing his hat-trick after capitalizing on a poor back pass. 'Big Jack' Charlton strolls up to nod home a Hunter cross before Jones completes the rout on his 300th league appearance. United conclude a master class performance by playing 'keep ball' to a chorus of 'Ole, Ole!' as despondent Southampton players chase forlornly around the pitch in the dying minutes.

ARSENAL 0 LEEDS UNITED 1
FA Cup final (at Wembley Stadium, London)
Saturday, 6 May 1972
Leeds United: Harvey, Reaney, Madeley, Bremner, Charlton, Hunter, Lorimer, Clarke, Jones, Giles, E Gray. Att: 100,000
'Sniffer' Clarke heads home on 53 minutes to clinch the 'Centenary' FA Cup for the first time in the club's history. Bremner lifts the famous trophy as Revie leads United to a full set of domestic honours. After Arsenal go close early on with a McLintock free kick, Reaney saves on the line from Ball before Bremer and Giles begin to win the midfield battle. Lorimer goes close before Clarke hits the bar with a smart header on half time. After Jones sets up his strike partner for the Leeds goal George strikes the crossbar on 75 minutes. In the final minute Jones dislocates an elbow before an unforgettable Wembley moment after the final whistle when he is determined to climb the 39 steps to receive his winners medal from the Queen.

WOLVES 2 LEEDS UNITED 1
Football League Division 1 (at Molineux, Wolverhampton)
Monday, 8 May 1972
Leeds United: Harvey, Reaney, Madeley, Bremner, Charlton, Hunter, Lorimer, Clarke (Yorath), Bates, Giles, E Gray. Att: 53,379

Two days after winning the Cup, Leeds are forced to play at Molineux in the final game of the season needing a draw to complete the league and FA Cup double. Revie gambles on the fitness of key players and Wolves open up a 2–0 lead before Bremner scores to set up a pulsating finish. Attacking non-stop, two cast-iron penalties are turned down as United go down to a heartbreaking defeat. For the third season running Leeds finish runners-up but thousands of fans turn out for a civic reception to celebrate FA Cup glory.

DERBY COUNTY 0 LEEDS UNITED 1
FA Cup quarter-final (at Baseball Ground, Derby)
Saturday, 17 March 1973
Leeds United: Harvey, Reaney, Cherry, Bremner (Bates), Madeley, Hunter, Lorimer, Clarke, Jones, Giles, E Gray. Att: 38,350
After losing out in the title race to Derby in 1971–72, United claim a league double over Brian Clough's team 5–0 at Elland Road and 3–2 at the Baseball Ground. For good measure they also knock Cloughie's team out of the FA Cup courtesy of a Lorimer special on 28 minutes. Cloughie boasts his team will win but Revie's Leeds silence him for a sixth semi-final spot in nine seasons after a professional display with Bremner and Giles superb in midfield.

HADJUK SPLIT 0 LEEDS UNITED 0–0 (Leeds win on aggregate 1–0)
European Cup Winners Cup semi final second leg (at Plinaric Stadium, Split)
Wednesday, 25 April 1973
Leeds United: Harvey, Reaney, Cherry, Bremner, Yorath, Hunter, Lorimer, Jordan, Jones, Giles, Madeley. Att: 30,000
United come into the tie a goal ahead from the first leg courtesy of a Clarke strike but Leeds' sharpshooter is later sent off in a stormy affair after retaliating when he was hacked down. In an intimidating atmosphere in Split, United soak up enormous pressure in an imperious display as Hajduk find it impossible to break through. Madeley and Hunter are outstanding in defence but this is a supreme team effort to reach a fourth European final.

LEEDS UNITED 0 SUNDERLAND 1
FA Cup final (at Wembley Stadium, London)
Saturday, 5 May 1973
Leeds United: Harvey, Reaney, Cherry, Bremner, Madeley, Hunter, Lorimer, Clarke, Jones, Giles, E Gray (Yorath). Att: 100,000
Heartbreak for Revie as odds-on favourites Leeds endure the biggest shock in FA Cup final history. A 32nd minute volley by Ian Porterfield wins the

Cup for the underdogs who become the first Division 2 team to win the trophy for 42 years. Sunderland match United in midfield but are indebted to a miraculous double-save by 'keeper Montgomery to prevent a shell-shocked Leeds from equalising following a Cherry header and Lorimer first time effort.

AC MILAN 1 LEEDS UNITED 0
European Cup Winners Cup final (Kaftantzoglio Stadium, Salonika)
Wednesday, 16 May 1973
Leeds United: Harvey, Reaney, Cherry, Bates, Madeley, Hunter, Lorimer, Jordan, Jones, F Gray (McQueen), Yorath. Att: 40,154
With Bremner suspended and Clarke, Giles and Gray out due to injury, preparations are shambolic as news filters through Everton are to offer Revie the managerial post. AC Milan score from a controversial fourth minute free kick by Chiarugi, which brings jeers from local fans who get more irate as Greek referee Christos Michas ignores blatant penalty appeals firstly for handball then when Jones and Reaney are scythed down as United pummel a packed defence. In the final minute, an altercation between Hunter and Sogliano, after Rivera hacks down the United stopper, sees both sent off while Rivera escapes punishment. Milan lift the trophy to a chorus of boos while UEFA suspend Michas, who is branded a disgrace in the media as Leeds suffer one of European football's darkest nights of shameful officiating.

LEEDS UNITED 3 EVERTON 1
Football League Division 1 (at Elland Road, Leeds)
Saturday, 25 August 1973
Leeds United: Harvey, Reaney, Madeley, Bremner, McQueen, Hunter, Lorimer, Clarke, Jones, Giles, E Gray. Att: 39,325
Revie turns down Everton overtures to become boss and with critics writing his team off, sets his players the unprecedented target of going through a league campaign unbeaten. Bremner gets Leeds off to a flyer before second half strikes by Giles and Jones settle the match. The message from Elland Road is loud and clear, United are back. Breaking records galore, Revie's lads rattle up seven consecutive wins before a 2–1 win at Chelsea makes it 20 unbeaten games breaking Liverpool's 24-year-old post-war record. The run reaches 29 matches until a visit to Stoke City in February '74.

HIBERNIAN 0 LEEDS UNITED 0 (aggregate score 0–0 after extra time, Leeds win penalty shoot out 5–4)
UEFA Cup second round second leg (at Easter Road, Edinburgh)
Wednesday, 7 November 1973
Leeds United: Shaw (Letheren), Reaney, Cherry, Bremner, Ellam, Yorath, Lorimer, Clarke, Jordan, Bates, E Gray. Att: 36,051
A shade lucky to draw the first leg, Revie's goalkeeper resources are stretched to the limit for the return. Kicking off at Easter Road with 19-year-old third choice 'keeper John Shaw, United restart the second half with 17-year-old youth 'keeper Letheren after Shaw breaks two fingers. Bremner relishes the challenge to shield his rookie 'keeper and United's goal is intact after extra time. In the club's first ever penalty shoot out Letheren instantly creates history as Stanton strikes a post with his team's first effort. In an era when shoot-outs are rare Lorimer, Gray, Bates and Clarke score before Bremner smashes home the winner.

LEEDS UNITED 3 IPSWICH TOWN 2
Football League Division 1 (at Elland Road, Leeds)
Saturday, 20 April 1974
Leeds United: Harvey, Reaney, Cherry, Bremner, McQueen, Hunter, Lorimer, Clarke, Jones, Madeley, E Gray. Att: 44,015
After dominating the league all season Revie watches with increasing concern as his team scrape one win in six games following a 3–2 defeat at Stoke City. Desperate for a victory over Ipswich in the penultimate game, Lorimer and Bremner, who sealed a win over Derby County to get Leeds back on track, settle jittery home nerves by putting Leeds 2–0 ahead after a number of hair-raising moments in a nervy United defence. Talbot cranks up the tension inside Elland Road with a goal and the home crowd is silenced when Hamilton equalises before the hour. But urged on from the Leeds dugout, Bremner drives his team forward and Clarke is coolness personified as he fires home a crucial winning goal on 70 minutes. United are in the box seat for the Division 1 title and are crowned champions when Arsenal defeat Liverpool at Anfield midweek. In Revie's last game as manager Clarke scores a second-half winner at Queens Park Rangers to round off the title-winning season in style.

BIBLIOGRAPHY

Bremner, Billy, 1969, *You Get Nowt for Being Second*, Souvenir Press

Edwards, Gary, 2011, *No Glossing Over It: How Football Cheated Leeds United*, Mainstream

Golesworthy, Maurice, 1972, *We Are The Champions: A History Of The Football League Champions 1888–1972*, Pelham Books

Hunter, Norman, 2004, *Biting Talk*, Hodder & Stoughton

Jarred, Martin and Macdonald, Malcolm, 1990, *Leeds United: The European Record*, Breedon

Jarred, Martin and Macdonald, Malcolm, 1991, *Leeds United Cup Book, 1920–1991*, Breedon

Jarred, Martin and Macdonald, Malcolm, 2009, *Leeds United: For Club And Country*, Breedon

Leeds United Book of Football No 1, Souvenir Press, 1969

Leeds United Book of Football No 2, Souvenir Press, 1970

Leeds United Book of Football No 3, Souvenir Press, 1971

McConnell, Peter, 2008, *Nice One Skip: From Elland Road to Brunton Park*, Print Graphic

Mourant, Andrew 1990, *Don Revie: Portrait of a Footballing Enigma*, Mainstream

Mourant, Andrew, 1992, *Leeds United: Player by Player*, Guinness

Saffer, David and Shepherd, Gary, 2005, *'and we've had our ups and downs' 100 Years: Leeds United and Leeds City* 1905–2005, Vertical Editions,

Saffer, David, 2004, *Leeds Legends*, Tempus

Saffer, David, 2005, *Boys of 72*, Tempus

Sutcliffe, Richard, 2010, *Revie: Revered And Reviled*, Great Northern Books

Warters, Don, 1979, *Leeds United: The Official History of the Club*, Wensum Books

REVIE'S BOYS' PLAYING STATISTICS 1960–61 TO 1973–74

Please note: Player statistics in pages 16–179 refer to their total appearances and goals. The tables of player statistics on pages 181–223 show data for the period of Don Revie's tenure as manager only. This means that players representing Leeds United before or after Revie's appointment have different statistics in the text when compared to the tables.

Mike Addy

Season	League			FA Cup			League Cup			Europe			Other			Total		
	Apps	Subs	Goals	Apps	Subs	Goals	Apps	Subs	Goals	Apps	Subs	Goals	Apps	Subs	Goals	Apps	Subs	Goals
1960-61																0	0	0
1961-62							1									1	0	0
1962-63	2						1									3	0	0
1963-64																0	0	0
1964-65																0	0	0
1965-66																0	0	0
1966-67																0	0	0
1967-68																0	0	0
1968-69																0	0	0
1969-70																0	0	0
1970-71																0	0	0
1971-72																0	0	0
1972-73																0	0	0
1973-74																0	0	0
TOTAL	2	0	0	0	0	0	2	0	0	0	0	0	0	0	0	4	0	0

Mick Bates

Season	League			FA Cup			League Cup			Europe			Other			Total		
	Apps	Subs	Goals	Apps	Subs	Goals	Apps	Subs	Goals	Apps	Subs	Goals	Apps	Subs	Goals	Apps	Subs	Goals
1960-61																0	0	0
1961-62																0	0	0
1962-63																0	0	0
1963-64																0	0	0
1964-65																0	0	0
1965-66							1									1	0	0
1966-67	8	1			1			1		1						9	3	0
1967-68	6	1						3			3					6	7	0
1968-69	3	1		2				1		1	1					6	3	0
1969-70	13	3	1		1		1	1		2	3					16	8	1
1970-71	29	1		2	1		1			8	2	1				40	4	1
1971-72	6	3		2						2						10	3	0
1972-73	26	3	1	4	1	1	4			6		1				40	4	3
1973-74	9	1	2							5		1				14	1	3
TOTAL	100	14	4	10	4	1	7	6	0	25	9	3	0	0	0	142	33	8

Rod Belfitt

Season	League			FA Cup			League Cup			Europe			Other			Total		
	Apps	Subs	Goals	Apps	Subs	Goals	Apps	Subs	Goals	Apps	Subs	Goals	Apps	Subs	Goals	Apps	Subs	Goals
1960-61																0	0	0
1961-62																0	0	0
1962-63																0	0	0
1963-64																0	0	0
1964-65	8		4				2		1							10	0	5
1965-66	3						3		2							6	0	2
1966-67	10	2	3	5		3	1			7		3				23	2	9
1967-68	11	3	2				5	1	2	2	2	1				18	6	5
1968-69	6	2	3		1		3			2		1				11	3	4
1969-70	6	1	1							4		2				10	1	3
1970-71	3	10	3				1	1		6		1				10	11	4
1971-72	10	1	1	1			2			2			1			16	1	1
1972-73																0	0	0
1973-74																0	0	0
TOTAL	57	19	17	6	1	3	17	2	5	23	2	8	1	0	0	104	24	33

Willie Bell

Season	League			FA Cup			League Cup			Europe			Other			Total		
	Apps	Subs	Goals	Apps	Subs	Goals	Apps	Subs	Goals	Apps	Subs	Goals	Apps	Subs	Goals	Apps	Subs	Goals
1960-61	3		1													3	0	1
1961-62	23		1	2			3									28	0	1
1962-63	32		2	3			1									36	0	2
1963-64	35		2	3			3		1							41	0	3
1964-65	35		4	7			2									44	0	4
1965-66	33		2	2			1			9		1				45	0	3
1966-67	38		3	7		1	4			8						57	0	4
1967-68	3						1									4	0	0
1968-69																0	0	0
1969-70																0	0	0
1970-71																0	0	0
1971-72																0	0	0
1972-73																0	0	0
1973-74																0	0	0
TOTAL	202	0	15	24	0	1	15	0	1	17	0	1	0	0	0	258	0	18

Billy Bremner

	League			FA Cup			League Cup			Europe			Other			Total		
	Apps	Subs	Goals	Apps	Subs	Goals	Apps	Subs	Goals	Apps	Subs	Goals	Apps	Subs	Goals	Apps	Subs	Goals
1960-61	9		2													9	0	2
1961-62	39		11	2			4		1							45	0	12
1962-63	24		10													24	0	10
1963-64	39		2	3		1	1									43	0	3
1964-65	40		6	8		2	1									49	0	8
1965-66	41		8	2						11		3				54	0	11
1966-67	36	1	1	6			4		1	10		1				56	1	3
1967-68	36		3	5			6			11		1				58	0	4
1968-69	42		6	2			2			8		1				54	0	7
1969-70	35		4	9		1	2			8		3	1			55	0	8
1970-71	26		3	2			1			10		4				39	0	7
1971-72	41		5	7			4			1			1			54	0	5
1972-73	38		4	7		1	5			7						57	0	5
1973-74	42		10	5		1	1			4						52	0	11
TOTAL	488	1	75	58	0	6	31	0	2	70	0	13	2	0	0	649	1	96

Bobby Cameron

	League			FA Cup			League Cup			Europe			Other			Total		
	Apps	Subs	Goals	Apps	Subs	Goals	Apps	Subs	Goals	Apps	Subs	Goals	Apps	Subs	Goals	Apps	Subs	Goals
1960-61	1															1	0	0
1961-62	7															7	0	0
1962-63																0	0	0
1963-64																0	0	0
1964-65																0	0	0
1965-66																0	0	0
1966-67																0	0	0
1967-68																0	0	0
1968-69																0	0	0
1969-70																0	0	0
1970-71																0	0	0
1971-72																0	0	0
1972-73																0	0	0
1973-74																0	0	0
TOTAL	8	0	0	0	0	0	0	0	0	0	0	0	0	0	0	8	0	0

Terry Carling

Season	League Apps	League Subs	League Goals	FA Cup Apps	FA Cup Subs	FA Cup Goals	League Cup Apps	League Cup Subs	League Cup Goals	Europe Apps	Europe Subs	Europe Goals	Other Apps	Other Subs	Other Goals	Total Apps	Total Subs	Total Goals
1960-61	4	0	0	0	0	0	0	0	0	0	0	0	0	0	0	4	0	0
1961-62	1	0	0	0	0	0	0	0	0	0	0	0	0	0	0	1	0	0
1962-63	0	0	0	0	0	0	0	0	0	0	0	0	0	0	0	0	0	0
1963-64	0	0	0	0	0	0	0	0	0	0	0	0	0	0	0	0	0	0
1964-65	0	0	0	0	0	0	0	0	0	0	0	0	0	0	0	0	0	0
1965-66	0	0	0	0	0	0	0	0	0	0	0	0	0	0	0	0	0	0
1966-67	0	0	0	0	0	0	0	0	0	0	0	0	0	0	0	0	0	0
1967-68	0	0	0	0	0	0	0	0	0	0	0	0	0	0	0	0	0	0
1968-69	0	0	0	0	0	0	0	0	0	0	0	0	0	0	0	0	0	0
1969-70	0	0	0	0	0	0	0	0	0	0	0	0	0	0	0	0	0	0
1970-71	0	0	0	0	0	0	0	0	0	0	0	0	0	0	0	0	0	0
1971-72	0	0	0	0	0	0	0	0	0	0	0	0	0	0	0	0	0	0
1972-73	0	0	0	0	0	0	0	0	0	0	0	0	0	0	0	0	0	0
1973-74	0	0	0	0	0	0	0	0	0	0	0	0	0	0	0	0	0	0
TOTAL	5	0	0	0	0	0	0	0	0	0	0	0	0	0	0	5	0	0

Terry Casey

Season	League Apps	League Subs	League Goals	FA Cup Apps	FA Cup Subs	FA Cup Goals	League Cup Apps	League Cup Subs	League Cup Goals	Europe Apps	Europe Subs	Europe Goals	Other Apps	Other Subs	Other Goals	Total Apps	Total Subs	Total Goals
1960-61	0	0	0	0	0	0	0	0	0	0	0	0	0	0	0	0	0	0
1961-62	3	0	0	0	0	0	1	0	0	0	0	0	0	0	0	4	0	0
1962-63	0	0	0	0	0	0	0	0	0	0	0	0	0	0	0	0	0	0
1963-64	0	0	0	0	0	0	0	0	0	0	0	0	0	0	0	0	0	0
1964-65	0	0	0	0	0	0	0	0	0	0	0	0	0	0	0	0	0	0
1965-66	0	0	0	0	0	0	0	0	0	0	0	0	0	0	0	0	0	0
1966-67	0	0	0	0	0	0	0	0	0	0	0	0	0	0	0	0	0	0
1967-68	0	0	0	0	0	0	0	0	0	0	0	0	0	0	0	0	0	0
1968-69	0	0	0	0	0	0	0	0	0	0	0	0	0	0	0	0	0	0
1969-70	0	0	0	0	0	0	0	0	0	0	0	0	0	0	0	0	0	0
1970-71	0	0	0	0	0	0	0	0	0	0	0	0	0	0	0	0	0	0
1971-72	0	0	0	0	0	0	0	0	0	0	0	0	0	0	0	0	0	0
1972-73	0	0	0	0	0	0	0	0	0	0	0	0	0	0	0	0	0	0
1973-74	0	0	0	0	0	0	0	0	0	0	0	0	0	0	0	0	0	0
TOTAL	3	0	0	0	0	0	1	0	0	0	0	0	0	0	0	4	0	0

John Charles

Season	League Apps	Subs	Goals	FA Cup Apps	Subs	Goals	League Cup Apps	Subs	Goals	Europe Apps	Subs	Goals	Other Apps	Subs	Goals	Total Apps	Subs	Goals
1960-61																0	0	0
1961-62																0	0	0
1962-63	11		3													11	0	3
1963-64																0	0	0
1964-65																0	0	0
1965-66																0	0	0
1966-67																0	0	0
1967-68																0	0	0
1968-69																0	0	0
1969-70																0	0	0
1970-71																0	0	0
1971-72																0	0	0
1972-73																0	0	0
1973-74																0	0	0
TOTAL	11	0	3	0	0	0	0	0	0	0	0	0	0	0	0	11	0	3

Jack Charlton

Season	League Apps	Subs	Goals	FA Cup Apps	Subs	Goals	League Cup Apps	Subs	Goals	Europe Apps	Subs	Goals	Other Apps	Subs	Goals	Total Apps	Subs	Goals
1960-61	9		5													9	0	5
1961-62	34		9	2			3		3							39	0	12
1962-63	38		2	3			1		1							42	0	3
1963-64	25		3				2									27	0	3
1964-65	39		9	8		1	2									49	0	10
1965-66	40		6	2			1			11		2				54	0	8
1966-67	28		5	6		1				11		1				45	0	7
1967-68	34		5	4		1	9			7		2				54	0	8
1968-69	41		3	2			2		2	7		2				52	0	7
1969-70	32		3	9		2	3			7		1				51	0	6
1970-71	41		6	4						10		2	1		1	56	0	9
1971-72	41		5	5		1	5									51	0	6
1972-73	18		3	1		1	3			2			1			25	0	4
1973-74																0	0	0
TOTAL	420	0	64	46	0	7	31	0	6	55	0	10	2	0	1	554	0	88

Trevor Cherry

Season	League Apps	League Subs	League Goals	FA Cup Apps	FA Cup Subs	FA Cup Goals	League Cup Apps	League Cup Subs	League Cup Goals	Europe Apps	Europe Subs	Europe Goals	Other Apps	Other Subs	Other Goals	Total Apps	Total Subs	Total Goals
1960-61																		
1961-62																		
1962-63																		
1963-64																		
1964-65																		
1965-66																		
1966-67																		
1967-68																		
1968-69																		
1969-70																		
1970-71																		
1971-72																		
1972-73	38	1	1	8			5		1	8		1				59	1	3
1973-74	37	1	1	5			1			6		1				49	1	2
TOTAL	75	2	2	13	0	0	6	0	1	14	0	2	0	0	0	108	2	5

Allan Clarke

Season	League Apps	League Subs	League Goals	FA Cup Apps	FA Cup Subs	FA Cup Goals	League Cup Apps	League Cup Subs	League Cup Goals	Europe Apps	Europe Subs	Europe Goals	Other Apps	Other Subs	Other Goals	Total Apps	Total Subs	Total Goals
1960-61																		
1961-62																		
1962-63																		
1963-64																		
1964-65																		
1965-66																		
1966-67																		
1967-68																		
1968-69																		
1969-70	28		17	9		7				5		2	1			43	0	26
1970-71	41		19	4		1	1			10		3				56	0	23
1971-72	35		11	6		4	2									43	0	15
1972-73	36		18	8		6	4			5		2				53	0	26
1973-74	34		13	2	1					5		3				41	1	16
TOTAL	174	0	78	29	1	18	7	0	0	25	0	10	1	0	0	236	1	106

Bobby Collins

	League			FA Cup			League Cup			Europe			Other			Total		
	Apps	Subs	Goals	Apps	Subs	Goals	Apps	Subs	Goals	Apps	Subs	Goals	Apps	Subs	Goals	Apps	Subs	Goals
1960-61																0	0	0
1961-62	11		1													11	0	1
1962-63	41		8	3		1										44	0	9
1963-64	41		6	2			1									44	0	6
1964-65	39		9	8			1		1							48	0	10
1965-66	10									2						12	0	0
1966-67	7									1						8	0	0
1967-68																0	0	0
1968-69																0	0	0
1969-70																0	0	0
1970-71																0	0	0
1971-72																0	0	0
1972-73																0	0	0
1973-74																0	0	0
TOTAL	149	0	24	13	0	1	2	0	1	3	0	0	0	0	0	167	0	26

Terry Cooper

	League			FA Cup			League Cup			Europe			Other			Total		
	Apps	Subs	Goals	Apps	Subs	Goals	Apps	Subs	Goals	Apps	Subs	Goals	Apps	Subs	Goals	Apps	Subs	Goals
1960-61																0	0	0
1961-62																0	0	0
1962-63																0	0	0
1963-64	2															2	0	0
1964-65	16			4			1									21	0	0
1965-66	15	3	2				2		1	4		1				21	3	4
1966-67	20	4	1	2	1					6						28	5	1
1967-68	37			5			6		1	12		1				60	1	2
1968-69	34	1	1				3			5						42	1	1
1969-70	29	1	1	9			3			7			1			49	1	1
1970-71	41		1	3			1			10						55	0	1
1971-72	34		1	5			3			1						43	0	1
1972-73																0	0	0
1973-74	1	1		2												3	1	0
TOTAL	229	10	7	30	1	0	19	0	2	45	0	2	1	0	0	324	11	11

Nigel Davey

Season	League			FA Cup			League Cup			Europe			Other			Total		
	Apps	Subs	Goals	Apps	Subs	Goals	Apps	Subs	Goals	Apps	Subs	Goals	Apps	Subs	Goals	Apps	Subs	Goals
1960-61																0	0	0
1961-62																0	0	0
1962-63																0	0	0
1963-64																0	0	0
1964-65																0	0	0
1965-66																0	0	0
1966-67							1									1	0	0
1967-68	2															2	0	0
1968-69																0	0	0
1969-70	5															5	0	0
1970-71	6	1		1						3	1					10	2	0
1971-72							1						1			2	0	0
1972-73											1					0	1	0
1973-74																0	0	0
TOTAL	13	1	0	1	0	0	2	0	0	3	2	0	1	0	0	20	3	0

Keith Edwards

Season	League			FA Cup			League Cup			Europe			Other			Total		
	Apps	Subs	Goals	Apps	Subs	Goals	Apps	Subs	Goals	Apps	Subs	Goals	Apps	Subs	Goals	Apps	Subs	Goals
1960-61																0	0	0
1961-62																0	0	0
1962-63																0	0	0
1963-64																0	0	0
1964-65																0	0	0
1965-66																0	0	0
1966-67																0	0	0
1967-68																0	0	0
1968-69																0	0	0
1969-70																0	0	0
1970-71		1														0	1	0
1971-72																0	0	0
1972-73																0	0	0
1973-74																0	0	0
TOTAL	0	1	0	0	0	0	0	0	0	0	0	0	0	0	0	0	1	0

Roy Ellam

	League			FA Cup			League Cup			Europe			Other			Total		
	Apps	Subs	Goals	Apps	Subs	Goals	Apps	Subs	Goals	Apps	Subs	Goals	Apps	Subs	Goals	Apps	Subs	Goals
1960-61																0	0	0
1961-62																0	0	0
1962-63																0	0	0
1963-64																0	0	0
1964-65																0	0	0
1965-66																0	0	0
1966-67																0	0	0
1967-68																0	0	0
1968-69																0	0	0
1969-70																0	0	0
1970-71																0	0	0
1971-72																0	0	0
1972-73	6	1					1			2						9	1	0
1973-74	3	1		2			1			4						10	1	0
TOTAL	9	2		2			2			6						19	2	0

John Faulkner

	League			FA Cup			League Cup			Europe			Other			Total		
	Apps	Subs	Goals	Apps	Subs	Goals	Apps	Subs	Goals	Apps	Subs	Goals	Apps	Subs	Goals	Apps	Subs	Goals
1960-61																0	0	0
1961-62																0	0	0
1962-63																0	0	0
1963-64																0	0	0
1964-65																0	0	0
1965-66																0	0	0
1966-67																0	0	0
1967-68																0	0	0
1968-69																0	0	0
1969-70	2															2	0	0
1970-71																0	0	0
1971-72										2						2	0	0
1972-73																0	0	0
1973-74																0	0	0
TOTAL	2									2						4	0	0

Peter Fitzgerald

Season	League Apps	League Subs	League Goals	FA Cup Apps	FA Cup Subs	FA Cup Goals	League Cup Apps	League Cup Subs	League Cup Goals	Europe Apps	Europe Subs	Europe Goals	Other Apps	Other Subs	Other Goals	Total Apps	Total Subs	Total Goals
1960-61	3															3	0	0
1961-62																0	0	0
1962-63																0	0	0
1963-64																0	0	0
1964-65																0	0	0
1965-66																0	0	0
1966-67																0	0	0
1967-68																0	0	0
1968-69																0	0	0
1969-70																0	0	0
1970-71																0	0	0
1971-72																0	0	0
1972-73																0	0	0
1973-74																0	0	0
TOTAL	3	0	0	0	0	0	0	0	0	0	0	0	0	0	0	3	0	0

Gerry Francis

Season	League Apps	League Subs	League Goals	FA Cup Apps	FA Cup Subs	FA Cup Goals	League Cup Apps	League Cup Subs	League Cup Goals	Europe Apps	Europe Subs	Europe Goals	Other Apps	Other Subs	Other Goals	Total Apps	Total Subs	Total Goals
1960-61	4															4	0	0
1961-62	4															4	0	0
1962-63																0	0	0
1963-64																0	0	0
1964-65																0	0	0
1965-66																0	0	0
1966-67																0	0	0
1967-68																0	0	0
1968-69																0	0	0
1969-70																0	0	0
1970-71																0	0	0
1971-72																0	0	0
1972-73																0	0	0
1973-74																0	0	0
TOTAL	8	0	0	0	0	0	0	0	0	0	0	0	0	0	0	8	0	0

Chris Galvin

Season	League Apps	League Subs	League Goals	FA Cup Apps	FA Cup Subs	FA Cup Goals	League Cup Apps	League Cup Subs	League Cup Goals	Europe Apps	Europe Subs	Europe Goals	Other Apps	Other Subs	Other Goals	Total Apps	Total Subs	Total Goals
1960-61																0	0	0
1961-62																0	0	0
1962-63																0	0	0
1963-64																0	0	0
1964-65																0	0	0
1965-66																0	0	0
1966-67																0	0	0
1967-68																0	0	0
1968-69																0	0	0
1969-70	3										1					3	1	0
1970-71					1						1					0	2	0
1971-72	2		1		1					2	1		1			5	2	1
1972-73	1						1			1						3	0	0
1973-74																0	0	0
TOTAL	6		1		2		1			3	3		1			11	5	1

Johnny Giles

Season	League Apps	League Subs	League Goals	FA Cup Apps	FA Cup Subs	FA Cup Goals	League Cup Apps	League Cup Subs	League Cup Goals	Europe Apps	Europe Subs	Europe Goals	Other Apps	Other Subs	Other Goals	Total Apps	Total Subs	Total Goals
1960-61																0	0	0
1961-62																0	0	0
1962-63																0	0	0
1963-64	40			3			2									45	0	7
1964-65	39			7												46	0	8
1965-66	40			2			1			11						54	0	6
1966-67	29			7			3			9						48	0	18
1967-68	20			5			3			7						35	0	10
1968-69	32			2						5						39	0	8
1969-70	32			7			4			7						50	0	19
1970-71	34			4						7			1			46	0	16
1971-72	38			7			4			1			1			51	0	10
1972-73	33			8						7	1					48	1	8
1973-74	17			2												19	0	2
TOTAL	354		86	54	0	14	17		1	54	1	11	2	0		481	1	112

191

Freddie Goodwin

	League			FA Cup			League Cup			Europe			Other			Total		
	Apps	Subs	Goals	Apps	Subs	Goals	Apps	Subs	Goals	Apps	Subs	Goals	Apps	Subs	Goals	Apps	Subs	Goals
1960-61	6															6	0	0
1961-62	41			2			4									47	0	0
1962-63	8															8	0	0
1963-64	12			1			1									14	0	0
1964-65																0	0	0
1965-66																0	0	0
1966-67																0	0	0
1967-68																0	0	0
1968-69																0	0	0
1969-70																0	0	0
1970-71																0	0	0
1971-72																0	0	0
1972-73																0	0	0
1973-74																0	0	0
TOTAL	67	0	0	3	0	0	5	0	0	0	0	0	0	0	0	75	0	0

Colin Grainger

	League			FA Cup			League Cup			Europe			Other			Total		
	Apps	Subs	Goals	Apps	Subs	Goals	Apps	Subs	Goals	Apps	Subs	Goals	Apps	Subs	Goals	Apps	Subs	Goals
1960-61	2															2	0	0
1961-62																0	0	0
1962-63																0	0	0
1963-64																0	0	0
1964-65																0	0	0
1965-66																0	0	0
1966-67																0	0	0
1967-68																0	0	0
1968-69																0	0	0
1969-70																0	0	0
1970-71																0	0	0
1971-72																0	0	0
1972-73																0	0	0
1973-74																0	0	0
TOTAL	2	0	0	0	0	0	0	0	0	0	0	0	0	0	0	2	0	0

Eddie Gray

Season	League Apps	League Subs	League Goals	FA Cup Apps	FA Cup Subs	FA Cup Goals	League Cup Apps	League Cup Subs	League Cup Goals	Europe Apps	Europe Subs	Europe Goals	Other Apps	Other Subs	Other Goals	Total Apps	Total Subs	Total Goals
1960-61																0	0	0
1961-62																0	0	0
1962-63																0	0	0
1963-64																0	0	0
1964-65																0	0	0
1965-66	3	1	1							2						5	1	1
1966-67	29		4	4			1			6						40	0	4
1967-68	32		6	3			7		1	8		2				50	0	9
1968-69	32	1	5	2			2			5	1					41	2	5
1969-70	30		9	6	1		2			5			1		1	44	1	10
1970-71	18		1	1						5		3				24	0	4
1971-72	25	1	6	6				1		2						31	2	6
1972-73	16	1	1	3			3			2						24	1	1
1973-74	8									1						9	0	0
TOTAL	193	4	33	25	1	0	15	1	1	34	1	5	1	0	1	268	7	40

Frank Gray

Season	League Apps	League Subs	League Goals	FA Cup Apps	FA Cup Subs	FA Cup Goals	League Cup Apps	League Cup Subs	League Cup Goals	Europe Apps	Europe Subs	Europe Goals	Other Apps	Other Subs	Other Goals	Total Apps	Total Subs	Total Goals
1960-61																0	0	0
1961-62																0	0	0
1962-63																0	0	0
1963-64																0	0	0
1964-65																0	0	0
1965-66																0	0	0
1966-67																0	0	0
1967-68																0	0	0
1968-69																0	0	0
1969-70																0	0	0
1970-71																0	0	0
1971-72																0	0	0
1972-73	3	1	1							1	1					4	2	1
1973-74	3	3		1				1		5	1	1				9	5	1
TOTAL	6	4	1	1	0	0	0	1	0	6	2	1	0	0	0	13	7	2

Jimmy Greenhoff

Season	League Apps	League Subs	League Goals	FA Cup Apps	FA Cup Subs	FA Cup Goals	League Cup Apps	League Cup Subs	League Cup Goals	Europe Apps	Europe Subs	Europe Goals	Other Apps	Other Subs	Other Goals	Total Apps	Total Subs	Total Goals
1960-61																0	0	0
1961-62																0	0	0
1962-63	2															2	0	0
1963-64	2						1									3	0	0
1964-65	9		2	1		1	1									11	0	3
1965-66	10	2	1	1		1				3						14	2	2
1966-67	27	2	7	5	1		3		1	5		2				40	3	10
1967-68	35	2	11	3			7		3	10	1	4				55	3	18
1968-69	3															3	0	0
1969-70																0	0	0
1970-71																0	0	0
1971-72																0	0	0
1972-73																0	0	0
1973-74																0	0	0
TOTAL	88	6	21	10	1	2	12	0	4	18	1	6	0	0	0	128	8	33

Grenville Hair

Season	League Apps	League Subs	League Goals	FA Cup Apps	FA Cup Subs	FA Cup Goals	League Cup Apps	League Cup Subs	League Cup Goals	Europe Apps	Europe Subs	Europe Goals	Other Apps	Other Subs	Other Goals	Total Apps	Total Subs	Total Goals
1960-61	8															8	0	0
1961-62	38		1	2			3									43	0	1
1962-63	26			3		1	1									30	0	1
1963-64	8						2									10	0	0
1964-65																0	0	0
1965-66																0	0	0
1966-67																0	0	0
1967-68																0	0	0
1968-69																0	0	0
1969-70																0	0	0
1970-71																0	0	0
1971-72																0	0	0
1972-73																0	0	0
1973-74																0	0	0
TOTAL	80	0	1	5	0	1	6	0	0	0	0	0	0	0	0	91	0	2

Tom Hallett

	League			FA Cup			League Cup			Europe			Other			Total		
	Apps	Subs	Goals	Apps	Subs	Goals	Apps	Subs	Goals	Apps	Subs	Goals	Apps	Subs	Goals	Apps	Subs	Goals
1960-61																0	0	0
1961-62																0	0	0
1962-63							1									1	0	0
1963-64																0	0	0
1964-65																0	0	0
1965-66																0	0	0
1966-67																0	0	0
1967-68																0	0	0
1968-69																0	0	0
1969-70																0	0	0
1970-71																0	0	0
1971-72																0	0	0
1972-73																0	0	0
1973-74																0	0	0
TOTAL	0	0	0	0	0	0	1	0	0	0	0	0	0	0	0	1	0	0

Peter Hampton

	League			FA Cup			League Cup			Europe			Other			Total		
	Apps	Subs	Goals	Apps	Subs	Goals	Apps	Subs	Goals	Apps	Subs	Goals	Apps	Subs	Goals	Apps	Subs	Goals
1960-61																0	0	0
1961-62																0	0	0
1962-63																0	0	0
1963-64																0	0	0
1964-65																0	0	0
1965-66																0	0	0
1966-67																0	0	0
1967-68																0	0	0
1968-69																0	0	0
1969-70																0	0	0
1970-71																0	0	0
1971-72																0	0	0
1972-73	2															2	0	0
1973-74										1						1	0	0
TOTAL	2	0	0	0	0	0	0	0	0	1	0	0	0	0	0	3	0	0

David Harvey

Season	League Apps	Subs	Goals	FA Cup Apps	Subs	Goals	League Cup Apps	Subs	Goals	Europe Apps	Subs	Goals	Other Apps	Subs	Goals	Total Apps	Subs	Goals
1960-61																0	0	0
1961-62																0	0	0
1962-63																0	0	0
1963-64																0	0	0
1964-65																0	0	0
1965-66	2						1									3	0	0
1966-67	3						2									5	0	0
1967-68	6									4						10	0	0
1968-69																0	0	0
1969-70	5			2			2				1					9	1	0
1970-71	8									3	1					11	1	0
1971-72	7			2			2									11	0	0
1972-73	41			8			5			9						63	0	0
1973-74	39			4			1			4						48	0	0
TOTAL	111	0	0	16	0	0	13	0	0	20	2	0	0	0	0	160	2	0

Dennis Hawkins

Season	League Apps	Subs	Goals	FA Cup Apps	Subs	Goals	League Cup Apps	Subs	Goals	Europe Apps	Subs	Goals	Other Apps	Subs	Goals	Total Apps	Subs	Goals
1960-61																0	0	0
1961-62																0	0	0
1962-63																0	0	0
1963-64																0	0	0
1964-65																0	0	0
1965-66							1									1	0	0
1966-67	1															1	0	0
1967-68	1						1									2	0	0
1968-69																0	0	0
1969-70																0	0	0
1970-71																0	0	0
1971-72																0	0	0
1972-73																0	0	0
1973-74																0	0	0
TOTAL	2	0	0	0	0	0	2	0	0	0	0	0	0	0	0	4	0	0

John Hawksby

	League			FA Cup			League Cup			Europe			Other			Total		
	Apps	Subs	Goals	Apps	Subs	Goals	Apps	Subs	Goals	Apps	Subs	Goals	Apps	Subs	Goals	Apps	Subs	Goals
1960-61	2															2	0	0
1961-62	25						4									29	0	0
1962-63	5						2									7	0	0
1963-64				1			1									2	0	0
1964-65																0	0	0
1965-66																0	0	0
1966-67																0	0	0
1967-68																0	0	0
1968-69																0	0	0
1969-70																0	0	0
1970-71																0	0	0
1971-72																0	0	0
1972-73																0	0	0
1973-74																0	0	0
TOTAL	32	0	0	1	0	0	7	0	0	0	0	0	0	0	0	40	0	0

Tommy Henderson

	League			FA Cup			League Cup			Europe			Other			Total		
	Apps	Subs	Goals	Apps	Subs	Goals	Apps	Subs	Goals	Apps	Subs	Goals	Apps	Subs	Goals	Apps	Subs	Goals
1960-61																0	0	0
1961-62																0	0	0
1962-63	20			1		3										23	0	1
1963-64	2			1		3	2									7	0	1
1964-65	2						2									4	0	0
1965-66																0	0	0
1966-67																0	0	0
1967-68																0	0	0
1968-69																0	0	0
1969-70																0	0	0
1970-71																0	0	0
1971-72																0	0	0
1972-73																0	0	0
1973-74																0	0	0
TOTAL	24	0	0	2	0	6	4	0	0	0	0	0	0	0	0	34	0	2

Terry Hibbitt

Season	League Apps	League Subs	League Goals	FA Cup Apps	FA Cup Subs	FA Cup Goals	League Cup Apps	League Cup Subs	League Cup Goals	Europe Apps	Europe Subs	Europe Goals	Other Apps	Other Subs	Other Goals	Total Apps	Total Subs	Total Goals
1960-61																0	0	0
1961-62																0	0	0
1962-63																0	0	0
1963-64																0	0	0
1964-65																0	0	0
1965-66		1	1													0	1	1
1966-67	3	1	1							1						4	1	1
1967-68	12	4	2	1			2			3						18	4	2
1968-69	9	3	3				1			2	2					12	5	3
1969-70	8	3	2				2			1		2				11	3	4
1970-71		3								1						1	3	0
1971-72																0	0	0
1972-73																0	0	0
1973-74																0	0	0
TOTAL	32	15	9	1	0	0	5	0	0	8	2	2	0	0	0	46	17	11

Alan Humphreys

Season	League Apps	League Subs	League Goals	FA Cup Apps	FA Cup Subs	FA Cup Goals	League Cup Apps	League Cup Subs	League Cup Goals	Europe Apps	Europe Subs	Europe Goals	Other Apps	Other Subs	Other Goals	Total Apps	Total Subs	Total Goals
1960-61	5															5	0	0
1961-62	9						1									10	0	0
1962-63																0	0	0
1963-64																0	0	0
1964-65																0	0	0
1965-66																0	0	0
1966-67																0	0	0
1967-68																0	0	0
1968-69																0	0	0
1969-70																0	0	0
1970-71																0	0	0
1971-72																0	0	0
1972-73																0	0	0
1973-74																0	0	0
TOTAL	14	0	0	0	0	0	1	0	0	0	0	0	0	0	0	15	0	0

Norman Hunter

Season	League Apps	League Subs	League Goals	FA Cup Apps	FA Cup Subs	FA Cup Goals	League Cup Apps	League Cup Subs	League Cup Goals	Europe Apps	Europe Subs	Europe Goals	Other Apps	Other Subs	Other Goals	Total Apps	Total Subs	Total Goals
1960-61																0	0	0
1961-62																0	0	0
1962-63	36		2	3			2									41	0	2
1963-64	42		2	3			2									47	0	2
1964-65	41		2	8			2		1							51	0	3
1965-66	41		5	2			1			11						55	0	5
1966-67	40			7			3			10						60	0	0
1967-68	40		2	5			7			12						64	0	2
1968-69	42			2			2			8		1				54	0	1
1969-70	35		1	7			2			6			1			51	0	1
1970-71	42		1	4		1	1			11			1			58	0	2
1971-72	42			7			4			1	1		1			55	1	0
1972-73	32		1	7			5			9						53	0	1
1973-74	42			5			1			1						49	0	0
TOTAL	475	0	16	60	0	1	32	0	1	69	1	1	2	0	0	638	1	19

Albert Johanneson

Season	League Apps	League Subs	League Goals	FA Cup Apps	FA Cup Subs	FA Cup Goals	League Cup Apps	League Cup Subs	League Cup Goals	Europe Apps	Europe Subs	Europe Goals	Other Apps	Other Subs	Other Goals	Total Apps	Total Subs	Total Goals
1960-61	5															5	0	0
1961-62	13		3				1									14	0	3
1962-63	41		13	3		1										44	0	14
1963-64	37		13	2			2		2							41	0	15
1964-65	30		9	5			1		3							36	0	12
1965-66	12		2				1			2		1				15	0	3
1966-67	22		7	2		1	2		2	2		2				28	0	12
1967-68	8	1	2				1		1	1	1	3				10	2	6
1968-69		1		2		3										2	1	3
1969-70	2															2	0	0
1970-71																0	0	0
1971-72																0	0	0
1972-73																0	0	0
1973-74																0	0	0
TOTAL	170	2	49	14	0	5	8	0	8	5	1	6	0	0	0	197	3	68

Rod Johnson

Season	League Apps	League Subs	League Goals	FA Cup Apps	FA Cup Subs	FA Cup Goals	League Cup Apps	League Cup Subs	League Cup Goals	Europe Apps	Europe Subs	Europe Goals	Other Apps	Other Subs	Other Goals	Total Apps	Total Subs	Total Goals
1960-61																0	0	0
1961-62																0	0	0
1962-63	4		1				2									6	0	1
1963-64																0	0	0
1964-65	9	3	2	1		1	1		1							11	3	4
1965-66	2		1				2									4	0	1
1966-67	3															3	0	0
1967-68		1					1	1								1	2	0
1968-69																0	0	0
1969-70																0	0	0
1970-71																0	0	0
1971-72																0	0	0
1972-73																0	0	0
1973-74																0	0	0
TOTAL	18	4	4	1	0	1	6	1	1	0	0	0	0	0	0	25	5	6

Alf Jones

Season	League Apps	League Subs	League Goals	FA Cup Apps	FA Cup Subs	FA Cup Goals	League Cup Apps	League Cup Subs	League Cup Goals	Europe Apps	Europe Subs	Europe Goals	Other Apps	Other Subs	Other Goals	Total Apps	Total Subs	Total Goals
1960-61	1															1	0	0
1961-62	5															6	0	0
1962-63							1									0	0	0
1963-64																0	0	0
1964-65																0	0	0
1965-66																0	0	0
1966-67																0	0	0
1967-68																0	0	0
1968-69																0	0	0
1969-70																0	0	0
1970-71																0	0	0
1971-72																0	0	0
1972-73																0	0	0
1973-74																0	0	0
TOTAL	6	0	0	0	0	0	1	0	0	0	0	0	0	0	0	7	0	0

Mick Jones

Season	League Apps	League Subs	League Goals	FA Cup Apps	FA Cup Subs	FA Cup Goals	League Cup Apps	League Cup Subs	League Cup Goals	Europe Apps	Europe Subs	Europe Goals	Other Apps	Other Subs	Other Goals	Total Apps	Total Subs	Total Goals
1960-61																0	0	0
1961-62																0	0	0
1962-63																0	0	0
1963-64																0	0	0
1964-65																0	0	0
1965-66																0	0	0
1966-67																0	0	0
1967-68	25		8	5		2				8		2				38	0	12
1968-69	40		14	2			3		2	8		1				53	0	17
1969-70	32		15	9		3	3			8		8	1			53	0	26
1970-71	40		6	3		1	1		2	9		1				53	0	10
1971-72	24		11	5		1	1		1							30	0	13
1972-73	27	1	9	8		4	4	1		6		3				45	2	16
1973-74	28	3	14	4		1	1			3		2				36	3	17
TOTAL	216	4	77	36	0	12	13	1	5	42	0	17	1	0	0	308	5	111

Joe Jordan

Season	League Apps	League Subs	League Goals	FA Cup Apps	FA Cup Subs	FA Cup Goals	League Cup Apps	League Cup Subs	League Cup Goals	Europe Apps	Europe Subs	Europe Goals	Other Apps	Other Subs	Other Goals	Total Apps	Total Subs	Total Goals
1960-61																0	0	0
1961-62																0	0	0
1962-63																0	0	0
1963-64																0	0	0
1964-65																0	0	0
1965-66																0	0	0
1966-67																0	0	0
1967-68																0	0	0
1968-69																0	0	0
1969-70																0	0	0
1970-71											2					0	2	0
1971-72	5	7		1	1		1		1							7	8	1
1972-73	16	10	9	1	1	2		1		6	1	1				23	13	12
1973-74	25	8	7	3	1	1				3	1		1		1	32	10	9
TOTAL	46	25	16	5	3	3	1	1	1	9	4	1	1	0	1	62	33	22

David Kennedy

Season	League			FA Cup			League Cup			Europe			Other			Total		
	Apps	Subs	Goals	Apps	Subs	Goals	Apps	Subs	Goals	Apps	Subs	Goals	Apps	Subs	Goals	Apps	Subs	Goals
1960-61																0	0	0
1961-62																0	0	0
1962-63																0	0	0
1963-64																0	0	0
1964-65																0	0	0
1965-66																0	0	0
1966-67																0	0	0
1967-68																0	0	0
1968-69																0	0	0
1969-70	2		1													2	0	1
1970-71																1	0	0
1971-72										1						1	0	0
1972-73																0	0	0
1973-74																0	0	0
TOTAL	2	0	1	0	0	0	0	0	0	1	0	0	0	0	0	3	0	1

John Kilford

Season	League			FA Cup			League Cup			Europe			Other			Total		
	Apps	Subs	Goals	Apps	Subs	Goals	Apps	Subs	Goals	Apps	Subs	Goals	Apps	Subs	Goals	Apps	Subs	Goals
1960-61	9															9	0	0
1961-62	6						2									8	0	0
1962-63																0	0	0
1963-64																0	0	0
1964-65																0	0	0
1965-66																0	0	0
1966-67																0	0	0
1967-68																0	0	0
1968-69																0	0	0
1969-70																0	0	0
1970-71																0	0	0
1971-72																0	0	0
1972-73																0	0	0
1973-74																0	0	0
TOTAL	15	0	0	0	0	0	2	0	0	0	0	0	0	0	0	17	0	0

Ian Lawson

	League			FA Cup			League Cup			Europe			Other			Total		
	Apps	Subs	Goals	Apps	Subs	Goals	Apps	Subs	Goals	Apps	Subs	Goals	Apps	Subs	Goals	Apps	Subs	Goals
1960-61																0	0	0
1961-62	11		1													11	0	1
1962-63	6		5				2									8	0	5
1963-64	24		11	3		1	2					3				29	0	15
1964-65	3															3	0	0
1965-66																0	0	0
1966-67																0	0	0
1967-68																0	0	0
1968-69																0	0	0
1969-70																0	0	0
1970-71																0	0	0
1971-72																0	0	0
1972-73																0	0	0
1973-74																0	0	0
TOTAL	44	0	17	3	0	1	4	0	0	0	0	3	0	0	0	51	0	21

Glan Letheren

	League			FA Cup			League Cup			Europe			Other			Total		
	Apps	Subs	Goals	Apps	Subs	Goals	Apps	Subs	Goals	Apps	Subs	Goals	Apps	Subs	Goals	Apps	Subs	Goals
1960-61																0	0	0
1961-62																0	0	0
1962-63																0	0	0
1963-64																0	0	0
1964-65																0	0	0
1965-66																0	0	0
1966-67																0	0	0
1967-68																0	0	0
1968-69																0	0	0
1969-70																0	0	0
1970-71																0	0	0
1971-72																0	0	0
1972-73											1					0	1	0
1973-74																0	0	0
TOTAL	0	0	0	0	0	0	0	0	0	0	1	0	0	0	0	0	1	0

Gary Liddell

Season	League Apps	League Subs	League Goals	FA Cup Apps	FA Cup Subs	FA Cup Goals	League Cup Apps	League Cup Subs	League Cup Goals	Europe Apps	Europe Subs	Europe Goals	Other Apps	Other Subs	Other Goals	Total Apps	Total Subs	Total Goals
1960-61																0	0	0
1961-62																0	0	0
1962-63																0	0	0
1963-64																0	0	0
1964-65																0	0	0
1965-66																0	0	0
1966-67																0	0	0
1967-68																0	0	0
1968-69																0	0	0
1969-70																0	0	0
1970-71																0	0	0
1971-72	1															1	0	0
1972-73										1	1	1				1	1	1
1973-74		1					1									1	1	0
TOTAL	1	1	0	0	0	0	1	0	0	1	1	1	0	0	0	3	2	1

Peter Lorimer

Season	League Apps	League Subs	League Goals	FA Cup Apps	FA Cup Subs	FA Cup Goals	League Cup Apps	League Cup Subs	League Cup Goals	Europe Apps	Europe Subs	Europe Goals	Other Apps	Other Subs	Other Goals	Total Apps	Total Subs	Total Goals
1960-61																0	0	0
1961-62																0	0	0
1962-63	1															1	0	0
1963-64																0	0	0
1964-65	1															1	0	0
1965-66	34		13	2		3				9		3				45	0	19
1966-67	27	2	9	5	1	2	2		2	5		1				39	3	14
1967-68	36	1	16	5		2	6		4	12		8				59	1	30
1968-69	25	4	9	4		1	1			6	1	3				36	5	13
1969-70	36	3	14	8		2	3			7		3	1	1		55	4	19
1970-71	37		12	4		2	1			10		5				52	0	19
1971-72	42		23	8		3	4		2	2		1				56	0	29
1972-73	41		15	8		3	5		3	9		2				63	0	23
1973-74	37		12	2		2	3			5						47	0	14
TOTAL	317	10	123	46	1	20	25	0	11	65	1	26	1	1	0	454	13	180

Jimmy Lumsden

Season	League Apps	League Subs	League Goals	FA Cup Apps	FA Cup Subs	FA Cup Goals	League Cup Apps	League Cup Subs	League Cup Goals	Europe Apps	Europe Subs	Europe Goals	Other Apps	Other Subs	Other Goals	Total Apps	Total Subs	Total Goals
1960-61																0	0	0
1961-62																0	0	0
1962-63																0	0	0
1963-64																0	0	0
1964-65																0	0	0
1965-66																0	0	0
1966-67	1															1	0	0
1967-68	1															1	0	0
1968-69																0	0	0
1969-70	1	1														1	1	0
1970-71																0	0	0
1971-72																0	0	0
1972-73																0	0	0
1973-74																0	0	1
TOTAL	3	1	0	0	0	0	0	0	0	0	0	0	0	0	0	3	0	1

Billy McAdams

Season	League Apps	League Subs	League Goals	FA Cup Apps	FA Cup Subs	FA Cup Goals	League Cup Apps	League Cup Subs	League Cup Goals	Europe Apps	Europe Subs	Europe Goals	Other Apps	Other Subs	Other Goals	Total Apps	Total Subs	Total Goals
1960-61																0	0	0
1961-62	11			2		3			1							13	0	4
1962-63																0	0	0
1963-64																0	0	0
1964-65																0	0	0
1965-66																0	0	0
1966-67																0	0	0
1967-68																0	0	0
1968-69																0	0	0
1969-70																0	0	0
1970-71																0	0	0
1971-72																0	0	0
1972-73																0	0	0
1973-74																0	0	0
TOTAL	11	0	0	2	0	3	0	0	1	0	0	0	0	0	0	13	0	4

John McCole

Season	League Apps	League Subs	League Goals	FA Cup Apps	FA Cup Subs	FA Cup Goals	League Cup Apps	League Cup Subs	League Cup Goals	Europe Apps	Europe Subs	Europe Goals	Other Apps	Other Subs	Other Goals	Total Apps	Total Subs	Total Goals
1960-61	5		4													5	0	4
1961-62	10		3				1		4							11	0	7
1962-63																0	0	0
1963-64																0	0	0
1964-65																0	0	0
1965-66																0	0	0
1966-67																0	0	0
1967-68																0	0	0
1968-69																0	0	0
1969-70																0	0	0
1970-71																0	0	0
1971-72																0	0	0
1972-73																0	0	0
1973-74																0	0	0
TOTAL	15	0	7	0	0	0	1	0	4	0	0	0	0	0	0	16	0	11

Peter McConnell

Season	League Apps	League Subs	League Goals	FA Cup Apps	FA Cup Subs	FA Cup Goals	League Cup Apps	League Cup Subs	League Cup Goals	Europe Apps	Europe Subs	Europe Goals	Other Apps	Other Subs	Other Goals	Total Apps	Total Subs	Total Goals
1960-61	9		1													9	0	1
1961-62	23		3	2			3		1							28	0	4
1962-63																0	0	0
1963-64																0	0	0
1964-65																0	0	0
1965-66																0	0	0
1966-67																0	0	0
1967-68																0	0	0
1968-69																0	0	0
1969-70																0	0	0
1970-71																0	0	0
1971-72																0	0	0
1972-73																0	0	0
1973-74																0	0	0
TOTAL	32	0	4	2	0	3	3	0	1	0	0	0	0	0	0	37	0	5

Billy McGinley

	League			FA Cup			League Cup			Europe			Other			Total		
	Apps	Subs	Goals	Apps	Subs	Goals	Apps	Subs	Goals	Apps	Subs	Goals	Apps	Subs	Goals	Apps	Subs	Goals
1960-61																0	0	0
1961-62																0	0	0
1962-63																0	0	0
1963-64																0	0	0
1964-65																0	0	0
1965-66																0	0	0
1966-67																0	0	0
1967-68																0	0	0
1968-69																0	0	0
1969-70																0	0	0
1970-71																0	0	0
1971-72																0	0	0
1972-73		1														0	1	0
1973-74											1					0	1	0
TOTAL	0	1	0	0	0	0	0	0	0	0	1	0	0	0	0	0	2	0

Gordon McQueen

	League			FA Cup			League Cup			Europe			Other			Total		
	Apps	Subs	Goals	Apps	Subs	Goals	Apps	Subs	Goals	Apps	Subs	Goals	Apps	Subs	Goals	Apps	Subs	Goals
1960-61																0	0	0
1961-62																0	0	0
1962-63																0	0	0
1963-64																0	0	0
1964-65																0	0	0
1965-66																0	0	0
1966-67																0	0	0
1967-68																0	0	0
1968-69																0	0	0
1969-70																0	0	0
1970-71																0	0	0
1971-72																0	0	0
1972-73	6									2	1	1				8	1	0
1973-74	36			3						3						42	0	0
TOTAL	42	0	0	3	0	0	0	0	0	5	1	1	0	0	0	50	1	1

Paul Madeley

	League Apps	Subs	Goals	FA Cup Apps	Subs	Goals	League Cup Apps	Subs	Goals	Europe Apps	Subs	Goals	Other Apps	Subs	Goals	Total Apps	Subs	Goals
1960-61																0	0	0
1961-62																0	0	0
1962-63																0	0	0
1963-64	4			2												6	0	0
1964-65	6						1									7	0	0
1965-66	9	4	1	1			2		1	4						16	4	2
1966-67	27	1	2	4	1	1	4			8		1				43	2	4
1967-68	33	3	7	3	2	1	5			10	1	2				51	6	10
1968-69	31		3	2			2		1	7						42	0	4
1969-70	39			8		1	3			8		1	1		1	59	0	1
1970-71	41	5	4	4		1	1			12		1				58	0	6
1971-72	42		2	7			4		1	1						54	0	2
1972-73	34			8			4			6						52	0	2
1973-74	39			1			1			2						47	0	2
TOTAL	305	8	22	44	3	2	27	0	3	58	1	4	1	0	0	435	12	31

Jimmy Mann

	League Apps	Subs	Goals	FA Cup Apps	Subs	Goals	League Cup Apps	Subs	Goals	Europe Apps	Subs	Goals	Other Apps	Subs	Goals	Total Apps	Subs	Goals
1960-61																0	0	0
1961-62																0	0	0
1962-63																0	0	0
1963-64																0	0	0
1964-65																0	0	0
1965-66																0	0	0
1966-67																0	0	0
1967-68																0	0	0
1968-69																0	0	0
1969-70																0	0	0
1970-71																0	0	0
1971-72	1								1	1		1				2	1	0
1972-73	1									1						1	0	0
1973-74																0	0	0
TOTAL	2	0	0	0	0	0	0	0	1	2	0	1	0	0	0	4	1	0

Cliff Mason

	League			FA Cup			League Cup			Europe			Other			Total		
	Apps	Subs	Goals	Apps	Subs	Goals	Apps	Subs	Goals	Apps	Subs	Goals	Apps	Subs	Goals	Apps	Subs	Goals
1960-61																0	0	0
1961-62	11															11	0	0
1962-63	20						2									22	0	0
1963-64																0	0	0
1964-65																0	0	0
1965-66																0	0	0
1966-67																0	0	0
1967-68																0	0	0
1968-69																0	0	0
1969-70																0	0	0
1970-71																0	0	0
1971-72																0	0	0
1972-73																0	0	0
1973-74																0	0	0
TOTAL	31	0	0	0	0	0	2	0	0	0	0	0	0	0	0	33	0	0

Derek Mayers

	League			FA Cup			League Cup			Europe			Other			Total		
	Apps	Subs	Goals	Apps	Subs	Goals	Apps	Subs	Goals	Apps	Subs	Goals	Apps	Subs	Goals	Apps	Subs	Goals
1960-61																0	0	0
1961-62	20		5	2			2									24	0	5
1962-63																0	0	0
1963-64																0	0	0
1964-65																0	0	0
1965-66																0	0	0
1966-67																0	0	0
1967-68																0	0	0
1968-69																0	0	0
1969-70																0	0	0
1970-71																0	0	0
1971-72																0	0	0
1972-73																0	0	0
1973-74																0	0	0
TOTAL	20	0	5	2	0	0	2	0	0	0	0	0	0	0	0	24	0	5

Mike O'Grady

Season	League Apps	League Subs	League Goals	FA Cup Apps	FA Cup Subs	FA Cup Goals	League Cup Apps	League Cup Subs	League Cup Goals	Europe Apps	Europe Subs	Europe Goals	Other Apps	Other Subs	Other Goals	Total Apps	Total Subs	Total Goals
1960-61																		
1961-62																		
1962-63																		
1963-64																		
1964-65																		
1965-66	29		4	1						7		1				37		5
1966-67	14		1	2		1	2			4						22		2
1967-68	6			1						1						8		
1968-69	38		8	1			3			7		1				49		9
1969-70	3	1								1		1				4	1	1
1970-71																		
1971-72																		
1972-73																		
1973-74																		
TOTAL	90	1	13	5	0	1	5	0	0	20	0	3	0	0	0	120	1	17

Jimmy O'Neill

Season	League Apps	League Subs	League Goals	FA Cup Apps	FA Cup Subs	FA Cup Goals	League Cup Apps	League Cup Subs	League Cup Goals	Europe Apps	Europe Subs	Europe Goals	Other Apps	Other Subs	Other Goals	Total Apps	Total Subs	Total Goals
1960-61																0	0	0
1961-62																0	0	0
1962-63																0	0	0
1963-64																0	0	0
1964-65																0	0	0
1965-66																0	0	0
1966-67																0	0	0
1967-68																0	0	0
1968-69																0	0	0
1969-70																0	0	0
1970-71																0	0	0
1971-72																0	0	0
1972-73																0	0	0
1973-74								1			2					0	0	0
TOTAL	0	0	0	0	0	0	0	0	0	0	0	0	0	0	0	0	3	0

Alan Peacock

	League			FA Cup			League Cup			Europe			Other			Total		
	Apps	Subs	Goals	Apps	Subs	Goals	Apps	Subs	Goals	Apps	Subs	Goals	Apps	Subs	Goals	Apps	Subs	Goals
1960-61																0	0	0
1961-62																0	0	0
1962-63																0	0	0
1963-64	14		8													14	0	8
1964-65	10		6	4		2										14	0	8
1965-66	24		10	1						3		1				28	0	11
1966-67	6		2	1			2		1							9	0	3
1967-68																0	0	0
1968-69																0	0	0
1969-70																0	0	0
1970-71																0	0	0
1971-72																0	0	0
1972-73																0	0	0
1973-74																0	0	0
TOTAL	54	0	26	6	0	2	2	0	1	3	0	1	0	0	0	65	0	30

Paul Peterson

	League			FA Cup			League Cup			Europe			Other			Total		
	Apps	Subs	Goals	Apps	Subs	Goals	Apps	Subs	Goals	Apps	Subs	Goals	Apps	Subs	Goals	Apps	Subs	Goals
1960-61																0	0	0
1961-62																0	0	0
1962-63																0	0	0
1963-64																0	0	0
1964-65																0	0	0
1965-66																0	0	0
1966-67																0	0	0
1967-68																0	0	0
1968-69																0	0	0
1969-70	3															3	0	0
1970-71		1														0	1	0
1971-72																0	0	0
1972-73																0	0	0
1973-74																0	0	0
TOTAL	3	1	0	0	0	0	0	0	0	0	0	0	0	0	0	3	1	0

Noel Peyton

Season	League Apps	League Subs	League Goals	FA Cup Apps	FA Cup Subs	FA Cup Goals	League Cup Apps	League Cup Subs	League Cup Goals	Europe Apps	Europe Subs	Europe Goals	Other Apps	Other Subs	Other Goals	Total Apps	Total Subs	Total Goals
1960-61	6		1													6	0	1
1961-62	37		5	2		1	4									43	0	6
1962-63	6						2									8	0	0
1963-64																0	0	0
1964-65																0	0	0
1965-66																0	0	0
1966-67																0	0	0
1967-68																0	0	0
1968-69																0	0	0
1969-70																0	0	0
1970-71																0	0	0
1971-72																0	0	0
1972-73																0	0	0
1973-74																0	0	0
TOTAL	49	0	6	2	0	1	6	0	0	0	0	0	0	0	0	57	0	7

Paul Reaney

Season	League Apps	League Subs	League Goals	FA Cup Apps	FA Cup Subs	FA Cup Goals	League Cup Apps	League Cup Subs	League Cup Goals	Europe Apps	Europe Subs	Europe Goals	Other Apps	Other Subs	Other Goals	Total Apps	Total Subs	Total Goals
1960-61																0	0	0
1961-62																0	0	0
1962-63	35		1	3			1									39	0	1
1963-64	41			3			2									46	0	0
1964-65	41			8		1										49	0	1
1965-66	41		1	2		1	1			11						55	0	2
1966-67	41			7			4			9						61	1	0
1967-68	40	1	1	5			7			12						64	1	1
1968-69	42			2			3			7						54	0	0
1969-70	37			7			3			7			1			55	0	0
1970-71	18	3		4						6	1					28	4	0
1971-72	29	2		5	1		4			2	2					40	5	0
1972-73	29		1	8			1			8		1				47	0	1
1973-74	36		1	3			1			4						44	0	1
TOTAL	430	6	5	57	1	2	27	0	0	66	3	0	2	0	0	582	10	7

Don Revie

	League			FA Cup			League Cup			Europe			Other			Total		
	Apps	Subs	Goals	Apps	Subs	Goals	Apps	Subs	Goals	Apps	Subs	Goals	Apps	Subs	Goals	Apps	Subs	Goals
1960-61																0	0	0
1961-62	7					1										7	0	1
1962-63																0	0	0
1963-64																0	0	0
1964-65																0	0	0
1965-66																0	0	0
1966-67																0	0	0
1967-68																0	0	0
1968-69																0	0	0
1969-70																0	0	0
1970-71																0	0	0
1971-72																0	0	0
1972-73																0	0	0
1973-74																0	0	0
TOTAL	7	0	0	0	0	1	0	0	0	0	0	0	0	0	0	7	0	1

John Shaw

	League			FA Cup			League Cup			Europe			Other			Total		
	Apps	Subs	Goals	Apps	Subs	Goals	Apps	Subs	Goals	Apps	Subs	Goals	Apps	Subs	Goals	Apps	Subs	Goals
1960-61																0	0	0
1961-62																0	0	0
1962-63																0	0	0
1963-64																0	0	0
1964-65																0	0	0
1965-66																0	0	0
1966-67																0	0	0
1967-68																0	0	0
1968-69																0	0	0
1969-70																0	0	0
1970-71																0	0	0
1971-72										1						1	0	0
1972-73										1						1	0	0
1973-74																0	0	0
TOTAL	0	0	0	0	0	0	0	0	0	2	0	0	0	0	0	2	0	0

Bobbie Sibbald

Season	League Apps	Subs	Goals	FA Cup Apps	Subs	Goals	League Cup Apps	Subs	Goals	Europe Apps	Subs	Goals	Other Apps	Subs	Goals	Total Apps	Subs	Goals
1960-61																		
1961-62																		
1962-63																		
1963-64																		
1964-65																		
1965-66																		
1966-67	1															1		
1967-68		1															1	
1968-69																		
1969-70																		
1970-71																		
1971-72																		
1972-73																		
1973-74																		
TOTAL	1	1	0	0	0	0	0	0	0	0	0	0	0	0	0	1	1	0

Eric Smith

Season	League Apps	Subs	Goals	FA Cup Apps	Subs	Goals	League Cup Apps	Subs	Goals	Europe Apps	Subs	Goals	Other Apps	Subs	Goals	Total Apps	Subs	Goals
1960-61	8															8		
1961-62	41		1	2			3									46		1
1962-63	6															6		
1963-64							1									1		
1964-65																		
1965-66																		
1966-67																		
1967-68																		
1968-69																		
1969-70																		
1970-71																		
1971-72																		
1972-73																		
1973-74																		
TOTAL	55	0	1	2	0	0	4	0	0	0	0	0	0	0	0	61	0	1

Gary Sprake

Season	League Apps	Subs	Goals	FA Cup Apps	Subs	Goals	League Cup Apps	Subs	Goals	Europe Apps	Subs	Goals	Other Apps	Subs	Goals	Total Apps	Subs	Goals
1960-61																0	0	0
1961-62	1															1	0	0
1962-63	33			3			2									38	0	0
1963-64	41			3			3									47	0	0
1964-65	41			8												49	0	0
1965-66	40			1			1			11						53	0	0
1966-67	39			7			2			10						58	0	0
1967-68	36			5			7			8						56	0	0
1968-69	42			2			3			8						55	0	0
1969-70	37			7			1			8			1			54	0	0
1970-71	34			4			1			9	1					48	1	0
1971-72	35			5			2			1	1		1			44	1	0
1972-73	1									1						1	0	0
1973-74																1	0	0
TOTAL	380	0	0	45	0	0	22	0	0	56	2	0	2	0	0	505	2	0

David Stewart

Season	League Apps	Subs	Goals	FA Cup Apps	Subs	Goals	League Cup Apps	Subs	Goals	Europe Apps	Subs	Goals	Other Apps	Subs	Goals	Total Apps	Subs	Goals
1960-61																0	0	0
1961-62																0	0	0
1962-63																0	0	0
1963-64																0	0	0
1964-65																0	0	0
1965-66																0	0	0
1966-67																0	0	0
1967-68																0	0	0
1968-69																0	0	0
1969-70																0	0	0
1970-71																0	0	0
1971-72																0	0	0
1972-73																0	0	0
1973-74	3			1												4	0	0
TOTAL	3	0	0	1	0	0	0	0	0	0	0	0	0	0	0	4	0	0

Jim Storrie

Season	League			FA Cup			League Cup			Europe			Other			Total		
	Apps	Subs	Goals	Apps	Subs	Goals	Apps	Subs	Goals	Apps	Subs	Goals	Apps	Subs	Goals	Apps	Subs	Goals
1960-61	38		25	3		1	2		1							43	0	27
1961-62	15		3				2		1							17	0	4
1962-63	37		16	8		2	1		1							46	0	19
1963-64	30		13	1			2		1	9		1				42	0	15
1964-65	3	3	1				1		1	1						5	3	2
1965-66																0	0	0
1966-67																0	0	0
1967-68																0	0	0
1968-69																0	0	0
1969-70																0	0	0
1970-71																0	0	0
1971-72																0	0	0
1972-73																0	0	0
1973-74																0	0	0
TOTAL	123	3	58	12	0	3	8	0	5	10	0	1	0	0	0	153	3	67

Don Weston

Season	League			FA Cup			League Cup			Europe			Other			Total		
	Apps	Subs	Goals	Apps	Subs	Goals	Apps	Subs	Goals	Apps	Subs	Goals	Apps	Subs	Goals	Apps	Subs	Goals
1960-61																0	0	0
1961-62																0	0	0
1962-63	15		7	3												18	0	7
1963-64	35		13	1			2		1							38	0	14
1964-65	15		4	3		1										18	0	5
1965-66	3						1									4	0	0
1966-67																0	0	0
1967-68																0	0	0
1968-69																0	0	0
1969-70																0	0	0
1970-71																0	0	0
1971-72																0	0	0
1972-73																0	0	0
1973-74																0	0	0
TOTAL	68	0	24	7	0	1	3	0	1	0	0	0	0	0	0	78	0	26

Brian Williamson

	League			FA Cup			League Cup			Europe			Other			Total		
	Apps	Subs	Goals	Apps	Subs	Goals	Apps	Subs	Goals	Apps	Subs	Goals	Apps	Subs	Goals	Apps	Subs	Goals
1960-61																0	0	0
1961-62																0	0	0
1962-63	3															3	0	0
1963-64	1															1	0	0
1964-65	1						2									3	0	0
1965-66				1												1	0	0
1966-67																0	0	0
1967-68																0	0	0
1968-69																0	0	0
1969-70																0	0	0
1970-71																0	0	0
1971-72																0	0	0
1972-73																0	0	0
1973-74																0	0	0
TOTAL	5	0	0	1	0	0	2	0	0	0	0	0	0	0	0	8	0	0

Barrie Wright

	League			FA Cup			League Cup			Europe			Other			Total		
	Apps	Subs	Goals	Apps	Subs	Goals	Apps	Subs	Goals	Apps	Subs	Goals	Apps	Subs	Goals	Apps	Subs	Goals
1960-61																0	0	0
1961-62																0	0	0
1962-63	3															3	0	0
1963-64	2															2	0	0
1964-65							2									2	0	0
1965-66							1									1	0	0
1966-67																0	0	0
1967-68																0	0	0
1968-69																0	0	0
1969-70																0	0	0
1970-71																0	0	0
1971-72																0	0	0
1972-73																0	0	0
1973-74																0	0	0
TOTAL	5	0	0	0	0	0	3	0	0	0	0	0	0	0	0	8	0	0

Terry Yorath

Season	League Apps	League Subs	League Goals	FA Cup Apps	FA Cup Subs	FA Cup Goals	League Cup Apps	League Cup Subs	League Cup Goals	Europe Apps	Europe Subs	Europe Goals	Other Apps	Other Subs	Other Goals	Total Apps	Total Subs	Total Goals
1960-61																0	0	0
1961-62																0	0	0
1962-63																0	0	0
1963-64																0	0	0
1964-65																0	0	0
1965-66																0	0	0
1966-67																0	0	0
1967-68	1															1	0	0
1968-69	7	4														7	4	0
1969-70	3	4	1				3			2	2					8	6	1
1970-71	3															3	0	0
1971-72	16	6		2	2		1	1		4	3					23	12	0
1972-73	23	5	2	3	1	1	1			6	1					33	7	3
1973-74																0	0	0
TOTAL	53	19	3	5	3	1	5	1		12	6	0	0	0	0	75	29	4

Tommy Younger

Season	League Apps	League Subs	League Goals	FA Cup Apps	FA Cup Subs	FA Cup Goals	League Cup Apps	League Cup Subs	League Cup Goals	Europe Apps	Europe Subs	Europe Goals	Other Apps	Other Subs	Other Goals	Total Apps	Total Subs	Total Goals
1960-61	31			2			3									36	0	0
1961-62	6															6	0	0
1962-63																0	0	0
1963-64																0	0	0
1964-65																0	0	0
1965-66																0	0	0
1966-67																0	0	0
1967-68																0	0	0
1968-69																0	0	0
1969-70																0	0	0
1970-71																0	0	0
1971-72																0	0	0
1972-73																0	0	0
1973-74																0	0	0
TOTAL	37	0	0	2	0	0	3	0	0	0	0	0	0	0	0	42	0	0

Revie's Playing Record at Leeds United

COMPETITION/PLACING	SEASON	APPEARANCES	GOALS
LEAGUE - Div 1 15TH		20	2
FA CUP - ROUND 3	1958-59	1	
TOTAL		21	2
LEAGUE - Div 1 21ST	1959-60	35	7
TOTAL		35	7
LEAGUE - Div 2 - 14TH		14	1
LEAGUE CUP - ROUND 4	1960-61	3	1
TOTAL		17	2
LEAGUE - Div 2 - 19TH	1961-62	7	1
TOTAL		7	1
LEAGUE TOTAL		76	11
FA CUP TOTAL	1958-59 to 1961-62	1	
LEAGUE CUP TOTAL		3	1
ALL COMPETITIONS - TOTAL		80	12

Revie's Managerial Record at Leeds United

COMPETITION / PLACING	SEASON	PLAYED	WON	DRAWN	LOST	GOALS FOR	GOALS AGAINST	POINTS
LEAGUE (FROM 18 MARCH 1961) - Div 2 14TH	1960-61	9	1	4	4	16	15	6
TOTAL		9	1	4	4	16	15	6
LEAGUE - Div 2 19TH		42	12	12	18	50	61	36
FA CUP - ROUND 3	1961-62	2	0	1	1	3	5	1
LEAGUE CUP - ROUND 4		4	2	1	1	9	6	5
TOTAL		48	14	14	20	62	72	42
LEAGUE - Div 2 5TH		42	19	10	13	79	53	48
FA CUP - ROUND 5	1962-63	3	2	0	1	5	4	4
LEAGUE CUP - ROUND 3		2	1	0	1	2	5	2
TOTAL		47	22	10	15	86	62	54
LEAGUE - Div 2 CHAMPIONS		42	24	15	3	71	34	63
FA CUP - ROUND 4	1963-64	3	1	1	1	2	3	3
LEAGUE CUP - ROUND 4		3	2	0	1	8	4	4
TOTAL		48	27	16	5	81	41	70
LEAGUE - Div 1 RUNNERS UP		42	26	9	7	83	52	61
FA CUP - RUNNERS UP	1964-65	8	5	2	1	13	4	12
LEAGUE CUP - ROUND 3		2	1	0	1	5	5	2
TOTAL		52	32	11	9	101	61	75
LEAGUE - Div 1 RUNNERS UP		42	23	9	10	79	38	55
FA CUP - ROUND 4		2	1	0	1	6	1	2
LEAGUE CUP - ROUND 3	1965-66	2	1	0	1	6	6	2
EUROPE - SEMI FINAL		11	5	4	2	14	10	14
TOTAL		57	30	13	14	105	55	73
LEAGUE - Div 1 4TH		42	22	11	9	62	42	55
FA CUP - SEMI FINAL		7	4	2	1	13	4	10
LEAGUE CUP - ROUND 4	1966-67	4	2	1	1	5	8	5
EUROPE - RUNNERS UP		10	5	3	2	16	8	13
TOTAL		63	33	17	13	96	62	83
LEAGUE - Div 1 4TH		42	22	9	11	71	41	53
FA CUP - SEMI FINAL		5	4	0	1	7	2	8
LEAGUE CUP - WINNERS	1967-68	7	7	0	0	15	3	14
EUROPE - WINNERS		12	7	5	0	26	4	19
TOTAL		66	40	14	12	119	50	94
LEAGUE - Div 1 CHAMPIONS		42	27	13	2	66	26	67
FA CUP - ROUND 3		2	0	1	1	2	4	1
LEAGUE CUP - ROUND 4	1968-69	3	2	0	1	4	3	4
EUROPE - ROUND 4		8	4	1	3	12	9	9
TOTAL		55	33	15	7	84	42	81

Revie's Managerial Record at Leeds United (Continued)

COMPETITION / PLACING	SEASON	PLAYED	WON	DRAWN	LOST	GOALS FOR	GOALS AGAINST	POINTS
LEAGUE - Div 1 RUNNERS UP		42	21	15	6	84	49	57
FA CUP - RUNNERS UP		9	5	3	1	16	5	13
LEAGUE CUP - ROUND 3	1969-70	3	1	1	1	2	3	3
EUROPE - SEMI FINAL		8	6	0	2	25	3	12
OTHER (CHARITY SHIELD) - WINNERS		1	1	0	0	2	1	2
TOTAL		**63**	**34**	**19**	**10**	**129**	**61**	**87**
LEAGUE - Div 1 RUNNERS UP		42	27	10	5	72	30	64
FA CUP - ROUND 5		4	2	1	1	9	5	5
LEAGUE CUP - ROUND 2	1970-71	1	0	0	1	0	1	0
EUROPE - WINNERS		12	7	4	1	24	9	18
TOTAL		**59**	**36**	**15**	**8**	**105**	**45**	**87**
LEAGUE - Div 1 RUNNERS UP		42	24	9	9	73	31	57
FA CUP - WINNERS		7	6	1	0	14	2	13
LEAGUE CUP - ROUND 3	1971-72	4	1	2	1	2	1	4
EUROPE - ROUND 1		2	1	0	1	2	4	2
OTHER (FAIRS CUP PLAY OFF) - RUNNERS UP		1	0	0	1	1	2	0
TOTAL		**56**	**32**	**12**	**12**	**92**	**40**	**76**
LEAGUE - DIV 1. 3RD		42	21	11	10	71	45	53
FA CUP - RUNNERS UP		8	5	2	1	13	4	12
LEAGUE CUP - ROUND 4	1972-73	5	2	2	1	9	4	6
EUROPE - RUNNERS UP		9	5	3	1	13	3	13
TOTAL		**64**	**33**	**18**	**13**	**106**	**56**	**84**
LEAGUE - Div 1 CHAMPIONS		42	24	14	4	66	31	62
FA CUP - ROUND 5		5	2	2	1	7	4	6
LEAGUE CUP - ROUND 2	1973-74	1	0	0	1	0	2	0
EUROPE - ROUND 3		6	2	3	1	9	5	7
TOTAL		**54**	**28**	**19**	**7**	**82**	**42**	**75**
LEAGUE TOTAL	1960-61 TO 1973-74	555	293	151	111	943	548	737
FA CUP TOTAL		65	37	16	12	110	47	90
LEAGUE CUP TOTAL		41	22	7	12	67	51	51
EUROPE TOTAL		78	42	23	13	141	55	107
OTHER TOTAL	1969-70 & 1971-72	2	1	0	1	3	3	2
ALL COMPETITIONS - TOTAL	1960-61 TO 1973-74	*741*	*395*	*197*	*149*	*1264*	*704*	*987*

Note: Points have been attributed to all competitions in a statistical illustration of Leeds United's overall team performance.

Revie's Boys' 'First' Game Appearance Record

PLAYER	SEASON	MATCH DATE	GAME	H/A	COMPETITION	SCORE
Billy Bremner	1960-61	18-Mar-1961	Portsmouth	A	Division 2	1-3
Bobby Cameron	1960-61	18-Mar-1961	Portsmouth	A	Division 2	1-3
Jack Charlton	1960-61	18-Mar-1961	Portsmouth	A	Division 2	1-3
Peter Fitzgerald	1960-61	18-Mar-1961	Portsmouth	A	Division 2	1-3
Gerry Francis	1960-61	18-Mar-1961	Portsmouth	A	Division 2	1-3
Freddie Goodwin	1960-61	18-Mar-1961	Portsmouth	A	Division 2	1-3
Colin Grainger	1960-61	18-Mar-1961	Portsmouth	A	Division 2	1-3
Alan Humphreys	1960-61	18-Mar-1961	Portsmouth	A	Division 2	1-3
Alf Jones	1960-61	18-Mar-1961	Portsmouth	A	Division 2	1-3
John Kilford	1960-61	18-Mar-1961	Portsmouth	A	Division 2	1-3
Peter McConnell	1960-61	18-Mar-1961	Portsmouth	A	Division 2	1-3
Grenville Hair	1960-61	25-Mar-1961	Sheffield United	H	Division 2	1-2
John McCole	1960-61	25-Mar-1961	Sheffield United	H	Division 2	1-2
Eric Smith	1960-61	25-Mar-1961	Sheffield United	H	Division 2	1-2
Terry Carling	1960-61	1-Apr-1961	Luton Town	A	Division 3	1-1
John Hawksby	1960-61	1-Apr-1961	Luton Town	A	Division 3	1-1
Noel Peyton	1960-61	3-Apr-1961	Scunthorpe United	A	Division 2	2-3
Albert Johanneson	1960-61	8-Apr-1961	Swansea Town	A	Division 2	2-2
Willie Bell	1960-61	22-Apr-1961	Lincoln City	A	Division 2	7-0
Derek Mayers	1961-62	19-Aug-1961	Charlton Athletic	H	Division 2	1-0
Don Revie	1961-62	6-Sep-1961	Norwich City	A	Division 2	0-2
Tommy Younger	1961-62	30-Sep-1961	Preston North End	H	Division 2	1-2
Terry Casey	1961-62	12-Dec-1961	Rotherham United	A	League Cup R4	1-1
Billy McAdams	1961-62	16-Dec-1961	Charlton Athletic	A	Division 2	1-3
Mike Addy	1961-62	15-Jan-1962	Rotherham United	H	League Cup R4 replay	1-2
Ian Lawson	1961-62	3-Mar-1962	Huddersfield Town	A	Division 2	1-2
Bobby Collins	1961-62	10-Mar-1962	Swansea Town	H	Division 2	2-0
Cliff Mason	1961-62	10-Mar-1962	Swansea Town	H	Division 2	2-0
Gary Sprake	1961-62	17-Mar-1962	Southampton	A	Division 2	1-4
John Charles	1962-63	18-Aug-1962	Stoke City	A	Division 2	1-0
Jim Storrie	1962-63	18-Aug-1962	Stoke City	A	Division 2	1-0
Norman Hunter	1962-63	8-Sep-1962	Swansea Town	A	Division 2	2-0
Rod Johnson	1962-63	8-Sep-1962	Swansea Town	A	Division 2	2-0
Paul Reaney	1962-63	8-Sep-1962	Swansea Town	A	Division 2	2-0
Peter Lorimer	1962-63	29-Sep-1962	Southampton	H	Division 2	1-1
Tom Hallett	1962-63	17-Oct-1962	Blackburn Rovers	A	League Cup R3	0-4
Tommy Henderson	1962-63	10-Nov-1962	Grimsby Town	A	Division 2	1-1
Don Weston	1962-63	15-Dec-1962	Stoke City	H	Division 2	3-1
Brian Williamson	1962-63	30-Mar-1963	Grimsby Town	H	Division 2	3-0
Barrie Wright	1962-63	13-Apr-1963	Preston North End	H	Division 2	4-1
Jimmy Greenhoff	1962-63	13-May-1963	Southampton	A	Division 2	1-3
John Giles	1963-64	31-Aug-1963	Bury	H	Division 2	3-0
Paul Madeley	1963-64	11-Jan-1964	Manchester City	H	Division 2	1-0
Alan Peacock	1963-64	8-Feb-1964	Norwich City	A	Division 2	2-2
Terry Cooper	1963-64	11-Apr-1964	Swansea Town	A	Division 2	3-0
Rod Belfitt	1964-65	23-Sep-1964	Huddersfield Town	H	League Cup R2	3-2
Mick Bates	1965-66	22-Sep-1965	Hartlepools United	H	League Cup R2	4-2
Nigel Davey	1965-66	13-Oct-1965	West Brom	H	League Cup R3	2-4
David Harvey	1965-66	13-Oct-1965	West Brom	H	League Cup R3	2-4
Dennis Hawkins	1965-66	13-Oct-1965	West Brom	H	League Cup R3	2-4
Mike O'Grady	1965-66	16-Oct-1965	Northampton Town	H	Division 1	6-1
Eddie Gray	1965-66	1-Jan-1966	Sheffield Wednesda	H	Division 1	3-0
Terry Hibbitt	1965-66	19-Feb-1966	Nottingham Forest	H	Division 1	4-0
Bobby Sibbald	1966-67	4-Feb-1967	Everton	A	Division 1	0-2
Jimmy Lumsden	1966-67	15-May-1967	Sheffield Wednesda	H	Division 1	1-0
Mick Jones	1967-68	23-Sep-1967	Leicester City	H	Division 1	3-2

Revie's Boys' 'First' Game Appearance Record (Continued)

PLAYER	SEASON	MATCH DATE	GAME	H/A	COMPETITION	SCORE
Terry Yorath	1967-68	11-May-1968	Burnley	A	Division 1	0-3
Allan Clarke	1969-70	2-Aug-1969	Manchester City	H	Charity Shield	2-1
Chris Galvin	1969-70	26-Nov-1969	Ferencvaros	A	European Cup R2 2nd le	3-0
David Kennedy	1969-70	30-Mar-1970	Derby County	A	Division 1	1-4
Paul Peterson	1969-70	30-Mar-1970	Derby County	A	Division 1	1-4
John Faulkner	1969-70	4-Apr-1970	Burnley	H	Division 1	2-1
Joe Jordan	1970-71	10-Mar-1971	Vitoria Setubal	H	Fairs Cup R4 1st leg	2-1
Keith Edwards	1971-72	25-Sep-1971	Huddersfield Town	A	Division 1	1-2
Jimmy Mann	1971-72	27-Sep-1971	Derby County	H	League Cup R2 replay	2-0
John Shaw	1971-72	29-Sep-1971	SK Lierse	H	Fairs Cup R1 2nd leg	0-4
Trevor Cherry	1972-73	12-Aug-1972	Chelsea	A	Division 1	0-4
Roy Ellam	1972-73	12-Aug-1972	Chelsea	A	Division 1	0-4
Frank Gray	1972-73	10-Feb-1973	Leicester City	A	Division 1	0-2
Gordon McQueen	1972-73	3-Mar-1973	Derby County	A	Division 1	3-2
Peter Hampton	1972-73	28-Apr-1973	Southampton	A	Division 1	1-3
Gary Liddell	1972-73	30-Apr-1973	Birmingham City	A	Division 1	1-2
Billy McGinley	1972-73	30-Apr-1973	Birmingham City	A	Division 1	1-2
Jimmy O'Neill	1973-74	3-Oct-1973	Stromsgodset	H	UEFA Cup R1 2nd leg	6-1
Glan Letheren	1973-74	7-Nov-1973	Hibernian	A	UEFA Cup R2 2nd leg	0-0* 5-4 pens
David Stewart	1973-74	9-Jan-1974	Wolves	H	FA Cup R3 replay	1-0